From Generation
to Generation

OTHER BOOKS BY JOHN LEITH

Introduction to the Reformed Tradition:
   A Way of Being the Christian Community

The Church: A Believing Fellowship (Rev.)

The Reformed Imperative:
   What the Church Has to Say That No One
      Else Can Say

John Calvin's Doctrine of the Christian Life

BOOKS EDITED BY JOHN LEITH

Creeds of the Churches:
   A Reader in Christian Doctrine from the Bible
      to the Present

Guides to the Reformed Tradition:
   Worship
   The Church

BV
600.2
.L452
1990

From Generation to Generation

THE RENEWAL OF THE CHURCH ACCORDING TO ITS OWN THEOLOGY AND PRACTICE

The 1989 Annie Kinkead Warfield Lectures

John H. Leith

GOSHEN COLLEGE LIBRARY
GOSHEN, INDIANA

Westminster/John Knox Press
Louisville, Kentucky

© 1990 John H. Leith

All rights reserved—no part of this book may be reproduced in any form without permission in writing from the publisher, except by a reviewer who wishes to quote brief passages in connection with a review in magazine or newspaper.

Scripture quotations are from the Revised Standard Version of the Bible, copyrighted 1946, 1952, © 1971, 1973 by the Division of Christian Education of the National Council of the Churches of Christ in the U.S.A., and are used by permission.

Book design by Polebridge Press

First edition

Published by Westminster/John Knox Press
Louisville, Kentucky

PRINTED IN THE UNITED STATES OF AMERICA
9 8 7 6 5 4 3 2 1

Library of Congress Cataloging-in-Publication Data

Leith, John H.
    From generation to generation : the renewal of the church according to its own theology and practice / John H. Leith. — 1st ed.
        p.   cm. — (The 1989 Annie Kinkead Warfield lectures)
    Includes bibliographical references.
    ISBN 0-664-25122-6

    1. Church renewal.   2. Protestant churches—United States.
3. United States—Church history—20th century.   4. Theology,
Pastoral—Reformed Church.   5. Reformed Church—United States—
Clergy.   6. Reformed Church—United States—Membership   I. Title
II. Series: Annie Kinkead Warfield lectures ; 1989.
BV600.2.L452   1990
262'.001'7—dc20
                                                          90-32390
                                                               CIP

For Caroline

Contents

Preface   9

1. Heritage and Trust   19

2. The Church and the Ministry   55

3. Preaching   82

4. Teaching   115

5. Pastoral Care   141

6. The Christian Witness in the World   162

Epilogue   177

Notes   181

Preface

The stipulated purpose of the Annie Kinkead Warfield Lectures and my own situation in life and in the church, when the invitation was received, determined the theme. The task of handing on the faith from generation to generation is appropriate to the purpose of the lectures, to the vocation of the author as a minister who teaches theology, and to the situation in the church.

> One generation shall laud thy works to another,
>   and shall declare thy mighty acts. . . .
> The LORD is gracious and merciful,
>   slow to anger and abounding in steadfast love.
> The LORD is good to all,
>   and his compassion is over all that he has made.
>   Psalm 145:4, 8–9

Benjamin Breckinridge Warfield (1851–1921), who was for thirty-four years Charles Hodge Professor of Didactic and Polemic Theology at Princeton Theological Seminary, established the lectures in memory of his wife, Annie Kinkead Warfield. His will provided that the lectures should discuss some central doctrine in the theological thought of Reformed churches. Warfield had a broad understanding of the Reformed faith, including not only the Westminster Confession and catechisms but also the Heidelberg Catechism and the Thirty-nine Articles. He specified that the lectures could focus on the exposition and defense of these doctrines as well as their historical and systematic formulation.

As these lectures are published, their author has been a minister in the Presbyterian Church for forty-seven years, including three as pastor of the Second Presbyterian Church of Nashville, Tennessee, eleven as pastor of the First Presbyterian Church of Auburn, Alabama, and thirty years as a teacher at Union Theological Seminary in Virginia. The invitation was extended at a time when the Presbyterian Church has been in a period of unprecedented decline in a society that needs and by many evidences wants to hear the gospel of Jesus Christ as it has been spoken in Reformed churches for four centuries. These lectures attempt to combine experience in the pastorate and years of reading, studying, and teaching the Reformed faith. It is the writer's intention that nothing should appear in these lectures that has not been tested in the pastorate and certified in the mainstream of Reformed theology. The lectures seek to combine theology and practice.

The decline in the quantifiable measurements of mainline churches has inspired many grants by foundations and many studies by social scientists.[1] These studies are useful in providing data about population changes, about the impact of government and social forces on the church, about the opinions, activities, and movements of people within and out of the church. They are not, however, the heart of the matter. Many read like accounts of life in a foreign land.[2] Furthermore, social scientists may themselves be too much identified with the problems the church is experiencing to bring critical judgment to bear upon them.[3] Critical judgment on the crises of the church may also call in question some of the most cherished dogmas of the university. Today, as in the sixteenth century, it is very difficult for people to reform themselves, whether they are bureaucrats, preachers, theologians, or social scientists.

The thesis of this book is that the crisis in the church is theological, including church practices that develop out of theology. On a more basic level, the crisis in the church is a crisis of faith. Hence the reality of the church that is at issue today is hidden from the view of outside observers.[4] Observers can tell us a great deal about the symptoms, but they cannot diagnose the illness.

The heart of the matter—at least as it seems to me from

having lived through the crisis and reflected upon it—is to be found in the question Jesus put to his disciples, "But who do you say that I am?" Churches have been gathered, built up, and sent forth by those who have answered with Peter, "You are the Christ, the Son of the living God" (Matt. 16:15–16).

The confession that Jesus is the Christ comes only by the power of the Holy Spirit. Hence a renewed and vital church cannot be programmed, arranged, planned. It always comes as a gift of the Spirit, for which we have to wait. Over against the contemporary axioms that the renewal of the church begins with goal setting, with task forces, with organizing, the New Testament sets the command, Wait for the promised presence of the Holy Spirit (Acts 1:4–5). The church in its organized life lives from the commitment of faith. The renewal of the church depends on the integrity of the faith and on the practices by which the worshiping, believing community lives.

Academic theology also lives on the strength of the worshiping, believing community, but it has not in contemporary history given evidence of the power to gather, build, and send forth churches. German theology in the last hundred years has been prolific in the scholarly world, but church attendance in West Germany is very low.[5] In the last fifty years, Friedrich Schleiermacher (1768–1834) has become a widely studied theologian in all universities, but John Wesley (1703–1791) as a preacher-theologian has been far more influential in building Christian congregations, in converting people of the Enlightenment age, and in changing the social, political, and economic life of society. This whole problem of the relation of academic life to the believing community is stated in a very challenging way in a recent book on biblical theology.

> The underlying question here is the relationship between theology and secular biblical scholarship. The solution that dispenses with a genuinely theological Old and New Testament theology implies that theologians should follow the fluctuations of biblical scholarship, but not seek to influence their direction.
>
> That is a dangerous policy for theologians to pursue in a culture where the subject-matter of the Bible is contested. Historians and believers may read it very differently. The real justification for letting biblical scholarship set the agenda for theological interpreta-

tion of the Bible is that the scholars' questions are those of the contemporary culture which theology seeks to address. But that is only part of the truth. The world may have more to learn from the Bible than what the scholars are experts in unravelling. A theology (and so a theological interpretation of the Bible) which allowed itself to be directed by the discoveries of biblical scholarship alone would be starved of fresh air and suffocate. Believers have other interests in the Bible, and there is no reason why these too should not guide and motivate (though not compel) their biblical interpretation. These other interests may also draw upon the resources of scholarship. . . . Historical scholarship has its own agenda and its own secular university base, even if its numerical strength remains parasitic upon people's religious interests in these texts.[6]

The renewal of the church must begin with the decisions and acts of faith which on the human level constitute the church and with the grace of God which calls forth those decisions and acts. The truths of faith are perceived by faith and repentance, which are gifts of the Holy Spirit. Yet they are likewise human works. While waiting for the Holy Spirit, we can be at work claiming God's promise.[7]

These lectures attempt to indicate some of the things we can do as we wait and pray for the Spirit's presence. While we cannot command the Spirit, there is wisdom in placing our lives in the context of those means of grace by which, we have been promised in the New Testament, the Holy Spirit works. If we do these things, it is likely that the church shall be renewed by the power of the Spirit.

The renewal of the church begins on the human level with an act of remembrance. The Christian church has bequeathed to us the Bible, theology, worship, and the fellowship of the church. These have been handed on from generation to generation by the witnesses, by believing, worshiping people. In addition, we are the inheritors of buildings, of institutions embodying many services from education to care for those who need support, and of a culture and a political order which have been influenced for good by Christian faith. Yet a characteristic of our time, according to Czeslaw Milosz in his Nobel lecture, is "the refusal to remember."

Certainly, the illiterates of past centuries, then an enormous majority of mankind, knew little of the history of their respective countries and of their civilization. In the minds of modern illiterates, however, who know how to read and write and even teach in schools and at universities, history is present but blurred, in a state of strange confusion. . . . We are surrounded today by fictions about the past, contrary to common sense and to an elementary perception of good and evil.[8]

The renewal of the church will begin with a remembering of what has been bequeathed to us.

Remembering is closely related to the integrity of the church's witness. When theology becomes preoccupied with relevance and frantic in its search for concepts and language that will appeal to modern people, it is in danger of losing its identity and therefore its power. For the past forty years, theologians have been passionately concerned to write the new theology or a theology that would make sense to modern people. Today the theological landscape is strewn with discarded theologies that never gained a hearing. The theologies that have sought the most to accommodate contemporary society never themselves became persuasive. No theology is likely to be persuasive unless it has its origin in the worshiping, believing community which is the Christian church. The church lives by remembering, and so must persuasive theology and preaching.

The renewal of the church will require not only a remembering but also a faithful witness. The church lives by the gospel of what God has done for our salvation in the life, death, and resurrection of Jesus Christ. Without the gospel, the church is just another political party or therapeutic group, albeit claiming divine sanction for its secular wisdom. Theologians have been engaged for decades in a search to establish Christian faith upon some foundation that is accessible to human beings in their own experience and reasoning.[9] These efforts have not been successful, and there is little reason in the history of the church to believe they will be.

The foundation for Christian faith is Jesus Christ. Yet this foundation as a particular historical event has never seemed arbitrary to Christian believers; for they have found that faith in Jesus Christ as the revelation of God for our salvation enabled them to understand their experiences in the world as nothing else did. This faith enabled them to see what they had not seen, to hear what they had not heard, to discover meaning in what had been arbitrary fate. It gave them hope where they had only known despair. The church bears witness not to its own discovery but to a revelation that called it into existence. The Christian community cannot therefore be founded upon human reason and experience. Yet God's redemption in Jesus Christ can be proclaimed with the aid of reason so as to illuminate life and to persuade unbelievers. In remembering, the Christian community proclaims the gracious act of God which called it into existence.

The renewal of the church requires the application of the message, or the interpretation of life today in the light of the Christian faith. Here the theological or logical order is critically important. The church is in trouble in considerable measure because it has sometimes interpreted the faith in the light of experience in the world. The first step in the renewal of the church is recovering the proper order. The world and human experience are to be understood in the light of the faith, not the faith in the light of human experience.

The persuasiveness of the Christian message under the power of the Holy Spirit is in the exposition of the faith itself and in the power of that exposition to illuminate life. The ancient rubrics are still the guide to a persuasive theology: "We believe in order to understand";[10] "Faith seeks understanding (intelligibility)."[11] Karl Barth was surely right in insisting that the first task of theology is the integrity of the church's proclamation.[12] Heresy has become an ugly word because of acrimonious debates. Yet the fact is, heresy in the forms of the dilution, the distortion, the truncation of the faith always undercuts the Christian message.[13] In seeking to accommodate Christian faith to modernity the church may well have encouraged unbelief.

The persuasiveness of the Christian message in the Augustinian and Calvinist sense always presupposes a profound knowledge of the scriptures and of the church's reflection on scripture as well as life in the community itself. However, preaching and witnessing today are never simply the repetition of what was said yesterday. The explication of the Christian message must illuminate the contemporary situation so that those who hear understand in the context of their own experience and of their own language.[14] In the past the theologians and preachers have been ably assisted in the proclamation of the Christian faith by philosophy in the ancient church and in the thirteenth century, and by humanism in the sixteenth century. No modern philosophy or thought form has proved as effective for theology as did philosophy for Thomas Aquinas or humanism for Calvin. The task of proclaiming the Christian message, however, cannot await the ideal philosophy or conceptual tools. The task of the minister in good times and bad is first of all to know the scriptures and to master the theological wisdom of the church in proclaiming the gospel with conviction and competence. This task also requires the best knowledge available of the culture, the science, and the language of the people.[15] Moreover, the wisdom requisite for the effective application of Christian faith comes more from the breadth and depth of the experience of life than it does from textbook knowledge of philosophy, science, or psychology.

These lectures do not provide any new suggestions. They do advocate a return to the tested wisdom of the church's tradition and to the methods that have developed in the life of the church and have warrant in its theology. Theologies that have demonstrated their power to persuade and to build worshiping congregations are a surer base for church renewal than untested contemporary theologies that delight in novelty and idiosyncratic theological vocabularies.

The church is renewed by preaching, teaching, and pastoral care as they have been traditionally practiced in the church. Management skills, understanding of goal-setting processes, therapy, public relations, conflict management do not gather and build churches. Churches that serve basic human needs sometimes thrive without much theology, and modern communications techniques can turn ministers without education into excellent entertainers. I know of no evidence that these skills gather and build congregations of faith. The Protestant churches that endure are those that emphasize preaching, teaching, and pastoral care. There are no shortcuts.

Hence the renewal of the church rests upon two foundations. The first is the renewal of faith, the outpouring of the Holy Spirit that enables us to say that Jesus is the Christ, that enables us to experience the Bible as the Word of God, that makes us sensitive to the activity of God in nature and in history. The second foundation is the act of remembering and recovering our identity and persuasively proclaiming it in the life of the church, especially in the ministries of preaching, teaching, and pastoral care.

Every writer is indebted to countless persons, many of whom have slipped beyond conscious memory, and to countless books, many of which have been forgotten. This book is an occasion to remember all my teachers and my colleagues in the ministry who have taught me much and who have shared with me their faith. Albert Outler died on September 1, 1989. He was my teacher and friend, and only two weeks before his death I had discussed with him on the telephone some of the issues embodied in these lectures.

I am grateful for the confidence of the Charles Hodge Professor of Theology, David Willis-Watkins, and to the faculty of Princeton Theological Seminary in extending me the invitation to give the Warfield Lectures during the academic year 1989–90. President Thomas Gillespie and Barbara Gillespie were gracious, thoughtful hosts who, in addition, were interested in what these lectures were attempting to say. Patrick and Mary Ann Miller, Daniel and Margaret Migliore, James Armstrong, Sam and Eileen Moffett, Edward Dowey, and William Harris of Princeton Theological Seminary, Arthur and Margaret Link of Princeton University, William P. and Mary Thompson, Hughes and Mary Old all went beyond the call of duty to be helpful to me. Wallace and Alice Alston, as well as the staff and members of Nassau Presbyterian Church, gave me a warm welcome to Princeton.

I owe an especial debt of gratitude to James I. McCord and the Center of Theological Inquiry at Princeton for the invitation to be a member of the center as much as my schedule permitted during the academic year 1988–89. The center is a remarkable institution, and it provides an ideal environment for writing. These lectures would not have been possible without the time spent at the center.

Portions of the lectures on teaching and pastoral care were given as part of the Alumni Lectures at Columbia Theological Seminary in 1978. Davison Philips was my gracious host and friend who has encouraged me in this study.

My work would be impossible without the assistance and encouragement I receive at Union Theological Seminary in Virgina. The Union Theological Seminary library is a remarkable institution, and Martha Aycock is as persistent as any librarian has ever been in her helpfulness to those who make use of that library. Sally Hicks is not only a typist but an editor of manuscripts, whose competence relieves the writer of much laborious work. Norma Kuhn has always kept my work on schedule, at least as best she could, and handled my correspondence. Stacy Johnson, among others, read the manuscript. Among my students, Sam Warner, Michael Bush, Mary Catherine Miller, Gordon Turnbull, and Elizabeth Ayscue have assisted in reading proofs and checking references. For all those who have contributed to the writing of this book, I am very grateful.

Union Theological Seminary in Virginia　　　　　　J. H. L.

CHAPTER ONE

Heritage and Trust

The Christian church, from the viewpoint of an observer, has always been at risk in the world. In the second century, the Christian community, weak in human strength, faced many of the theological and social crises it does today. There was the human possibility, indeed probability, that it would disappear into the social mix.

Three centuries later, in the West, the Christian community was confronted with a major cultural transition, as well as the task of educating and evangelizing the various peoples of northern Europe. It was soon to be decimated in the eastern Mediterranean and in northern Africa by the Islamic advance. Again, there was the human possibility that the church would disappear or become an inconsequential community in the ongoing of the human race.

In the eighteenth century the prospects for the church were dim. Few if any would have predicted in 1760 that the nineteenth century would be, in Kenneth Scott Latourette's words, the great century in the "advance" of Christianity.[1]

Today in the industrialized West the church is at grave risk. In the United States, where Christian faith remains very much alive, the crisis of Protestant churches, which have their historic roots in European communities, has often enough been documented in quantifiable terms.[2]

Many factors in our society have put Protestant churches at risk. The thesis of these lectures, however, is that the primary reasons for the decline of churches are to be found within the community of faith itself, and are in part hidden from the observation of external observers—historians, psychologists, sociologists, anthropologists. The external observers have much to say which is important, but finally the diagnosis as well as renewal must come from within the community itself, and in the light of its own tradition and authorities. Those who have lived through the transitions of the church during the past forty years, while appreciating the studies of external observers, know that what they describe, largely in quantifiable terms, does not reach the depths of what has been experienced within the community itself.[3]

I

The elementary form of the crisis is a loss of identity as Presbyterians, as Protestants, as Christians. This loss of identity is closely related to the loss of the history that told us who we were. As the character in Steinbeck's novel put it, How will we know it is us without our past?[4] On the one hand, we have forgotten the history and failed to teach it to our children; on the other hand, the history has been put at risk by the increasingly secular and pluralistic society in which we live.

The history that gives us our identity is the history we have assimilated into our own personhood and made the story of our lives. This is the same history that historians study, analyze, and record, but it is perceived from a different perspective, from the perspective of our own personal history. Christians are those who know, whatever their biological ancestry, that Abraham, the prophets of Israel, the disciples in the upper room, the whole host of believers who have bequeathed to them the faith, and the Christian community are the family that gives them their deepest identity.[5]

H. Richard Niebuhr, in an influential book, *The Meaning of Revelation,* distinguished two ways of understanding history: history as seen and observed and history as lived and understood from within. History as remembered gives us our identity, shapes our lives, and forms the communities in which we live.

History as remembered is not a different history from that

which is objectively studied and analyzed. It is the same history, but a history personally remembered, with which one identifies as the story of his or her life. This does not mean that history as remembered is unreliable or wholly subjective. It is history that occurs in community and therefore is subject to the critical tests of the community's memory. Persons can refresh as well as criticize each other's memories of what has happened to them in their common life. True and false categories can be applied to history as remembered or to history as objectively studied. There are true and false appeals to memory as well as true and false external descriptions. Truth is not the exclusive claim or prerogative of either point of view.[6]

This history which has overwhelmingly shaped the formation of Western countries and in particular the formation of the United States, as well as Protestant churches, is threefold: (1) it is a cultural and political history that originated in Greece and in Rome; (2) it is the history of the Christian church in the formation of culture, especially of medieval culture and universities; (3) it is the story of faith itself, which had its beginning with the call of Abraham.

These three traditions have interacted for almost two thousand years. The shape of Western Christianity and the shape of Western culture cannot be understood apart from these histories. They were decisive influences in making us as persons what we are, and in making the social order of the nation what it has been. Without the histories of Greek culture, of the Roman world, of medieval civilization and universities, of the Christian faith, of Protestantism, of Puritanism, the United States would be a very different nation, and we as individuals would be different persons.[7]

Christians have perceived the convergence of Hebrew, Greek, and Roman cultures as the work of God's providence, and in part the meaning of the New Testament doctrine of the fullness of time (Eph. 1:10; cf. Gal. 4:4).[8] These philosophical, cultural, and political histories assume even greater significance in view of the fact that few peoples in human history have originated powerful philosophical traditions; that the literary traditions of Virgil, Cicero, Dante, Shakespeare, Milton have enabled human beings over centuries to understand themselves with a new clarity and depth; and that liberal political democracy in the contemporary world is a very remarkable and fragile achievement. Rome still stands as one of the greatest political and social achievements of the human spirit. Plato and Aristotle have their contemporary critics, but no one has, at least to the present, replaced them as stimulators of the philosophical enterprise.

For better or worse, we have been shaped by the history of human thought: Plato, Aristotle, the medieval universities, the Renaissance, the Enlightenment, and the scientific revolution. Our political institutions were not created *ex nihilo* in 1776, but have their origins in a great history: Pericles, Plato's *Republic,* Aristotle's *Politics,* Rome, the Magna Charta, and the rise of liberal political democracies.

Our understanding of human greatness has been shaped by great literature, drama, and art: Homer, Virgil, Michelangelo, Dante, Leonardo da Vinci, Rembrandt, the Gothic cathedrals, Shakespeare, and Milton.

Our identity has also been mightily shaped by the great army of Christian missionaries and the organized work of the church which helped to form the civilization that emerged in Europe after the decline of the Roman Empire. Herbert Butterfield has summarized the difference Christian faith made in the formation of European history in a very moving way.

> It pointed to a way of harnessing passion itself—harnessing the affective dispositions of men—to the cause of a higher righteousness. By their doctrine of a divine grace which brings a higher liberty the Christians bridged the ancient gulf between freedom and necessity. Against the wisdom of ancient Athens, against the claims of a natural reason that pretended to stand high and dry as it examined the world "objectively," they claimed that God was not an object to be examined in the way that mere inanimate things are so often presumed to be—but that belief in God was preliminary to intellectual inquiry itself; God was not to be found by the natural reason in the study of Nature, but Nature itself in reality was only to be discovered through God. . . .
>
> In all these ways Christianity seriously affected man's relations with the world and his responses to that world, as well as influencing his whole conception of humanity. And the transformation affected the subsequent centuries of European history.
>
> In any case, there is a further consequence that Christianity must have wherever it is preached, and the influence must be re-

garded as existing in every age—even in those periods when religion provides also sinister forces that counteract it. Christian teaching contains certain elements that are bound to operate in favour of what we might call a softening of manners; and in the ancient Roman empire it stressed the sanctity of human life, the importance of the family, the evils of sexual licence and divorce, and the wickedness of either suicide or the gladiatorial contests or the murder of infants. In all this Christianity was standing for a higher estimation of personality, based on the view of man as a spiritual creature. Furthermore, the organization of charity was carried by the Christian Church to the point at which we can regard it as an original contribution to the life of the time. And in the fundamental place which it gave to love, in its emphasis on gentleness, humility, joy, and peace, the Church was parting from the ethical ideals of the pagan world, and promoting a different kind of personality, a different posture for human beings under the sun.[9]

The other history was the story of faith. It began with the creation of the universe, in particular with the creation of Adam and Eve. It included their fall and God's covenant with Noah, his commitment to struggle with fallen human beings to achieve his purpose. It traced the history of God's grace from the call of Abraham and the covenant with him, that he should be a blessing to all people; to Moses, Joshua, and David. The prophets played their part in this history, and all of history found its fulfillment and the revelation of its meaning in Jesus Christ. This history was told not only in the Bible, not only in the teaching of the church, but also in the great literature, art, and architecture of Western culture.

The story included the remarkable spread of the Christian witness throughout the world. In about A.D. 50, Paul, wanting to go to Bithynia, but being directed to Troas, wanting to go to the east, but being destined to go west to Macedonia, changed the course of human history (see Acts 16:7–10). The remarkable spread of Christianity throughout the Mediterranean world and northern Europe reached its climax in the great missionary movement in the nineteenth century when the Christian community became the first truly universal community.

Within the larger stories of culture and faith, there were smaller stories. There were the special stories of Protestantism, of the Puritans, of the migration of people to the thirteen colonies, of the *Mayflower*, and of the events of 1776. There was the story of Presbyterians, with their roots in Zurich and Geneva, their history in Scotland and northern Ireland, and their settlement of the back country in the American colonies.

These were stories of a faith, not of races, nations, economic systems, or even cultures. Augustine in his old age came to understand as he had not earlier that the great human difference is faith.[10] Medieval Christianity emphasized that faith shapes human beings more decisively than race, tribe, or nation, and thereby gave to the disparate peoples of Europe a considerable measure of theological and cultural unity. Faith does constitute the most decisive difference between human beings. Augustine, the North African of Berber descent, is today the spiritual father of multitudes who are remote indeed from him racially, politically, and culturally. Augustine's conversion in 386–387, together with Paul's crossing the Aegean Sea to Macedonia about A.D. 50, are two crucial dates in Western history. The family line of faith is more determinative of destiny than the heritage of race or culture.

A new sensitivity to the dignity and significance of cultures and of the many remembered histories which have given identity to various people is a characteristic of our time. A new awareness exists in America of the particular histories of the Indian, black, Hispanic, and Asian Christians. This dignity of history, personhood, and conscience must be respected as a right guaranteed by the Creator. In addition, these stories have already become in varying degrees a part of the story of the Christian community in the United States. Yet the assimilation of stories is not simple. How different human history would be in the twentieth century if the people of northern Europe had repudiated the culture of Greece and Rome and the Christian faith of the Nicene Creed. Likewise, we owe many of the most precious qualities of our society to the fact that Augustine of Hippo is our father in a deeper sense than any biological father can be.

The critical issue for the traditioning of the faith is not culture, race, or nation as such, but the integrity of the faith itself. Repeatedly, the integrity of the faith has been put at risk by compromises with alien ideas and practices. In the pluralistic society of the second century Christianity could have been absorbed by alien practices and beliefs. In the fourth century, if Arianism had triumphed, Christianity would have become just another religion of the empire.[11] Again in northern Europe the Nordic religions of race, blood, and soil could have transformed Christian faith into a nature religion. National socialism in the recent past and an emergent paganism today reveal how these religions continue to live under the surface of society. The Christian community that has survived has always taken seriously the integrity of its own identity.

Today the histories of culture and of faith that have given us our identity are in danger of being forgotten, even by those whose lives have been shaped by them. We no longer adequately teach them in our schools and universities, and more particularly in the church and in our homes.

The problem, however, is not simply that the story is being forgotten. The story of Western culture and the story of faith are under attack. The visibility of this attack is seen, for example, in the protest against the reading of the great books and the courses on Western civilization on university campuses. Ironically, the chant "Ho, ho, ho, ho, Western culture has got to go" has been heard on university campuses, which are the products of the story and of the generosity of persons shaped by the tradition.[12] The story of faith has been eroded by the increasing secularism of the culture and by the pluralism of our society, which places all stories and traditions, cultural and theological, on the same level. The implicit assumption is that many roads lead to God, that one faith is essentially as good as another faith, one culture as another culture. This egalitarianism goes beyond the affirmation that values are to be found even in the most mean culture and that certain truths are expressed in all faiths, even witchcraft. It assumes that all cultures not only have their rights and places but are also equally good for the human race.

Few consequences in history are clearer, however, than the differences that faith and culture make in social, economic, and political life. Yet it is no longer part of the ethos of "civility" and "tolerance" in American cultural and social life to raise questions as to the validity and the consequences of faiths and culture. Even in the church there is a new hesitancy to declare that the

Christian faith is true, that the Nicene conviction that Jesus Christ is truly God is the truth, not simply a meaningful symbol.

The loss of the stories that gave us our identity is related not only to the pluralism and the civility that reign in our society but also to the lost dominance of Western civilization, and of the United States, as well as the lost cultural status of Protestantism in Western culture. While the decline of the United States and of Protestantism is no doubt greatly exaggerated, the perception of this decline, to say nothing of the threat, leads to anxiety and loss of confidence. The secularism of culture, pluralism, an ethos of tolerance, the loss of hegemony all play a part in the lost stories and the decline in the worshiping, believing congregations as a consequence of the lost story.

The history of the church has something to teach us in this crisis. First, the church has survived dramatic cultural crises and perils in the second century, in the fourth and sixth centuries, in the sixteenth and eighteenth centuries. Second, the church has survived changing economic, social, and political systems. Indeed, it has demonstrated more durability than any other segment of our society. Third, Protestantism has had more experience dealing with the "modern" world than any other faith. Fourth, the forms of Christian faith that have been most alive to and clear about their own identity have had the greatest survival power.

II

What, more specifically, is the faith we have lost? What is the heritage that has been entrusted to us? The simple but true answer is Jesus Christ: the history of God's works in creation, judgment, and redemption which Jesus Christ fulfilled. Faith in Jesus Christ as Savior and Lord constitutes the church. The decisive mark of the church, as Luther, Zwingli, and Calvin knew, is the proclamation of the gospel of Jesus Christ. Everything else is secondary. The admonition of Paul and the Pauline church to Timothy may be the text of these lectures. "O Timothy, guard what has been entrusted to you. Avoid the godless chatter and contradictions of what is falsely called knowledge, for by professing it some have missed the mark as regards the faith" (1 Tim. 6:20–21). There is no other gospel. Yet from the beginning there were those who sought to unsettle the minds of Christian people. "I am astonished," Paul wrote to the Galatians, "that you are so quickly deserting him who called you in the grace of Christ and turning to a different gospel—not that there is another gospel, but there are some who trouble you and want to pervert the gospel of Christ. But even if we, or an angel from heaven, should preach to you a gospel contrary to that which we preached to you, let him be accursed. As we have said before, so now I say again, If any one is preaching to you a gospel contrary to that which you received, let him be accursed"(Gal. 1:6–9).

The gospel of Jesus Christ is the heritage that has been entrusted to us. The church has always believed, confessed, and taught that Jesus Christ is the embodiment of the wisdom and power of God, the Word made flesh, or as the church would later say, fully God and fully man, who bearing our sins on the cross brings us forgiveness, and who sending his Spirit calls for faith and renews our lives according to his image. Moreover, his resurrection vouchsafes our resurrection from the dead, and our hope of a new heaven and a new earth. The gospel is the promise that nothing can separate us from the love of God in Jesus Christ, and that nothing which is committed to his keeping shall be finally lost. It has been embodied in lives of trust in God and in charity which has humanized life and society.

This is the heritage as Paul knew it and as it was reaffirmed by the great Reformers of the sixteenth century. Many practices, many dimensions of the life of the Christian community are derivative from this. The church's witness to the world on social, economic, and political matters is derivative. If the heritage is lost, the derivatives, the practices, the missions, and the witnesses become cut flowers which can only die.

The renewal of tradition is not so much the recovery of a Christian past as it is the return to that which originated the tradition. For Luther, tradition "involves the need for each generation to be reminded of the same unchanged body of knowledge whose binding force exists in its going back in origin to a divine message as its source. Specifically for the Christian tradition, the authority of Scripture derives from its proximity and witness to the divine source—Christ. For the early church made no distinction or separation between the content of Scripture and the content of tradi-

tion."[13] For Luther, the tradition is Jesus Christ, and the
continuity of the church is preserved in the proclamation of Christ
in baptism, in preaching, in the forgiveness of sins, in the Lord's
Supper. In preaching, the revelation of Christ and the work of the
Holy Spirit are united, and the Word of God proclaimed evokes
the crisis of faith and thus the reality of the church.[14]

This summary of Christian faith, with its references to the
triune God, to the person and work of Christ, to the giving of the
Holy Spirit, and to the consummation of all things by the power
of God, is found not only in the New Testament but in all the
creeds of the church and in the writings of the theologians who
have been the teachers of the church as a believing, worshiping
people. Yet this summary has its own particular idiom in its expression. It is Antiochene rather than Alexandrian, Protestant
rather than Roman Catholic or Orthodox. It reflects the Puritans
and the historical American Presbyterian way of giving expression to an Augustinian, Calvinist understanding of the faith. It
claims to be a true statement of the substance of the Christian
faith, but not *the* statement of the faith.

"The faith which was once for all delivered to the saints"
(Jude 3) has through Christian history maintained the clarity and
the specificity of its identity and of its references in a remarkable
way. Yet there has never been a final statement of the faith, one
form of words or set of categories that could win acceptance as
the statement of the faith. Efforts to state precisely the "essence"
of the faith or to define specifically the identity of the faith have
failed. Yet the continuity and the identifiability of the faith in its
various forms and in different times and places are clear enough.
It always has a reference to the triune God, to the Word made
flesh, to the decisiveness of the work of Jesus Christ for the salvation of all people, and to the consummation of all things, the
new heaven and new earth, by the power of God. It has always
affirmed the koinonia (the fellowship or community) of the
church and the diaconate, deeds of love and mercy. There is no
Christian creed that has received the approbation of the people of
God that has not included these references. There has been no
enduring Christian community that has not believed, confessed,
and taught this faith.

The continuity of the faith is such that Justin Martyr

(c. 100–c. 165), Augustine (354–430), Thomas Aquinas (1225–1274), Martin Luther (1483–1546), John Calvin (1509–1564), Jonathan Edwards (1703–1758), Charles Hodge (1797–1878), could all participate meaningfully in a Sunday service of a mainstream church. The cultural, economic, and political context would be very disconcerting, but they would all recognize and concur in the central acts of worship. This continuity is muted or denied in contemporary theological debates, but it is very visible in the believing, worshiping life of the church. The old theological rubric *lex orandi, lex credendi* has its validity even in Calvinistic churches, which emphasize the theological intelligibility of worship and subject worship to biblical and theological criticism.

The one critical question that the decline of the church raises is the one Jesus put to his disciples, "But who do you say that I am?" Congregations, the institutions and programs of the church, have always been built by those who answered as Peter did: "You are the Christ, the Son of the living God" (Matt. 16:16; cf. Mark 8:29 and Luke 9:20). Apart from Peter's answer there is no reason for the church to exist.

The Christian tradition is that which the church believes, confesses, and teaches as well as the practices that these actions entail and the fellowship they create. The boundaries of the tradition are hard to define, but the central core is clear enough. There has been no enduring Christian community that has not believed that Jesus Christ is the Word made flesh and that by his life, death, and resurrection we are saved. There has been no enduring Christian community that has not treasured the Bible as the Word of God written. There has been no enduring Christian community without the fellowship and the ministry of compassion. The tradition, as Albert Outler has so well pointed out, is Jesus Christ, and the various human statements of the tradition in theologies and communities of the faith are broken representations of it.[15]

III

The gospel that the Word of God became flesh in Jesus of Nazareth, full of grace and truth, is handed on to us in at least four concrete embodiments.

The first is the scriptures of the Old and New Testaments. The scriptures are, according to Barth, the original and authentic witness to the revelation of God.[16] The witness, however, cannot be separated from the revelation. We know the revelation only through the witness. The Christian revelation moved those who received it to express it in metaphors, images, sentences, and paragraphs. Revelation, William Temple insisted, is event and interpretation.[17] In this sense, the scriptures of the Old and New Testaments are an integral dimension of the Christian revelation. They are "the incarnation in written form of the living personal revelation of the living God in the history of revelation and salvation."[18]

The scripture, as the apostolic witness, impressed itself upon the church as the *true* witness. There were other ways to understand the Hebrew scriptures which became for Christians the Old Testament. There were other ways to understand who Jesus was—a prophet, a teacher, or a wise man, as some believed. The canon of the New Testament is the judgment of the church that the New Testament is the true and faithful witness. The overwhelming conviction of the church through the centuries has been that the God who revealed himself in Jesus Christ inspired the writing of the scriptures. For all Christians, but for Reformed Christians in particular, the Bible sets the boundaries for interpretation and orders the way the church's theology is shaped. As the narrative of the acts of the triune God for our salvation it provides the context in which Christians understand their lives.

The writings of the great leaders of the church in the second, third, and fourth centuries speak of the handing on of the faith with a certain awe as well as responsibility. Ignatius, Irenaeus, Tertullian, Origen received the tradition, the apostolic faith, in faith, and they handed it on in faith, from faith to faith as a treasure beyond value.[19] They stood under its judgment in rules of faith, in scripture, in the witness of tradition guarded by the bishop. They received the witness as believers who nevertheless with awe exercised critical judgment separating the false from the true. This awe-filled sense of responsibility in receiving the apostolic witness in its written form, receiving it in faith and handing it on in faith, has been a striking characteristic of the church until quite recently. The loss of a sense of awe in the presence of scripture and of awe-filled responsibility in the handing on of the faith is one of the great tragedies of contemporary church life.

The Bible, however, is more than the authority for the life of the church, the rule of faith and practice. It is, by the power of the Holy Spirit, the revelation of God. In the church, the Bible is experienced not simply as a piece of Near Eastern literature but as God's Word to the Christian in judgment and in mercy.

Hence the importance of the Bible in the traditioning of the faith in a Protestant context cannot be overestimated.[20] The reading and study of the Bible are necessary for faithful participation in the life of a Protestant church. The devotional reading of the Bible for Protestants is also essential for personal growth to Christian maturity. The faith is handed on when the church places the scriptures in the hands of a child and a believer.

The gospel is also embodied in the reflections of the community of faith, in interpretations and applications of scripture. These take the form of commentaries on scripture, of sermons, of catechetical material, of theology, of apologetics, and of creedal statements.

The accumulation of this material cannot replace the original and authentic witness of the Bible as the Word of God written. Yet it has significance. The promise of Jesus Christ is, "But the Counselor, the Holy Spirit, whom the Father will send in my name, he will teach you all things, and bring to your remembrance all that I have said to you" (John 14:26). The Holy Spirit is the Spirit of Christ whom we know in history.[21] The Spirit does not make us any less dependent on the Christ, but the Spirit illuminates our understanding. We are heirs of the Augustines, the Thomases, the Luthers, and the Calvins. Because they believed, our faith has a richness that would not be possible otherwise.

Karl Rahner, the Roman Catholic theologian, in reflecting on tradition, observed that no later reflection upon or scientific study of the experience of one person being in love with another can ever replace or become a substitute for the experience.[22] Yet reflection may clarify, correct, and deepen the meaning of the experience even for those who experience it. The reflection of the Christian community has had this significance for the community of faith.

The third concrete embodiment of the heritage is found in the practices of the church. These range from the "exercises" of personal piety to the formal services of worship which have had a fixed structure almost from the beginning. The exercises of Reformed piety were the public worship of God, scripture reading, prayer, table blessing, and the stewardship of money.[23] From the beginning, the Reformers were skeptical of rules and exercises. Calvin feared that exercises would become ends in themselves.[24] He apparently believed the practices clearly stated in the New Testament were adequate. His emphasis on the kingdom of God rather than the vision of God and on the personal, historical, and moral rather than the meditative and mystical made the routine activities of life the primary focus of faith.

Psalm- and hymn-singing is one of the most powerful practices of the church.[25] Certainly as many people learn their theology, and learn it in their hearts as well as in their minds, from the hymns they sing as they do from any other practice. Calvin knew that singing deeply moved the heart, and that the words that are sung shape personality. This is the reason he paid special attention to the music as well as to the language of the hymns. He maintained that the music of the church must be simple, so as not to obscure the spoken message, and that the words should be carefully chosen, indeed, that they should be the words of scripture, namely the psalms. Preaching, teaching, baptism, the Lord's Supper, eating together, the ministry of compassion, are practices that have their warrant in the ministry of Jesus. Christian conversation, which Luther designated a means of grace, likewise has its authority in the habit of Jesus. Daily Bible reading, prayer, and table blessings became exercises of piety in devout Reformed homes.

The Lord's Day has been of incalculable influence in transmitting the faith. For Calvin the gathering of the community to hear God's Word and to respond in faith was essential for the existence of the church.[26] Karl Barth has stated the significance of the Lord's Day very clearly.

> It speaks of a limiting of man's activity, . . . his own work, his own undertaking and achievement, the job he does for his livelihood and in the service of the community. It says that, in defer-

ence to God and to the heart and meaning of His work, there must be from time to time an interruption, a rest, a deliberate non-continuation, a temporal pause, to reflect on God and His work and to participate consciously in the salvation provided by Him and to be awaited from Him. It says that man's own work is to be performed as a work bounded by this continually recurring interruption. This interruption is the holy day.[27]

The Lord's Day, the gathering to worship in the company of the people of God, is the heart of the church's earthly existence. If the church does not happen here, it does not happen. When Christians absent themselves from the worship of the people, they engage in an evil and destructive practice. This has been the witness not only of the Puritans but of the non-Puritan theologians John Calvin in the sixteenth century and Karl Barth in the twentieth century. The task of maintaining space and time for worship and the renewal of faith is a great difficulty in our society.[28]

The fourth embodiment of the tradition is found in institutions, in buildings, in portraits, in communities. Even when the buildings have been reduced to a pile of rubble and the communities have faded from existence, they still bear a silent witness to the faith that was expressed in and through them.

But the heritage finally resides not in objects but in the hearts and minds of people, or, more particularly, in the life of a community of faith. Hence it is insufficient to point to the Bible, to the reflections of the community embodied in books, to the practices of the community, to the artifacts such as the ruins of church buildings or even magnificent churches that still stand. The primary form in which the heritage is passed on is the living community of faith in which the heritage is affirmed as the life of the community.

The church as community is a social reality that can be observed and studied. The knowledge of the observer is very useful. Church people can profit from the wisdom of sociologists, psychologists, anthropologists, and management experts.

The authentic reality of the church, however, is beyond the observation of the spectator. For this reason, Augustine and Calvin spoke of the invisible church, and the creed makes the existence of the church an article of faith.[29] Faith is a very personal act, and so also is the reality of the communion of the saints.

Indeed, the reality of the church is made visible in the communion of saints, the personal sharing in a common hope, faith, love, and in common graces, gifts, blessings, as well as sorrows.

The church lives, not by organization and techniques, but by the passionate conviction that Jesus Christ is the Word made flesh, full of grace and truth, that in his death on the cross our sins are forgiven, that God raised him from the dead for our salvation. No technique, skill, or wisdom can substitute for this passionate conviction. Furthermore, the Holy Spirit, who cannot be programmed by any technique or ritual, confirms faith in the heart. The faith is therefore traditioned on a level beyond observation and beyond the power of techniques. The traditioning of the faith is finally the work of the Holy Spirit.

IV

The traditioning of the faith on the human level has three dimensions.

First of all, it is individual. No one has ever become a Christian apart from a witness.[30] The witness may be a mother or a father, a friend or a stranger. Always someone tells the story. Until this is done, nothing happens in the traditioning of the faith.

Faith cannot be inherited as lands and houses are. Genetical inheritances fix much of life, and they may make it easier or more difficult for faith. Yet biological processes cannot transmit the faith. Culture may shape our lives and influence the idiom of our religious expressions and practices. Faith, however, involves decision, and Christian faith comes from hearing the Word. Unless they hear, how can they believe?

Second, this faith is always handed on not simply by individuals but also in community, in the fellowship of believing, worshiping people. The witness is a member of a community, and out of the communal context makes the Christian witness. The witness of the individual is undergirded by the witness of the church. Likewise the witness of the community does not exist apart from the witness of the persons who compose it. The handing on of the faith is the movement from the confession of the community to the confession of the person in the community.

This movement includes preaching and teaching on the one hand and the practices of faith in the community on the other.

William Temple, who as Archbishop of Canterbury was very much concerned with evangelism, declared:

> Before considering any question about methods of Evangelism we must recall the fact—the rather frightening fact—that the most potent evangelist for good or ill is the actual Church—not only the minister, but minister and congregation together. If the man who observes from outside sees no Christian graces in those who are inside, if congregations are quarrelsome or self-complacent, then no amount of preaching can counteract the harm that is done. The presupposition of effective evangelism, and the first step towards achieving it, is a truly dedicated Church.[31]

Third, the traditioning of the faith is generational. Generations play a significant role in the biblical account of history. The genealogies of the Pentateuch and of the history of Israel, as well as the genealogies of the birth of Jesus, serve numerous purposes. They provide identity, structure history, validate officeholders. They also reflect the descent and heritage that shape human personality. The genealogy of Jesus explains his significance. Genealogies are not a record of biological productivity (on this point, the biblical genealogies are frequently incorrect) but of God's providence. They reflect "the working out of God's plan of creation in a history of salvation." They are the way God exercises his Lordship in history.[32]

A person's biological history may be very different from the generational history of faith. For most Christians today, this is the case. In the decision of faith we decide for a generational history, a faith community with a common ethos, a history that continues to enrich our faith and the community of faith. The generations of faith play a significant role in biblical history and they, as well as succeeding generations, shape our lives today.

The biblical concern with generations has been supplemented by the study of sociologists. Robert Wuthnow, for example, has recently suggested that the generation of the '60s may now be significantly influencing the church of the 1980s and the 1990s.[33] In the past, generational movements, such as the role of young people in the revivals of the early nineteenth century, played an important part in the evangelization of the Western frontier. The influence of the Student Volunteer Movement on the Christian church and its worldwide witness is difficult to overestimate.[34]

The traditioning of the faith is always individual, communal, and generational. These dimensions of the Christian witness help shape everything we may do to transmit the faith.

The Christian tradition shares many characteristics with other human traditions. Traditions grow out of the experience of community and they take shape in time. They cannot be momentarily and rationally created, nor can they be imposed on a community.[35] The traditioning of the faith does not exhaustively or finally express what is believed, taught, and confessed. Handing on the faith is not static but alive with argument, correction, and fulfillment, trial and error.[36] The apostolicity of the church, the continuity of the faith, is personal and communal and never finally expressed in propositions or structures. Traditions grow slowly, taking at least three generations to become established or for practices to become an ongoing way of life.

The act of traditioning at its best enlarges the human understanding of that which is traditioned. The Christian witness cannot simply go back to the sources, cannot merely read the Bible, cannot just repeat what a previous generation has said. There is inescapably the translation of the tradition into the language and idiom of the time. The task of translation not only enhances the understanding of the tradition but also entails the possibility of the distortion, dilution, or corruption of the tradition. Ideally every Christian recapitulates the church's witness to and reflection upon Jesus Christ as the rite of passage into full membership in the community. Traditioning the faith is an awesome responsibility on the one hand to incorporate each new person and generation into the community of faith and on the other hand to do so in a self-critical manner which maintains the faith without distortion, dilution, or corruption.

V

A community of faith, which is particular in that it differentiates itself from other communities and which has its origin in ancient events, is confronted with many crises and problems in contemporary American society. These problems are today acute for the Christian church, which has as its fundamental conviction that the eternal God, creator of heaven and earth, became incarnate in Jesus of Nazareth.

Many factors in contemporary society are inhospitable to traditions generally and to Christian faith particularly. Hence it is increasingly important to ask how the Christian tradition and how the Christian community as a worshiping, believing people can survive in our particular society. The salient characteristics of our society that create difficulties for the Christian community, or any tradition, for that matter, are very apparent.

First, contemporary society lives in the present moment. For many, as one critic has put it, life begins in the present. The question of Eliphaz to Job can be put to people today: "Are you the first man that was born?" (Job 15:7). A pervasive characteristic of contemporary life is lack of interest in and even the rejection of history, "the refusal to remember." There is a general conviction that whatever exists is unsatisfactory, and that the new or the future will be better. Edward Shils has commented that increasingly the novel is normative.[37] People live by embracing the new. There is a passion not simply in society generally but in particular in many areas of church leadership to be on the cutting edge. In this culture of the present, it is permissible not to know Calvin or Augustine or Plato or Thomas, but it is impermissible not to know the latest work in theology, or not to be involved in the latest cause. The comment of Karl Popper is a proper judgment upon this effort to live in the present: "If everyone started where Adam started, they would get where Adam did."[38]

Tradition at its best is the tested wisdom of generations. Hence the rejection of tradition is always hazardous. One sign of human wisdom is modesty concerning one's judgments, especially when set over against the thought of the wisest persons who ever lived and against practices that have worked effectively over centuries. In the 1960s, theologians, church leaders, and committees were increasingly self-confident in substituting their own untested judgments for the wisdom of tradition. The results have not been reassuring. One theological trend has followed another and none has given evidence of the power to establish a community of faith. The new ecclesiastical devices have been less effective than the ones they replaced. Liturgical reforms have brought more satisfaction to the liturgists than to the congregations. Yet those who have sought to replace the wisdom of tradition with the untested judgments of the present moment have had influential roles in mainline churches and theological debates of the past twenty-five years, as the history of the churches and the actions of governing bodies indicate.

In the church, a very voluntary community of faith, constructive change comes slowly with the approbation of the people. Robert Heilbroner has illustrated how respect for tradition is the beginning of wisdom in human activities as diverse as agriculture and politics.[39] In every area of life, tradition is accumulated wisdom, and the most creative developments come out of tradition itself. Traditions, of course, can lose their wisdom or become corrupt. They, as all human achievements, must be subjected to criticism. Yet the criticism should come not only out of knowledge of the tradition but out of respect for its wisdom.

There is also a hedonistic dimension to this attempt to live in the present, concentrating all of life's energy in the fullest enjoyment of the moment. The old Puritan doctrine of the economical use of life, a doctrine that took time with utter seriousness, is forgotten.[40] Those who live in the present moment forget the future as readily as they forget the past. The failure to realize that what I do in the present moment determines what I shall be able to do twenty years from now is quite as disastrous as the attempt to live in the present moment without the wisdom of the past. Time, as Augustine taught us, is a dimension of the human soul.[41] Failure to take time seriously is a personal as well as a communal disaster.

The Christian faith, which is based on the conviction that God decisively disclosed himself in Jesus Christ in an event that occurred two thousand years ago, and which also believes that all of history is moving toward its consummation in the appearing of Jesus Christ, stands in contradiction to a culture determined to live in the present moment.

A second feature of this society which puts the church at risk is its secularity. Philosophers as well as church people became increasingly aware of the secular character of our society several generations ago, a drift that began six centuries ago.[42] Many church people welcomed secularism as a sign of the influence of Christian faith.[43] It was recognized that Christian faith had desacralized the world and had given it an independent character as the good creation of God. The proper attitude toward the world and nature is not fear, nor the anticipation that in the vitalities and energies of nature one will find the powers of the divine; but its acceptance as a created good. Hence nature and the world can be used by human beings not only without fear but also with joy.[44]

Secularism may be seen as the emancipation of human beings and institutions from the tyranny of the organized church. Education, medicine, social welfare, and the state in a secular society are governed by laws and regulations that evolve out of the activities and disciplines themselves. This new freedom of various areas of life from the control of religion greatly enhanced productivity and freedom.

The desacralization of the world and the emancipation of various areas of life from the control of the church also make possible living as if there were no God. The consequence has been a society that in considerable measure operates without any conscious reference to God, and that obscures the mysterious character of created existence and of human life in particular.

The extent to which contemporary society is secular is debated. Andrew Greeley, after surveying American religious life since the Second World War, concluded that it is remarkably stable. "Religion does not in general seem to have been notably weakened in the United States during the past half century, insofar as we are able to measure its strength from survey items."[45]

Secularism has come to dominate the centers of information such as the media and the universities. The media elite, according to one survey, is as secular a group as exists in American life. Fifty percent deny any religious affiliation. Only one in five identifies himself as a Protestant. Eighty-six percent seldom attend church or synagogue. Only 8 percent worship regularly.[46]

As late as the 1940s and 1950s, Protestant worship services were a significant activity in such universities as Yale, Harvard, and Princeton. The presidents of these institutions frequently read the scripture at the Sunday worship service. Today the university is increasingly secular and secularizing.[47]

It may be argued that state schools now have departments of religion. Yet there is no evidence I know that these departments contribute significantly to the vitality of the church. A secular society has now achieved a nontheological study of scripture as a piece of Near Eastern literature[48] and a faith-free study of religion and theology. It can be argued that if students regarded the Bible as a piece of Near Eastern literature the size of the departments of religion would be drastically reduced for lack of students. Religious studies are increasingly living parasitically on the community of faith.

The dominant secular influence in centers of information and in the media constitutes a challenge to the church we cannot yet estimate. For the first time the church will nurture young adults whose education from kindergarten to graduate school has been secular and who have watched and listened to a media which is as secular as any group in our society. Long ago Walter Lippmann wrote in another situation that censorship was exercised not so much by law or institutions but by the convictions of reporters which shaped what they saw, heard, and reported.[49]

The secularization of society has affected the church in at least three different ways.

1. It means that the church has to exist in a society that provides no support for the peculiar life of the church. For a millennium and a half, the Christian church had existed in Christendom, that is, a society whose basic and official allegiance was to God, and a society that gave many supports to life in the church. As late as a few decades ago, public schools in America were in many instances Protestant schools, which quite directly supported life within the church. Moreover, the structures of society aided church life. For example, society generally, until after the Second World War, closed businesses and other activities on Sunday. Today the church increasingly has difficulty maintaining its worship services, its youth activities, and other programs because of the various secular uses of Sunday.

2. Secularism has influenced the life of the church in the reduction of the church's influence on society generally. The tremendous increase in church pronouncements in recent years is in inverse proportion to the actual influence of the church as an institution on society. The state and secular agencies seldom con-

sider the convenience of the church as an organization in setting their agendas. On the other hand, the influence of the church as a people on society may be as great as ever. The greatest influence of the church on society has always been the indirect consequence of the activities that constitute the church.

3. Secularism has influenced the church in the secularization of the church's life itself. Almost every Protestant church has eagerly adopted the personnel policies of business.[50] There is no longer much difference between calling a minister and hiring a manager for General Motors, between calling a professor for a seminary and the hiring of a professor for a state university. We talk less and less about the call. In no area has the secularization of the church been more obvious than in the changed attitude toward the calling of ministers.

Many churches and theologians have sought to deal with "secularism" or "modernity" by embracing it. Just as liberals of a generation ago were embarrassed to be outflanked on the left, so many contemporary church people seem more concerned to be "contemporary" than to be Christian. By this accommodation, it can be argued, the churches themselves contributed to the rise of unbelief.[51]

A third dimension of contemporary society that puts the church at risk is pluralism. As is the case with secularism, pluralism has roots within the church itself, particularly in Puritanism.[52] Denominations, which were an invention of seventeenth-century Christianity, are based not only on the historical fact of pluralism but also on the conviction that no one is good enough or wise enough to tell another person what his or her religion ought to be, and that the Christian church finds its greatest catholicity when various forms of the church have freedom to exist side by side. Furthermore, when Christian theology has been true to itself, it has insisted upon a freedom of conscience and the responsibility of each one's answering for himself or herself before God.[53] Freedom of religion has its roots in the Christian doctrine of a person made in the image of God, though the church has not always been true to this conviction, or seen its implications. In Britain and in America, pluralism developed from the various forms of Protestantism to the various forms of Christian faith and finally to a pluralism of all religions and life-styles. America has always been a pluralistic society, but the decades since the Second World War have seen a radical increase in pluralism that is psychological as well as legal and that belongs to the ethos of the society.

Many factors have contributed to the increase in pluralism. In the past, the wars of religion convinced many people that there was a better way. The acrimony as well as the futility of theological debates likewise were in the end self-condemning. Furthermore, the simple historical fact of a plurality of religions has contributed to the ethos of pluralism. The breakdown of any comprehensive vision of human community and the freedom of the mass media from traditional loyalties have produced a radical individualism and a "loose bounded culture" in which almost all, if not all, life-styles are acceptable.

The affirmation of pluralism has become the ethos of society and even the mark of civility and sophistication.[54] The limits of pluralism have not been publicly assessed, nor has the importance of consensus for any democratic society. The consternation the recent assertiveness of Islamic groups in England and the United States created among the liberal establishment, especially in the media, is a warning that pluralism has been superficially accepted without critical examination. No community can survive with unlimited pluralism.

The Christian faith is rooted in the conviction that the Word, the mind, the intention of God who created heaven and earth became embodied in the life of a particular person, and that this person is the embodiment of the wisdom and the power of God. Some in a secular society deny there is any Word to become flesh, but in a pluralistic society, there is the pervasive conviction that there cannot be in any case a single Word; there must be many Words to become flesh. When the pluralism of civility becomes dominant, there is little reason why anyone should be invited to become a member of the Christian community, much less the Presbyterian Church.

Inclusivism, when it becomes the dominant virtue, is destructive of community. In the history of the church as well as in teaching the scripture, inclusivism is balanced by an emphasis upon the integrity of identity. In the Old Testament, Hebrew families did not want their sons to marry Canaanite women (Gen.

28:8; Deuteronomy 7; Ezra 9–10). Ezra was convinced that the very survival of the Hebrew community returning from exile depended upon an exclusivism of faith and life. In the Synoptic Gospels, as well as in the Fourth Gospel, faith causes separation and even conflict. The apostle Paul drew a sharp line between believers and unbelievers (2 Cor. 6:14–18). The integrity of the Christian community's own life and its security from alien influences is a persistent theme in the pastoral epistles, in 1 Peter, and in Revelation. In the history of the church, the inclusivism of the Christian faith has always been balanced by separation from the world and conflict against the world. Christian faith is inclusive in its affirmation that God created all human beings in his image, that God graciously offers salvation to all people through the life, death, and resurrection of Jesus Christ. Christian practice at its best has always been influenced by a humility that recognizes the finite limitations of human judgments and the corruption of all human judgments by sin, as well as by respect for the privacy, freedom, and responsibility of each person as a child of God. Yet the inclusivism of the Christian community must always maintain the integrity of its own faith as well as the awareness that many human practices, as well as beliefs, are destructive of human life and of human community.

A fourth characteristic of contemporary society that puts the church at risk is mobility. Until the Second World War, mobility was very limited. There were mass migrations, but the overwhelming tendency was for persons to continue to live in the communities in which they were born. Hence they were surrounded not only by a community structure, but also by family, grandparents, uncles and aunts, and cousins. The structure of a community in which a family had lived for generations and the family itself gave to an individual his or her identity, which frequently included membership in the church. This traditional structure also supported certain particular patterns of life.

All of this has come to an end in the second half of the twentieth century. This century has seen the mass uprooting of people, tremendous waves of migration and immigration, and the disruption of stable patterns of life generally. In a stable society, such as the United States, the ease of transportation and communication makes it possible for persons to move from one section of the country to another. The consequence is that young married couples, in particular, as well as single people, live at a distance from the support of the family or the traditional community. With this breakup of society, there has come the loss of the visible symbols of stability, namely, the family home, the family church, the family cemetery, as well as the identifying buildings and institutions of the community.

It was once argued that this new society was compatible with Christian faith because it enhanced human freedom. It is now apparent that while human freedom may have given to many persons an opportunity to develop their personal lives, it has loaded others with responsibilities for which they were ill-equipped.

The constant movement of people means that those on the move must continually reidentify themselves with local congregations. It also means that congregations have to assume new responsibilities for babies who were not baptized in their presence and for couples who were not married in their context.

A fifth factor in contemporary society that puts the church and tradition at risk is the pervasive influence of the mass media. The media contributed greatly to pluralism, presenting a great variety of life-styles, forms of worship, music as possible human options. For Christians, it brought into homes ways of living and believing that both undermined and contradicted the faith. Furthermore, television attracted Christians away from the programs of the church just as it undermined secular programs that depended on community meetings. Until now the churches have not found effective ways to make use of television. Television which "provides its audience with a sense that what it views is true and real far more than newspapers, radio, or the movies" greatly enhanced the power of the media to shape American life.[55]

Mobility combined with communication, especially television, helps produce what Richard Merelman calls a "loose bounded culture." The primordial ties to family, locality, church, and what is considered appropriate behavior eroded. Americans lost their sense of time and place. Merelman concludes:

> The contemporary weakness of the Puritan, democratic and class visions of America has released large numbers of Americans from

comprehensive group identifications and from firm social moorings. The liberated individual, not the social group, must therefore become the basic cultural unit. . . . Group membership . . . becomes voluntary, contingent and fluid, not "given," fixed, and rigid.[56]

A sixth factor that puts the church at risk is the scientific, technological character of society.[57] When divorced from faith in the Creator, a scientific culture becomes impersonal and without any final purpose. Moreover, contemporary technology makes it possible to invade the privacy which is necessary for personal existence and to control people in a way which undermines responsibility and freedom. It undermines the distinctive character of a person as one who hears the Word of God.

The listing of factors that put the church at risk must not obscure the fact that the church is at risk in all societies. Stable societies have also been the occasion for the decline of the church. The new developments in society can be opportunities. While external factors influence a community of faith positively and negatively, the crucial dimension, except in extraordinary situations, is found in the community of faith itself.

VI

How shall we respond to the crisis of the American churches with traditional roots in the Protestant Reformation?

Three responses are warranted by our own church tradition: (1) quiet confidence about the church as the people of God; (2) prayerful expectancy that the Holy Spirit will renew the church; (3) commitment to those activities for the building up of the church which have their warrant in the New Testament.

For the past several centuries, many commentators on human affairs have believed that religion would disappear. Some explained it away in terms of economics or how a person earns his or her living, or in terms of psychology, or in terms of historical development. It was expected that religion, no longer serving human needs, would disappear. There was considerable truth in the criticism. Insofar as religion existed to satisfy human needs that could be better met by human wisdom, religions have ceased

GOSHEN COLLEGE LIBRARY
GOSHEN, INDIANA

to exist. Harry Emerson Fosdick preached a famous sermon on the theme that science had not disproved religion, but made it unnecessary for many people. Whereas people who wanted good crops or babies or good fishing once prayed, they now use fertilizer or consult doctors or make use of scientific studies of fish life in the ocean.[58] The clear fact is that religion has not disappeared. There are good reasons why it has not.

The first is the theological conviction put so well by Augustine in the opening paragraph of the *Confessions:* "Thou hast made us for thyself and restless is our heart until it comes to rest in thee."[59]

Calvin likewise knew the arguments that religion had its origin in fraud or superstition, factors that in principle may be eliminated.[60] Yet Calvin was convinced that we know God with the immediacy that we know the world and our own selves.[61] God has created human beings with a sense of divinity, a seed of religion, and with a conscience which distinguishes right and wrong. Religion, for Calvin, belonged to the very structure of human existence, and the only options for human beings were faith in God or faith in idols.

Augustine and Calvin spoke out of theological convictions as well as out of observation. There is, however, abundant evidence today to confirm their theological convictions. First of all, religion continues to exist. Theodosius Dobzhansky, a biologist, quotes the observation of a distinguished historian, Crane Brinton, that religion is as much a part of life as sex.[62] As sex can be repressed, so can religion, but religion, like sex, always finds expression, sometimes in bizarre forms.

Daniel Bell, a sociologist, has concluded that religion is neither primitive nor fetish in origin. "Religion is not an ideology, or a regulative or integrative feature of society—though in its institutional forms, it has, at different times, functioned in this way. It is a constitutive aspect of human experience because it is a response to the existential predicaments which are the *ricorsi* of human culture." In addition, "religions, unlike technologies or social policies, cannot be manufactured or designed. They grow out of shared responses and shared experiences which one begins to endow with a sense of awe, expressed in some ritual form. Furthermore, religion is not of the moment. Religion returns to the past, seeks tradition, and searches for threads which give a person a set of ties that place them in the continuity of the dead and the living and those still to be born." Religion is a return to history, not to nature, and to the community of the living and the dead and those to be born, not to the self.[63]

These reflections of a sociologist are very similar to those of Augustine and Calvin, who, in addition to being theologians (indeed, because they were theologians), observed human nature and history and reflected upon it. Religion, as Augustine and Calvin knew, has its roots on the human level in the structure of human existence. Human beings are pressed by their own existence to find some coherent answer to the contradictions, the limits, the frustrations, and at the same time, the intimations of significance, of love, of value they know in everyday life. They must worship God or an idol. Religion has survived because it is rooted in human existence itself.

Karl Barth has emphasized that Christian faith rests not on human need that human observation may uncover but on the proclaiming of the gospel that awakens human needs which are not recognized by human reflection.[64] This is the reason Barth develops his doctrine of sin after he has reflected on the reconciliation brought by Jesus Christ. This qualification is implicit in Augustine and Calvin. It does not refute the conviction that God created human beings in the divine image. Barth insists that sin has obscured that image. For Barth as well as Augustine and Calvin, human existence is fully realized when human beings hear the Word of God.

The security of the church is not in the existential structure of human existence or in human work, but in the activity of God. The foundation of the church is "the secret election" of God. Calvin could write that "although the melancholy desolation which confronts us on every side may cry that no remnant of the church is left, let us know that Christ's death is fruitful, and that God miraculously keeps his church as in hiding places." The church "stands by God's election, and cannot waver or fail any more than his eternal promise can."[65] This conviction that the church is established by God should find expression in poise and dignity, but not in presumption. In the New Testament, those who presumed that they were children of Abraham were reminded that "God is able from . . . stones to raise up children to Abraham" (Matt. 3:9; Luke 3:8). Likewise, the promise does not mean that much of value in the church may not be lost. Presbyterianism, with its traditions and its way of being the Christian community, is not essential to the one holy catholic church, but its demise in American life today would impoverish the one holy catholic church as it would the nation and the culture.

The second response to the crisis is prayerful expectancy that the Holy Spirit, God in the power of the divine personhood, will mightily move the hearts of people enabling them to confess that Jesus is the Christ.

The church is finally not a human achievement but a gift for which we must wait. Hence the renewal of the church will come as we participate in the hearing, worshiping, believing people who are the church. In this sense, the first step toward the renewal of the church is participation in the communion of saints, in the worship of the church. In the book of Acts, the church was described in this way.

> So those who received his word were baptized, and there were added that day about three thousand souls. And they devoted themselves to the apostles' teaching and fellowship, to the breaking of bread and the prayers.
>
> And fear came upon every soul; and many wonders and signs were done through the apostles. And all who believed were together and had all things in common; and they sold their possessions and goods and distributed them to all, as any had need. And day by day, attending the temple together and breaking bread in their homes, they partook of food with glad and generous hearts, praising God and having favor with all the people. And the Lord added to their number day by day those who were being saved.
>
> Acts 2:41–47

Adding members to the church was integrally related to the life of the church as the communion of saints, as the worshiping, believing people of God. It is not likely that members will be added to the church in any other way today. Nor is it likely that the church's own interior life will be renewed except as the church gathers for worship.

John Calvin, in his epistle to Charles V, declared that the reformation of the church is God's work, and as much dependent on God as the raising of the dead.[66] The church as the people of God cannot be programmed or planned. It comes first of all as God's gracious gift. Yet Calvin, as did the Christians of the New Testament, concentrated all his energies in doing the work of the church. In this sense as in so many others, the church is 100 percent the human work of those who on earth are its members, but in a profound sense, it is entirely the work of God.

Christians can respond to the crisis of the church today in a third way by engaging in those works and activities for the upbuilding of the church which have warrant in the New Testament and which have been fruitful in the tradition.

The growth of the church cannot be described in precise ways and much less can it be quantified. The descriptions and the numbers must always be tentative and approximate. Church growth is growth in the communion of saints. The communion of saints is "a theological and confessional fellowship. It is a fellowship of thankfulness and thanksgiving." It is a fellowship of prayer, it is a fellowship of penitence leading to conversion.

> It takes place, in relationship to the world, as the fellowship of the need of those who are moved by the burdens of the world, and the promise given to it, as their own inmost concern; yet also, in this relationship, as the fellowship in arms of those who are determined, in order to be true to the world and meaningfully to address themselves to it, not in any sense to be conformed to the world. It takes place as the fellowship of service in which the saints assist and support one another, and in which they have also actively to attest to those outside what is the will of the One who has taken them apart and sanctified them. . . . It takes place as the fellowship of their proclamation of the Gospel, of the Word by which they are gathered and impelled and maintained. For this reason, and because it takes place as a fellowship of prayer, it takes place as the fellowship of divine service—a liturgical fellowship. And in and above all these things it takes place as the fellowship of worship, of the silent or vocal adoration and praise of Almighty God.[67]

The numerical growth of the church which can be reported in statistical tables cannot be separated from the upbuilding of the church as the communion of saints, which cannot be so precisely identified.

The human works that contribute to the upbuilding of the church are works that are done out of the community of faith, both for the community of faith itself and for the world.

The works that will enhance the church are always done out of the life of the church. This appears at first to be very simple, and yet it is not simple in a society in which church and world are so intermingled. The proper Christian dialogue is from the church to the world, not from the world to the church. This becomes a problem when the boundary between church and world becomes indistinct. For those within the church may and do speak as the world even within the organized church. The church is critically at risk when it does not recognize that those within the church frequently speak from the traditions and perspectives of the world.

The importance of this principle is illustrated theologically. Christians who speak from faith can make use of philosophical wisdom, as well as theological studies, to enlarge and strengthen faith. Even the so-called arguments for the existence of God can serve faith. Yet few if any persons ever move from philosophy, from theology, or from rational arguments for the existence of God to faith, particularly faith in the living God.

Christians who believe can make use of historical studies of the Bible to come to a deeper understanding of their own faith and to an enhancement of the Christian community. Yet few if any persons ever move from critical studies to faith. No historian or theologian can ever justify the Christian conviction that Jesus Christ is the Word of God incarnate. No historian or theologian can ever establish that the Bible is the Word of God. Whether or not we are confronted by Jesus Christ as the living God and whether or not we experience the Bible as God's Word to us is dependent upon the community of worship and faith in which we live, not upon classes which we may take in a university.

The integrity and indeed the life of the church are also destroyed when the politically committed on the right *and* left use the church for their party or cause. A Christian may constructively move from faith to political and social activity, but few, if any, ever move from political activity to faith. They may bring their own political and social allegiances under the judgment of the transcendent God. The best servants of the state, as Eustace

Percy once declared, have as their first allegiance God, not the state.[68]

Evangelism likewise illustrates the significance of the Christian community as the matrix of those activities which enhance the growth of the church. Evangelism is not an activity that has its source in organizations or in task forces or in techniques, even though all of these may contribute to its success. It is not a discrete, separate activity of the church. Evangelism is simply the reality of the church. To be evangelistic and to be the church is identical.[69]

Evangelism in any historic meaning of the word is proclaiming the gospel out of faith and inviting all people to participate in the community of faith, to place themselves in the context of the means of grace. Until there is within the community of faith the desire to proclaim the faith, and until there is within the community of faith the conviction that it is God's will that all persons participate in this community of faith, evangelistic effort is futile.

The upbuilding and the growth of the church depend on the church's being simply what it says it is, the people of God, and in carrying on those activities by which the church lives and for which all Christians are responsible, namely, preaching, teaching, the sacraments, and pastoral care.

When the church is the church, it grows. There is substantial evidence for this in church history. David Barrett, the editor of the *World Christian Encyclopedia,* estimates that in A.D. 500, 22 percent of the world population was Christian, in A.D. 1000, 18.7 percent; in A.D. 1500, 19 percent; and in A.D. 1900, 34.4 percent. In this century a slight decline has been reversed and in A.D. 2000 the percentage of Christians will be about as it was in 1900.[70] Here again Karl Barth has a pertinent comment.

> The communion of saints shows itself to be fruitful in the mere fact that as it exists it enlarges its own circle and constituency in the world. It produces new saints by those whose entry it has been enlarged and increased. Of course, we are not told, even by the parable of the seed, that it will become constantly greater in this way so that all living men may eventually become Christians. What we are told is that it has the supreme power to extend in this way, that it does not stand therefore under serious threat of dimi-

nution, and that as a subject which grows by definition, it has an astonishing capacity even for numerical increase. It is not self-evident that this should be the case; that it should have this capacity; that there should always be Christians raised up like stones to be Abraham's children. The more clearly we see the human frailty of the saints in their fellowship as it is palpable both at the very outside and in every effort, the more astonishing we shall find it that from the very first and right up to our own time it has continually renewed itself in the existence of men who have been reached by its feeble witness and have become Christians in consequence. . . . It does not matter whether the growth has been big or little. The fact remains that it has continually grown. And it still grows. It has the power to do so.[71]

The church has always grown. In some sense, 34 percent of the world's population is affiliated with the Christian community. Church growth is no inconsiderable fact, either in history or at the present time. This growth is subject to critical judgments, and the church must always ask if it is adding saints to saints or if it is only adding numbers to numbers. Yet the inescapable historical fact is that the church has always grown out of its own life as the people of God.

The Christian church, as a religion, is a human phenomenon and is the subject of study. The recent decline of the mainline churches and the public impact of television ministries have attracted the attention of sociologists, psychologists, historians in secular universities, and elicited numerous foundation grants for the study of the phenomena.

These studies, both inside and outside the church, provide much useful information, even though church statistics are very imprecise and not clearly defined.[72] It is good to know, for example, that there may be a connection between government expenditures and church participation, or that generations, for example, the '60s, may leave their mark on the church.[73] The data about young people, about the ratio of men and women, young and old, have their value. We need to know whether those who leave mainline churches simply disappear into the society or become members of other churches. Yet the methodological procedures and the stance of an observer preclude the possibility of any definitive understanding of the worshiping, believing community, either of its vitality or of its problems. The diagnosis and the cure for the traumas must come today, as they have in every previous crisis, from within the church.

The children of light should be as wise as the children of darkness. Hence in the church it is well to know the wisdom of the world and to be aware of what external observers think of the church. The human situation does make people more or less open to Christian faith. The social resources of the community either undergird or undermine the faith. Any discussion of the church as a community and of preaching, teaching, and pastoral care must take into account these factors. Yet all the wisdom that may come to us from observers and all the skills that we may acquire from management, communication, and therapy are secondary. The church is not just a religious community, much less a political community or an ethical society. The Christian church was brought into being by the life, death, and resurrection of Jesus Christ and the giving of the Holy Spirit. It lives on the human level by the conviction that Jesus Christ is the Word made flesh, God in his self-expression. The honest renewal of this confession is the beginning of the renewal of the church, the community that lives by hearing the Word of God in Jesus Christ as attested in scriptures. This hearing and receiving of the Word constitutes the church. In this the church differs from all other religious, ethical, and social communities.

The mission of the church grows out of the reality of the community of faith, the priesthood of believers. It expresses itself in preaching, teaching, pastoral care, and witnessing to Jesus Christ.

William Temple, in assessing the Christian witness in a secular world, declared that

> it must be active in two distinct ways. It must at all costs maintain its own spiritual life, the fellowship which this life creates, and the proclamation of the Gospel in all its fullness, wherein this life expresses itself. Here it must insist on all those truths from which its distinctive quality is derived.[74]

We have an increasing tendency today to complicate unduly the life and mission of the church. We invent or adopt from the secular order new jargons; we have endless study groups and task forces; we adopt the management style and the processes of the secular society in our frantic effort to reorganize the church. Nothing much seems to happen. The simple answer is that the foundation of the church's growth is not in the wisdom of the world, but in the study of the Bible, learning the theology of the church, and above all, engaging in the tasks of preaching, teaching, pastoral care, and in the concrete diaconal ministry of confession. Evangelism is not so complex as some would make it. It is preaching and teaching the gospel, visiting people, and bringing them into the context of the means of grace.

Calvin understood the Reformation of the church as the evangelization of the church. By the evangelization of the church Calvin meant the simplification of the church from all theatrical trifles so that the gospel could be communicated in sermon and sacrament, but also in the whole life of the community. Out of the evangelization of the church the faith has been handed on in preaching, teaching, and pastoral care. The renewal of the church begins not with getting organized or in establishing a program, but in the words of the risen Christ: "Receive the Holy Spirit," or with the question Jesus put to his disciples then and now, "But who do you say that I am?"

CHAPTER TWO

The Church and the Ministry

The first thesis of the Bern disputation (1528) that established the Protestant Reformation in Switzerland defined the church. "The holy Christian Church, whose only Head is Christ, is born of the Word of God, and abides in the same, and listens not to the voice of a stranger."[1] Protestantism began not simply with the question, How can I find the gracious God, or how can I discover meaning in life, but also with the question, Where can I find the true church? What is the essence of the church? How is the church as the people of God distinguished from false churches which listen to alien shepherds?[2] The later battles which Reformed Protestantism would fight over the question of polity reflect this concern. Yet questions about polity, or about the boundaries of the church, were always secondary to questions about the essence of the church. On the basic definition of the church, Reformed Protestants were clear from the beginning. The church is constituted by hearing the gracious Word of God. The church is the people of God.

Protestants in general and Reformed Protestants in particular were also clear about the definition of a minister. No Protestant ever understood the ministry to be essential to the existence of the church, however important the ministry may be to the well-being of the church. The only essential for the church is the Word of God. Wherever the Word of God is heard in faith and obeyed in love, there is the church. Or, as earlier Christians would say, where the Spirit of God is, there is the church. Yet within the church, the minister performs functions that are of decisive significance for the church's well-being. Hence clarity about the nature of the ministry is crucial for the renewal of the church and for the vitality of Protestant communities.

Reformed Christians have always emphasized that the polity and the ministry are subordinate to the gospel, and must serve the gospel. Furthermore, polity and the ministry are likewise subordinate to the existential reality, or to the essence of the church as the people of God. The polity and the ministry under God serve the people. The people do not serve the polity or the ministry.

Practical considerations, as well as historical precedents and theological considerations, indicate that the renewal of the church today must begin with a clearer understanding as to what the church is and what is the task and mission of the minister.

A striking fact about the church in our time is the obvious decline and the obvious growth of churches, both congregations and denominations, existing side by side in the same communities. Why is it that some congregations experience all the signs of Christian growth and renewal in contemporary American society and others do not? Why, for example, are some downtown Presbyterian churches stronger today in quantifiable terms than they have ever been in their history, while other downtown churches have difficulty maintaining their existence? Why is it that Presbyterian churches, which have traditionally emphasized the life of the mind in the service of God and an intellectual ministry, have been so ineffective in a society in which there are so many colleges and universities, so many college graduates?

There are significant data that indicate that changing conceptions of the church and of the ministry have been influential in the decline of mainline Protestant denominations.[3] Hence in any study of the transmission of the faith consideration has to be given to the formative understandings of the church and the ministry in Reformed churches and the relationship of that understanding to church practice today.

Demographic, economic, cultural, political, and generational factors have always influenced the growth, decline, and character of church life. A "scientific" culture can explain church growth or decline without remainder in these terms. The church, however, has always lived by the conviction that these quantifiable characteristics are the outward signs of the deeper reality of faith. The church needs the wisdom of the world but it cannot live by it. The church lives by hearing the Word of God.

The churches that are growing today, as the churches of the Reformation, are clear as to the identity of the church and the minister. They did not and they do not confuse the church with a civic club, a social agency, or a political party; or the minister with a political advocate, a therapist, or an executive. The Protestants knew the church was the priesthood of believers, the people of God, and the minister was called by God to preach and teach the gospel and to exercise pastoral care. It is not likely that churches which have experienced decline today will grow and become alive again without this clarity.

I

The Reformation was one of the greatest revivals in history of Christian faith and of the church. Roland Bainton concluded that it made religion once again the primary concern of common people, humanists, artists, merchants, and powerful political figures.[4] Three recent studies increase our understanding of the Reformation of the sixteenth century and throw light on our situation today.

The French historian Lucien Febvre discounted the explanations of the Reformation in terms of ecclesiastical institutions and political factors.[5] He also discounted the role of the theologian. Febvre especially objected to those who interpreted the Reformation in terms of the decline of the church or as a reaction to church abuses. Neither does he explain the Reformation in terms of economics, psychology, politics, and demographic changes, as important as these factors may be. The Reformation, Febvre insisted, had its origin in the spiritual aspirations of people. It developed out of the bruised spirits and wounded consciences as well as out of the oppression of the laity by the clergy. Steven Ozment concurs with Febvre, "The essential condition of the Reformation's success was aggrieved hearts and minds; a perceived need for reform and determination to grasp it are the only things without which it can be said categorically there would have been no Reformation."[6]

Febvre made two judgments about the Reformation that are particularly relevant to our concerns today.

The first judgment is that the Reformation was a response to deeply felt human needs. "The essential feature of the Reformation is that it was able to find a remedy for the disturbed consciences of a good number of Christians; it was able to propose to men, who seemed to have been waiting for it for years and who adopted it with a sort of haste and greed that is very revealing, a solution that really took account of their needs and spiritual conditions; yet offered the masses what they had anxiously been searching for: a simple, clear, and fully effective religion."[7] The reverse side of the wounded hearts of the people was the inability of the medieval church to mediate the grace of God to these bruised spirits and wounded hearts. It was out of this abyss that the Reformation was to arise. Whether we are speaking of the Lutheran, Zwinglian, or Catholic Reformation, two things were responsible for its success, two things it offered to men who were already thirsting for them in advance. One was the Bible in the vernacular, the other was justification through faith.

The second judgment of Febvre that has relevance for us is his emphasis upon the anticlerical character of the Reformation. "Anticlericalism was in fact so strong a desire on the part of the masses, so popular and so deep-seated, that several of its partisans, on finding that their leaders and their vanguard were not carrying it far enough, rose up against the faintheartedness of those same leaders and against the remains of that sacerdotalism which was still being maintained in public worship, with Luther foremost among the guilty ones."[8]

The words of Luther, "We are all priests, as many of us as are Christians,"[9] did away with the clerical structure of the medieval church. After the Reformation, the priests and the institutional church no longer controlled access to God. The laity heard the Word of God directly through the Bible, which they held in their hands and which they read. They prayed to God for themselves and were no longer obligated to buy services from the clergy.

The Reformation, Febvre observes, led to a new understanding of the church.

The church was no longer a place which, inhabited by the divinity, opened its doors at any hour and on any day to the individual believer who came to satisfy a personal need for prayer, or a place where the priests came to perform the sacrifice of the redeeming victim on the altar. As a result of a total revolution in habits and conceptions, it was the united mass of believers, the groups and not the individual that came to the Protestant chapel at a fixed hour on a fixed day, and it was nothing more than a meeting-house; it was the community that assembled there, constituting a cultural assembly, expressing aloud and directly, in the canticles, songs, and prayers which so deeply impressed themselves on Lefevre and Roussel at Strasbourg, this desire to reach God through the Word, without any consecrated priest to act as an intermediary. This was the last element in a logical, coherent system born out of the needs of an age that was developing fast, both socially and morally; all this and not a jot less lay behind the explicit words "la Bible en vulgaire" (the Bible in the vernacular).[10]

Febvre's judgments about the Reformation have been called in question by other historians,[11] but his basic affirmations are confirmed in the letters, the tracts, the *Institutes,* and the sermons of Calvin, as well as in the writings of Martin Luther and other Reformers. Luther and Calvin alike found that the basic human problem was theological, and they attempted to give a theological answer to that problem. They strenuously rejected every effort on the part of special interest groups and of the political structures to use the church. Calvin was exiled from Geneva for his insistence upon the independence of the church, and the Marxists have never forgiven Martin Luther his refusal to allow the theological cause to be identified with the peasants' movement. The Reformation was above all the evangelization of the church, the opening up of the life of the church so that the grace of God could heal the wounded spirits and the bruised hearts of human beings.

A second study of the Reformation, done by Professor Robert Kingdon, also throws light upon our situation today. Many contemporary studies of the Reformation have emphasized the importance of social factors such as the urbanization of life and social tensions between classes and social groups. Kingdon emphasized that the Reformation was "indeed a genuine social revolution, but that its main target was the Roman Catholic clergy, a highly privileged social elite. It was thus an anti-clerical revolution. I would further argue that the main social result of the Reformation was the creation of a new clerical class, an elite of a very different type."[12] Prior to the Reformation in Geneva there was a total of four hundred or more persons attached to the church, including members of religious orders, one hundred members of the cathedral staff in actual residence, and between one hundred and two hundred seculars, attached to seven parishes, and a number of chaplaincies and hospitals. If one adds the lay employees of the church, the total comes to one thousand. This number was radically reduced by the Protestant revolution. During Calvin's lifetime, the Protestant ministers in Geneva varied from nine to twenty-two.[13] In this sense, the Reformation was a revolt against the bureaucratization of the church, and in particular against a church structure and bureaucracy that lived oppressively off of the offerings and the fees that were collected from the people.

The third study that is useful in assessing our situation today is Jenny Wormald's *Court, Kirk, and Community: Scotland, 1470–1625.* Wormald's conclusions are cautious and well studied, running between the extremes of those who idealized the Reformation in Scotland and the highly critical comments of Gordon Donaldson, a historian with episcopal commitments. According to Wormald, the Reformation in Scotland provided not so much a new religion or even a purified church as it did a clear alternative. The church in Scotland was not dying, but the Reformation provided an alternative, which when vigorously presented was persuasive to Christian believers.

The church had neglected the local congregation for the sake of the religious institutions, the cathedrals, the monasteries, the collegiate churches, and the universities. The bulk of the revenue of the local parishes was appropriated not for the maintenance of the parish but for the maintenance of the church's institutions and organizations.[14]

The ministry of local parishes deteriorated under the impact of this emphasis. The priest of the local congregation had little prestige. The able people went to the institutions, the cathedrals, the universities. "The vicar to whom the religious institutions entrusted the parishes within their gift was likely to be the man who failed to make it to better things."[15] At the same time, there was an increasing literacy among the laity.

The poor priests in the local church worked always under the temptation to relieve this poverty by charging fees for services, "Na penny, na paternoster."[16] The exploitation of church services to relieve the poverty of the priests may be understandable, but it had devastating consequences in the life of the parish. The great tragedy is that this corruption of the priesthood occurred when there were adequate resources to provide care for local congregations. Leadership in monasteries, cathedrals, and schools was no substitute for lack of quality in the local church.

Wormald understands the Reformation as a vision of a new alternative. This alternative included the Bible in the vernacular. An act of the Scottish Parliament in 1543 made it lawful to read the Bible in English or Scots. This was rightly regarded as a notable triumph.

> The clerical estate in Parliament formally dissociated themselves from the act; Knox produced a wonderful passage extolling the act as "no small victory of Christ Jesus . . . no small comfort to such as were held in bondage. . . . Then might have been seen the Bible lying almost upon every gentleman's table. The New Testament was borne about in many men's hands . . . thereby did the knowledge of God wondrously increase, and God give his Holy Spirit to simple men in great abundance."[17]

Wormald concluded that the church lost out as a teacher of doctrine because the laity could read the Bible. A similar judgment was made by G. R. Elton, "If there is a single thread running through the whole story of the Reformation, it is the explosive and renovating and often disintegrating effect of the Bible, put into the hands of the commonality and interpreted no longer by the well-conditioned learned, but by faith and delusion, the common sense and the uncommon nonsense of all sorts of men. One country after another was to receive its vernacular Bible in this century and with it a new standard of its language."[18] Wormald goes on to comment that Alexander Scott summed up in brilliantly simple lines the horror of all of this for ecclesiastical authorities:

For limmer lads and little lassis, lo,
will argue baith with bishop, priest, and freir.[19]

The Reformation also provided a confession that power-fully expressed the faith.

> The Scottish Confession is an immensely moving and impressive document, not least because it is entirely positive. . . . It was never sidetracked from its basic purpose, to explain, in clear and unclut-tered language, basic beliefs. It set out its vision of the kirk, both the invisible community of all believers, "Catholik" because it contained the "elect of all ages, realms, nations, tongues, Jews and Gentiles," and the particular kirks now on this earth.[20]

Finally, the Reformation provided a new understanding of the church and of the ministry. "Language was consciously changed, 'parish' gave way to 'kirk' or 'congregation.' "[21] This new alternative for the church included a radical rejection of hier-archy.

> This was a new church, not a revised version of the old. It did have a strong sense of continuity with the past—the past of the early church (though not the Celtic church of legend). But it was a complete break with the immediate past in its distaste for hierar-chy, both in the original Greek sense of priest-rule, and in the more familiar connotation of acknowledged and unchanging sta-tus. Its initial three-fold order of ministers, bishops or preachers, elders, and deacons or distributors, and the later four-fold order including doctors, which was derived from Calvin, and also from Bucer and Bullinger, was in no sense hierarchical, for all were exercising a ministry, and all were answerable to the courts of the church. In practice, no society has ever succeeded in eradicating hierarchy, and the kirk was no exception. Nevertheless, the prin-ciple of parity was followed as far as possible, within the ranks of the kirk itself. No matter how much any individual minister be-came top dog in his congregation, he was not proof against the assembly's regular castigations of the ministry for lack of zeal.[22]

The new conception of the church called for a new concep-tion of the ministry. The ministry was now consciously under-stood as a calling rather than as a living. Its competence and its integrity were to be appropriate to the tasks of preaching, teach-ing, and pastoral care. "From the beginning, there was to be no compromise over the ministry. If no suitable candidates offered themselves as ministers or superintendents, then rather than have men incapable of preaching the Word, there would be no appointment." Wormald goes on to observe that "it was doctrine and preaching of the Word that gave the church its real unity"[23]; hence the great concern about a ministry with the personal and intellectual discipline competent to perform these tasks.

The social and historical factors in Geneva, France, and Scotland as well as theological commitments led Protestants in these countries to speak and to act in a different idiom from the Lutherans. Yet these three studies, with all their Reformed characteristics, are in harmony with the great Lutheran writings of 1520. They tell us very much about what was at the heart of the renewal of the church in the sixteenth century, and can thereby illuminate the renewal of the church in our time.

II

The importance of the task of the minister in the church has always been emphasized, but by no one more so than by Reformed Christians in general and John Calvin in particular. The function of the minister, but not the status of the minister, is necessary for the church's existence. The cruciality of the minister's task made the personal and theological qualifications of the minister of the highest importance. Reformed churches have maintained this emphasis upon a qualified ministry, albeit with corruptions, for four centuries. For much of this time, the Presbyterian minister was frequently the best trained and most highly qualified person in the community. Today, this emphasis upon the personal strength and the theological competence of the ministry is greatly at risk.

Neither William Farel (1489–1565) nor John Calvin (1509–1564) was a priest. There is no record of their ordination to the ministry. Alexandre Ganoczy has concluded that the memory of his baptism was enough to make Calvin fully a man of the church. His authority was in the prophetic call "to reestablish the faith by returning to the sources." He endeavored to integrate the call into the pastoral office, taking into account the priesthood of believers.[24] As a general rule for established churches

Calvin provided for a rite of ordination. Later Calvinists maintained that in emergencies the call of the people was sufficient. Calvin's correspondence with Du Tillet suggests that Calvin was also of this opinion.

The gospel, the message, is the crucial factor in the life of the church. The office and even the character of the minister are, in relation to the integrity of the message, of secondary importance. In the Donatist controversy, Augustine and the church generally declared that the holiness of the church resides neither in the people nor in the minister but in the Holy Spirit working through the appointed means of grace. The life of the minister on the human level adds credibility to the gospel. No one wanted to say this more vigorously than the Calvinists. Yet even they always knew, no doubt with less enthusiasm than Luther, that the most important human condition is that the minister must be a competent, faithful interpreter of scripture. The integrity of the gospel is more important than the holiness of the congregation or the minister. The Holy Spirit is not dependent on the broken and fragile character of minister or people.

The classic Reformed emphasis on the ministry is nowhere better illustrated than in the careful distinction that Calvin and later Reformed Christians made between the ministry as a calling and "a living" or "a benefice." Calvin specifically set the vocation of the pastor in contrast to "priestly living" and the "benefice." For Calvin, the pastorate is a calling, not a "living," a stewardship, not a benefice. Calvin knew that "it is fair and sanctioned also by the law of the Lord, that those who work for the church be supported at public expense; and some presbyters in that age also consecrating their inheritances to God made themselves voluntarily poor. . . . Yet provision was meanwhile made that the very ministers, who ought to give others an example of frugality, should not have so much as to abuse it to the point of luxury and indulgence, but only enough to meet their needs."[25]

The proper determination of the minister's compensation or life-style is not simple. First of all, there is no one clear line that distinguishes quantifiably between compensation which is appropriate to simple, frugal living, and compensation which makes ministers an elite and privileged group; between what is necessary to maintain the effectiveness of the work of a minister and what undermines the effectiveness of a minister's work. In addition, the question of a minister's manner of life is complicated by the basic incongruity between preaching the gospel, administering the sacraments, and exercising pastoral care and being paid to do so. Paul himself acknowledged something of this incongruity in that while he spoke of the entitlement of the minister to support, he himself earned his own living (2 Cor. 11:7–10). No contemporary person has expressed this difficulty better than Reinhold Niebuhr in 1924, when he recorded in his diary,

> The idea of a professionally good man is difficult enough for all of us who are professionally engaged as teachers of the moral ideal. Of course, "a man must live," and it is promised that if we seek first the kingdom and its righteousness, "all these things shall be added unto us." But I doubt whether Jesus had a $15,000 salary in mind. If the things that are added become too numerous, they distract your attention terribly. To try to keep your eye on the main purpose may only result in making you squint-eyed. I hope this new prophet won't begin his pastorate with a sermon on the text, "I count all things but loss."[26]

Protestants used to underscore the peculiar nature of the ministry by the refusal to accept payments, fees, or gifts for baptisms, for funerals, and for other pastoral services. The practice broke down on weddings, but traditionally the minister modified the acceptance of gifts for weddings by passing them on to his wife. Yet there were still ministers who considered weddings as a service of the church. All the services of the church were free and open for those who needed them. This was a basic Protestant principle.

The secularization of the church and the establishment of personnel policies on the corporate model make it very difficult to maintain this ancient Protestant understanding of the minister. "Negotiating" and "contracting" are written into the very process of the call today. Personal information forms, imposed on ministers by the system, lead to self-advertising and to the soliciting of positions very much as in the secular world. As recently as three decades ago, the open solicitation of a call to a church or a position on a seminary faculty would have been sufficient to have disqualified a person. Likewise, active campaigning to be Moderator of the General Assembly was regarded as obscene. While these developments have been taking place, presbyteries more and more come to resemble labor unions, not only establishing standards for salary and other compensation between pastors and churches, but even setting fees for the preaching of a sermon. All these changes and practices have led to a vision of the church as a corporation which has jobs to which persons are entitled, often without too much regard to ability or performance.

Calvinists have always known there must be checks and balances in all human activities. Congregations and governing bodies are made up of sinners. Hence there is need for policies protecting ministers and others who work for the church. Ministers are also sinners as well as human beings with limitations of finiteness. Therefore the protection of the minister must be balanced by checks on competence, performance, and effectiveness of leadership. In recent decades church councils have placed more emphasis on protection than performance.

The church must be organized, since we live in a very physical world and are not angels. No one ought to underestimate the difficulties of organizing the church, especially in the light of the essential nature of the church and the ministry. Yet it seems clear enough that the church in the last thirty years has been unduly secularized in its organization, and that this has had devastating consequences for the ministry.

Writing in 1948, Daniel Jenkins, a British Congregational minister, declared:

> Thus it is clear from scripture that the ministry of the church is, like that of its Lord, in the form of a servant, and that it loses its meaning whenever that is forgotten. "The authority within this community is based solely on service. When Paul calls himself, servant of Christ, he already makes a secondary derivation of the original conception of the diaconate. The disciples of Jesus are to be servants and bondsmen to one another and servants and bondsmen of mankind." . . . The ministry of the apostles is never conceived of as a thing in itself, but always in dependence upon, and as an expression of, the ministry of Jesus Christ.[27]

The minister, as Calvin described himself, is minister or servant of the Word. The crucial virtue for a minister is faithfulness to the Word of God.

The ministry of the Word and sacraments is not a job by which we support ourselves, at least in its basic thrust, but a calling to proclaim the gospel, to build up the church and the communion of saints. In this sense the ministry is different from the calling of a lawyer who has clients or a medical doctor who has patients. The ministry of Word and sacraments must be clearly distinguished from a staff position in a business or government.

The ministry's call is not to ministry in general, but to be a pastor. The ministry of the Word and sacraments must be carefully distinguished from the Christian ministry, to which all Christian people are ordained by their baptism.[28] In baptism, every Christian is commissioned to be a witness to the faith and to do deeds of love and mercy.

The calling to be a minister of the Word and sacraments is not a calling to the Christian life. It presupposes this. The ministry is a calling to perform certain functions of critical significance in the life of the Christian community. A call to be a minister in the Reformed tradition was a call to preach the gospel, to teach the faith, to administer the sacraments, and to exercise pastoral care in the context of the faith.

The early Reformers, Calvin in particular, endeavored to simplify the call to the ministry. The calling to be a pastor is quite specific, namely, to be a pastor of a particular congregation, or to work as a missionary in establishing new congregations. Calvin quotes with approval the action of the Council of Chalcedon when it decreed that there should be no ordinations free of pastoral obligations, that is, a place to be assigned to the person ordained where he is to exercise his office. "This decree is very valuable for two reasons. First, that the church may not be burdened with needless expense, and spend upon idle men what ought to be distributed to the poor. Secondly, that those ordained are not to think themselves promoted to an honor but charged with an office which they are with solemn attestation obligated to discharge." Calvin and other Protestants sought to reform the church by insisting that the pastor, including his family, live in the midst of the congregation. He rejected pluralities which provided responsibilities with compensation but divided the pastor's attention.[29] Thomas Cartwright put it this way: "Every church officer [minister] ought to execute the office committed unto him with all faithful diligence, and consequently to be continually resident upon his charge."[30] Richard Baxter would later insist, "When we are commanded to take heed to all the flock, it is plainly implied, that flocks ordinarily be no greater than we are capable of overseeing, or 'taking heed to.' "[31] Furthermore, pastors were expected in the early Reformed churches to give their undivided attention to the work of the ministry and not to be engaged in other activities. The ministry is too important to be distracted by other work. The Church of Scotland found it even "repugnant" for a minister to have a special responsibility in Parliament.[32]

The chief task of the minister as Calvin and Protestants generally understood was preaching the Word of God. The Genevan Confession of 1537 declared:

> We recognize no other pastors in the Church than faithful pastors of the Word of God, feeding the sheep of Jesus Christ on the one hand, with instruction, admonition, consolation, exaltation, deprecation; and on the other resisting all false doctrines and deceptions of the devil, without mixing with the pure doctrine of Scripture their dreams or their foolish imaginings. To these we accord no other power or authority but to conduct, rule, and govern the people of God committed to them by the same Word, in which they have power to command, defend, promise, and warn and without which they neither can nor ought to attempt anything.[33]

A little over a hundred years later the Westminster Larger Catechism would speak of the minister in similar words.

> Q. 158. By whom is the word of God to be preached?
> A. The word of God is to be preached only by such as are sufficiently gifted, and also duly approved and called to that office.
> Q. 159. How is the word of God to be preached by those that are called thereunto?
> A. They that are called to labor in the ministry of the word are to preach sound doctrine, diligently, in season, and out of season; plainly, not in the enticing word of man's wisdom, but in demonstration of the Spirit, and of power, faithfully, making known the

whole counsel of God; wisely, applying themselves to the necessities and capacities of the hearers; zealously, with fervent love to God, and the souls of his people; sincerely, aiming at his glory, and their conversion, edification, and salvation.

The Protestants of the sixteenth and seventeenth centuries emphasized the importance of preaching more than any other church function. The minister has no special power. Ordination does not give status or honor, but rather the responsibility above all to preach. The validity of what a minister does on the human level is guaranteed not by ordination but by competence to interpret and apply the Word of God. Lacking this competence, ordination has no validity.[34]

This great emphasis on preaching never diminished the responsibility of the minister to teach. The minister is always a teacher, even in preaching.[35] Pastoral work also, for Calvin and for the Reformed generally, was the minister's particular responsibility, along with the session or the consistory.[36] But for the Reformed of the sixteenth century, teaching and pastoral care were justified by preaching and determined by it.

Reformed Protestantism—the great Reformers of the sixteenth century, the Puritan movement of the seventeenth century, the great church theologians, church leaders, and revivalists of the nineteenth century—has always been convinced that (1) ministers are called to a stewardship, not to a living, and (2) the task of the minister is to preach the gospel, to teach the faith, and to exercise pastoral care in the light of the faith.

The ministry is a high calling beyond the strength and goodness of any human being. The calling to the ministry and justification by grace through faith must be held together. In the ministry as in every area of life, we live by the grace of God. In affirming justification by grace through faith all ministers must remember that the ministry belongs also to their sanctification. In the ministry as in life, "cheap grace" is a threat to human integrity. The awareness of the call to the ministry entails the minister's highest effort, however fragmented and flawed that effort may be.

The flawed and fragmented character of every ministry must not obscure the impressive and heroic achievements. There have been ministers in every age who embodied in their own calling the words of Martin Luther's great hymn.

> Let goods and kindred go,
> This mortal life also;
> The body they may kill:
> God's truth abideth still;
> His kingdom is forever.

In the words of Milton, good ministers have known in every time and place the call "to scorn delights and live laborious days" for the gathering and upbuilding of the church. Most of the institutions, the local congregations, and programs of the church that enrich our lives today have been bequeathed to us from the past. They are for the most part the consequence of the work of those who often without the security of a job, yet had a vision of what by the grace of God was possible. They went out on their own without the guarantees that are commonplace today. In a highly organized and security-conscious society, all ministers should have as a part of their memory the great achievements of those who traveled the American frontier for no greater reason than their conviction that God had called them to establish churches and to build congregations. Task forces, committees, funds for plane travel and hotel meetings, elaborately devised processes and structures, are no substitute for the sense of call and the willingness to commit life's energies to the fulfillment of that call in the gathering of congregations and in the building up of the communion of saints.[37]

III

The Reformation began not only with a new conception of the ministry but also with another understanding of the church. Martin Luther exclaimed that the curia is not the church.

> The Creed calls the holy Christian church a *communio sanctorum,* "a communion of saints." . . . The word *ecclesia* properly means an assembly. We, however, are accustomed to the term *Kirche,* "church," by which simple folk understand not a group of people but a consecrated house or building. But the house should not be called a church except for the single reason that the group of peo-

ple assembles there. For we who assemble select a special place and give the house its name by virtue of the assembly. Thus the word "church" (*Kirche*) really means nothing else than a common assembly; it is not of German but of Greek origin, like the word *ecclesia*. In that language the word is *kyria*, and in Latin *curia*. In our mother tongue therefore it ought to be called "a Christian congregation or assembly," or best and most clearly of all, "a holy Christian people." . . .

This is the sum and substance of this phrase: I believe that there is on earth a little holy flock or community of pure saints under one head, Christ. It is called together by the Holy Spirit in one faith, mind, and understanding. It possesses a variety of gifts, yet is united in love without sect or schism. Of this community I also am a part and member, a participant and co-partner in all the blessings it possesses. I was brought to it by the Holy Spirit and incorporated into it through the fact that I have heard and still hear God's Word, which is the first step in entering it. Before we had advanced this far, we were entirely of the devil; knowing nothing of God and of Christ. Until the last day the Holy Spirit remains with the holy community or Christian people. Through it he gathers us, using it to teach and preach the Word. By it he creates and increases sanctification, causing it daily to grow and become strong in the faith and in the fruits of the Spirit.[38]

The church is not the priesthood, not the curia, but the people. It is certainly not the building. The Puritans did not like to call the building a church, but rather the meetinghouse, the place where the church gathers.[39] The doctrine of the priesthood of all believers did away with the distinction of priest and people, clergy and people. The whole church is the clergy, the inheritants of the Lord (1 Peter 5:3). Calvin wished that those who were ministers were called by another title than clergy to indicate not a different status but a specific function to which they were called by the congregation.[40]

No one put this as clearly as Luther. Every Christian believer is a priest who answers for himself or herself in the presence of God. Each person can confess sins directly to God, and each Christian can hear a neighbor's confession and proclaim the promise of forgiveness. As Luther put it, "every man must believe for himself, because sooner or later every man dies by himself."[41] There is nothing a Protestant minister can do for a dying person which that person cannot do for himself or for herself, or that another Christian may not do in Christian ministry. Hence the priesthood is a responsibility as well as a privilege. The conviction that the Word of God, the gospel alone, is necessary for the existence of the church casts doubt on any church order that claims to be more than a human establishment.

Luther was subject to the criticism that his emphasis upon the priesthood of believers turned the church into an aggregation of individuals rather than a community. Luther, however, insisted that the Christian must be a Christ to the neighbor.[42] By this he meant that as God in Christ loves us, so we must love our neighbor. He also meant something more. As God in Christ has borne our sins, so we must bear our neighbor's sin. No Christian can be a spectator to the moral tragedy of another. To be a priest is to bear the neighbor's burdens and the neighbor's guilt.

Calvin does not emphasize the priesthood of believers as Luther did. The phrase seldom occurs in his writings.[43] The task of upbuilding the church in Calvin's day required ministers of competence, and it also required respect for the dignity and significance of their work. His pressing task was the maintenance of the ministry, and in doing so he sometimes made claims for the ministry which were extravagant. The ministry was a function, not a status, but it was also God's gift to the church.

Yet the awareness that the church is the people, not the ministry, not the organization, persisted. It was maintained in Puritanism and in the congregational polities of the Congregationalists and the Baptists. It reasserted itself in the church renewals which have invigorated the church from the seventeenth century to the twentieth. A recent study of Scotch-Irish piety and the Great Awakening, 1625–1760, was entitled *The Triumph of the Laity*.[44] The conditions of American life up through the nineteenth century enhanced the role of the laity in local congregations. Nathan Hatch has recently observed that the strength of the Christian community in America is due to this democratic character.

> What then is the driving force behind American Christianity if it is not the quality of its organization, the status of its clergy, or the power of its intellectual life? I would suggest that a central dy-

namic has been its democratic orientation. In America the principal mediator of God's voice has not been state, church, council, confession, ethnic group, university, college, or seminary; it has been, quite simply, the people. American Christianity, particularly its evangelical varieties, has not been something held aloof from the rank and file, a faith to be appropriated on someone else's terms. Instead, the evangelical instinct for two centuries has been to pursue people wherever they could be found, to embrace them without regard to social standing, to challenge them to think, interpret Scripture, and organize the church for themselves, and to endow their lives with the ultimate meaning of knowing Christ personally, being filled with the Spirit, and knowing with assurance the reality of eternal life. These democratic yearnings are among the oldest and deepest impulses in American religious life. Given this fact, what is surprising is not the continued dynamism of evangelical Christianity in this century. What is surprising is that analysts of religion and culture have paid so little attention to its democratic foundations and thus too readily assumed its demise.[45]

The churches which are growing are churches of the people.

The church as the priesthood of all believers has been put at risk by at least five developments.

First, the church is at risk because of the priorities of church life. According to the tradition, the first priority in the human activity of the church are those actions by which the church lives: namely, the hearing and receiving of the Word of God. This is the activity in which the church originates and by which its existence is maintained. It comes to a focus in the worship of the congregation but it includes the church school, pastoral care, and special activities with youth, women, men. Today the emphasis is not on the church's hearing the Word of God but on what the church does or its mission to the world.

Many of the slogans which have become current in the contemporary church mislead the church, such as "The church is mission," or "The church lives by mission as fire lives by burning," or that the church must be concerned not for itself, but for the world.[46] These slogans, which mesh with the ideologies of the time, are only partially true. They assume that there is a church to live by mission, or a fire to live by burning. They also assume that preaching, teaching, and pastoral care are self-centered actions, or that they are safe and secure and so we do not have to worry about them. They define the church as a religious society or a therapy center or an agency for social change.

The functions by which the church lives direct our attention, not to the self or to the society, but to God. John Calvin insisted that the salvation of the soul is not the chief end of human existence.[47] The salvation of the world, or even the survival of the world from a nuclear holocaust, as horrible as it might be, is not the chief end of the church's existence. That shrewd agnostic, Sidney Hook, was a good Calvinist when he declared that those who make the survival of human life the chief end of life are declaring there is not anything they would not do to survive.[48] As Calvin put it, and as the Westminster Shorter Catechism Question 1 reaffirmed, the chief end of human life is to glorify God and to enjoy him forever.

The church today must ask if it is giving priority to those works by which, on the human level, it lives. There are many additional activities that strengthen the life of the church and indeed strengthen any human organization. But the church must first ask not about management, not about the strategies of human wisdom, as important as they may be, but about those activities by which, according to its faith, it lives.

Second, the priority of the church as the priesthood of believers is also endangered by the church's absorption in so many good activities, such as social witness, which are derivative from the faith by which the church lives. Christian faith that is not concerned with justice is fraudulent, but a faith that is primarily concerned with justice is dead.[49]

Much of the leadership of the church today came to consciousness when faith, the church, the Christian way of life could be taken for granted. What may have been at risk in 1950 was the church's relevance to some critical social issues. Today the reverse is true. The social witness of the church is not so much at risk as those human activities by which the church lives.

Third, the priesthood of all believers is also put at risk by the increasingly coercive role of the *Book of Order*.[50] In the late 1960s voices were raised in advocacy of strict construction of the *Book of Order*, but loose construction of the creed.[51] This to my knowledge was the first time in the history of Protestantism for any such idea to have been voiced as a serious opinion. In actual fact, American Presbyterianism existed for more than a century, one third of its history, without a *Book of Order*.

The burning of the canon law was one of the decisive acts of the Protestant Reformation. On June 15, 1520, Pope Leo published the bull *Exsurge Domine,* condemning Luther as a wild boar in the vineyard and giving him sixty days in which to recant. In response to the bull and to the burning of Luther's books, faculty and students at Wittenberg burned books on scholastic theology *and* the canon law in a bonfire on December 10.[52]

Canon law arises almost inevitably in the life of the church. The Christian community, being made up of human beings, cannot live without order and regulations. There is also an innate tendency for "clergy" and staff to define the church more in terms of themselves than of the people. Hence there have to be, even in Protestant and congregational churches, periodic reforms such as the Protestant Reformation's emphasis that the church is the people. In the twentieth century the Reformed theologians Karl Barth[53] and Emil Brunner[54] have made the church as the community of the people an essential part of their theologies. Neither was at home in the contemporary bureaucratization of the church.

The *Book of Order* began in a very simple form. Calvin's *Ordinances,* the *Books of Discipline* of the Church of Scotland, the Form of Presbyterial Government of the Westminster Assembly, and the old books of church order in American Presbyterian were all small books, enunciating principles more than prescriptions.[55] These books did not need to be revised every year. Today the *Book of Order* is more and more a manual of operations rather than a church policy. Increasingly, the statements of the book are prescriptions, "must" replacing "may."

There are historical reasons for the changed character of the *Book of Order.* For example, it followed the replacement of clerks by executives in presbytery, synod, and General Assembly. In the earlier centuries, Presbyterians conveyed their understanding of any continuing office in the church by entitling the official a clerk, that is, a secretary. Since the Second World War, the image of clerks has frequently been replaced by the corporate image of the executive. The language of the executive, even the chief executive, crept into the vocabulary of the church, surely representing the high point of the secularization of the church itself.

The new form of the *Book of Order* can also be understood as a response to the increasingly voluntary character of the church in a secular, pluralistic, mobile, mass-media-dominated society. As such, it is comparable to the fundamentalist reaction to the Enlightenment and the nineteenth-century cultural developments. A fundamentalism of the *Book of Order* has replaced a theological fundamentalism. There is no evidence that a fundamentalism of the *Book of Order* will be any more successful in dealing with the problems of the church in the world today than theological fundamentalism.

The church must consider whether the organizational structure of the church today must not be modified to enhance the priesthood of all believers.

1. It must be modified to guarantee the right of the people to elect those who govern them and who serve as their pastors. This right of the people, especially in Presbyterianism, was won in a long struggle that began with Calvin in Geneva and reached heights of intensity in seventeenth- and eighteenth-century Scotland.[56] Yet the changes in the *Book of Order* in recent years have significantly restricted both freedoms. Again, there is no convincing evidence that these restrictions have led either to better officers or to better pastors. The evidence, as seen in quantifiable ways, seems to point in a negative direction.

2. There needs to be a restoring of the freedom of local churches and ministers to engage in creative and spontaneous action in church mission, such actions as the establishment of chapels and churches, so long as they carry on these activities with funds which they themselves have given. There are many mission projects which can only be thought of, developed, and supported by creative action on the congregational level.

3. There needs to be greater freedom for Christians in the church to have a choice in how their benevolent gifts are spent.[57] Of course, some church activities are the responsibility of all church people to support. However, the increasing restriction upon the freedom of church people to make any decision in the use of their benevolent offerings, or even how special offerings are to be spent, can only lead to a decline in giving. In the

church, as in civil society, money is more likely to be used responsibly when its expenditure is close to the surveillance of those who give it and who have earned it.

4. The church must ask what it means for the priesthood of believers that the leaders of the Presbyterian Church never have to face the people. Leaders in civil government, legislators, mayors, congressmen, presidents, all finally have to face the people and be voted upon. In contrast, Presbyterian leadership is increasingly elected by delegated committees and bodies whose own freedom is restricted by processes and regulations. Any secular politician knows that the more a body is delegated, the more its actions can be controlled. The church must be concerned that those elected by delegated bodies and appointed to staff positions have the approbation of the people who are the church. No test of church leadership is infallible, but the old tests of the approbation of the people and the demonstrated gift to proclaim persuasively the gospel and build up the church are the most reliable yet devised.

Fourth, the priesthood of believers has also been put at risk by the bureaucratization of the church. The bureaucratization of the Protestant church is very recent, largely during the last hundred years, and especially during the years since the Second World War.[58] In the nineteenth century, much of the church's work beyond the local congregation was done through voluntary organizations, such as the American Board of Commissioners for Foreign Missions, the American Bible Society, the American Sunday School Union, and the Christian Endeavor. Charles Hodge[59] of Princeton Theological Seminary and James Henley Thornwell[60] of Columbia Theological Seminary carried on a brilliant series of debates in the General Assembly of the Presbyterian Church in the 1840s on the nature of church organization. Neither Hodge nor Thornwell could have conceived of the modern bureaucratic structure, yet in the church of the 1840s Thornwell opposed and Hodge supported boards. Thornwell insisted on committees immediately responsible to the people. The congregation is a missionary society. The work of the church must be the work of the people. The functions of the church are those which the congregation must do and from which they cannot be relieved by any board. From today's perspective, the debate between Hodge and Thornwell is mostly about words. Hodge won the debate, and in terms of practice was persuasive. Thornwell's warnings are justified by the conflict between bureaucracy and congregations today.

A bureaucracy is necessary for the life of the church today, and the work of staff is highly useful. For church staff we must be grateful. Yet all bureaucracies have built-in tendencies to be self-perpetuating, to think of themselves as the church and also to become remote from the church.

In one of the first studies of the crisis in the church, Jeffrey Hadden emphasized the voluntary character of the church. "It is a fundamental sociological principle that the leadership of a voluntary organization can only be so far out of line with the expectations of its constituency before that leadership is questioned."[61] The negative side of this principle is that the people may not be qualified to exercise this power. The great advocates of Presbyterianism John Calvin[62] and James Henley Thornwell[63] developed their polity on theological grounds. They opposed congregationalism because the people in general lack the wisdom and constructive experience. They opposed episcopal governments (oligarchy or monarchy) because no one is good enough or wise enough for that much power. Hence they advocated conciliar or presbyterial government. Calvin wanted, in civil as well as ecclesiastical government, democracy tempered by aristocracy, that is the qualified. Effective conciliar government depends upon the members of the councils being qualified and *truly* representative of the people.

Effective church leadership from congregation to presbytery, to synod, to General Assembly, to ecumenical council must come out of the authentic life of local congregations and must be shaped in style and substance by participating in the worship and work of the congregation. Moreover, in a far greater degree than is true of any other organization in our society, the church lives by moral suasion. Church people are free to follow or not to follow the actions of church organizations. The old notion that demonstrated ability to build up and lead a congregation was a condition for leadership in the church on the conciliar level was a sound principle. Effective church leaders are those who, having the confidence of the people, are able to persuade them.

Peter Berger, in a very challenging paper, has related "the new class" to the life of the church.[64] The new class is composed of service people, information people, managers, bureaucracies, teachers. The new class does much useful work, but to use a secular term, it does not produce wealth. The new class makes money without producing money. Berger suggests that the church today also has a new class who manage the life of the church, who are concerned with ideas, who teach, who service the functions of the church.

The new class in the church and in society has the common characteristic of not producing wealth. In the civil order, this means money or goods. In the church, it means congregations, church members, church budgets. The secular order can support the new class because of the very rapid increase in productivity. For example, the hours of labor required on farms decreased from 9.8 billion in 1960 to 3.6 billion in 1985. Two hundred years ago families had difficulty producing enough to take care of themselves. The increased productivity of goods in our society has been phenomenal. In the church, there has been a great expansion of the new class, but there has been no increase in productivity, that is, in new churches, new members, and raised budgets; rather, a dramatic decline in productivity.

Fifth, the church as the priesthood of believers is put at risk by the loss of consensus in the life of the church.[65] Many activities within the church have contributed to this loss as well as the pressures of a secular, pluralistic, mobile society. Partisan positions on political, social, and economic issues destroy the catholicity of the church. The plethora of theologies reveling in novelties and coining new jargons has likewise broken down consensus. Random changes in the rituals and revisions in the language of worship have not, as their proponents argued, brought people together in worship. Finally, there has been the loss of a common language of Christian discourse. This was once supplied by creeds and catechisms so that Christians across cultural, national, and language barriers spoke one language of faith. The basis for this consensus in language, thought, and life was the Bible, read in the church and by believers as the account of what the triune God has done for us in creation and redemption. The recovery of the consensus of the faith will of necessity begin in

Protestant churches with the reading and devotional study of the Bible as the Word of God.

IV

The trends that put at risk the church as the priesthood of believers, as the people, are serious from a theological perspective. They are disastrous on the practical level. The church from the point of view of a human organization is a highly voluntary society. There are fewer and fewer psychological and social pressures to move a person to be an active member of the church. In addition to membership, work in the church is likewise highly voluntary, and in competition with the pressures of other community organizations.

The voluntary financial support of the church was one of the great achievements of the Protestant church in America.[66] American churches have been supported not by the state, and not by persons in particular classes or social groups, but by the people. No characteristic of American church life was more typical than the every member canvass, an American invention. The church by its very nature, as the residues of the Constantinian church disappear, will depend on voluntary contributions.

The only thing in our society which is freer than being a member of the church is not putting any money in the collection plate when it passes. This is the crisis of the church today.

The voluntary character of the church affects more than members, church work, and financial support. It also lies at the root of the viability of the system of church courts or governing bodies. We speak of governing bodies in the life of the church, but except for a minimal authority over ministers, these governing bodies live and govern by moral suasion. The church is in very great contrast to the government. The government has a Marine Corps, and perhaps more significantly, an Internal Revenue Service to impose its will and to secure its support. The church has neither. Furthermore, the old psychological and social supports for church membership, activity, and financial support are disappearing. People are freer today to be or not to be the church, to support or not to support the church than they have been in many areas of Western society since the fifth century.

John Calvin in Geneva believed that the only power which he really needed was the freedom to preach the Word of God, to create a godly public opinion. This is now the *only* power sessions, presbyteries, synods, and General Assemblies have. Hence it is increasingly important that the sessions, the presbyteries, the synods, the General Assembly be representative of the people, and that this representation must not be curtailed by church policies, strategies, or quota systems.

The conclusion of the matter is that the renewal of the church in our time must begin with a recovery of the church as the priesthood of believers, and with an understanding of the ministry as a calling, not a living, concentrating upon the task of a pastor. Luther insisted that only the gospel is necessary for the existence of the church. The church can exist without a building, a clergy, or a bureaucracy. On the level of human history, the well-being of the church depends above all else on the people who are hearing the gospel, the church, and upon the competence and dedication of ministers whom the people call to preach, teach, and exercise pastoral care.

CHAPTER THREE

Preaching

During the centennial celebration of Fifth Avenue Presbyterian Church, New York (1908), A. F. Schauffler thanked the Session of the church for its concern to provide excellent preaching. His words are worth quoting:

> The management of this church is of such an intelligent nature that they place in this pulpit men of national and international reputation during June, July and August, so that these pews and galleries are full, never mind what the thermometer says, that is a benediction to this great town of ours; that is letting your light so shine that men see your good works, and glorify your Father who is in Heaven, and the gathering here, the securing here, not during the summer season only, but at times during the regular season, of men like "Gypsy" Smith, and other men we can mention—Campbell Morgan and Hugh Black and the like—the gathering of these men is something for which the city ought to be thankful, and of which this church has just reason to be sanctifiedly proud.
>
> On behalf of many who come here, who are not members of this church, to whom you have thus ministered, I desire to bring a token of gratitude, and to render in their behalf to this church and its pastor and elders, thanks for this careful ministry to the wants of the great spiritual public.[1]

No higher tribute can be paid a session than that it provided preaching of the highest excellence and integrity.

It is no longer clear that many church people attend church services with the conviction that they shall hear a good sermon, that is, good in its depth and breadth, in its utilization of the resources of the Christian community, in its clarity about what the church is, and in its delivery by a person who is passionate in conviction and trained in the art of explicating and applying the Word of God in a sermon. Yet there is overwhelming evidence that congregations want two competencies in their pastors. First, they want persons who are able to explicate and apply the Word of God with power. Second, they want pastors who know how to incorporate persons into the worshiping, believing community and bring to them the treasures of the gospel in the passages and crises of life as well as support when life is routine and boring. With amazing unanimity, pulpit committees want a pastor who can preach.

Yet most pulpit committees would have a difficult time explaining what is a good sermon. Some have never heard good preaching in the classical definition of the term, and have a difficult time distinguishing the preaching of the gospel from entertainment, or therapy, or moral exhortation, or political advice. Indeed, many congregations may require a period of time to become acclimated to a really good preacher. James Hastings Nichols, in a study of Reformed worship, noted that church services in the Reformed tradition were dependent upon a theologically and biblically informed congregation.[2] There is a paucity of such congregations. Yet congregations can be educated. A decisive test of the effectiveness of a minister is the difference between the sermon taste of the congregation when the minister arrives and the sermon taste of the congregation when the minister leaves. A second test is the power of preaching to gather a congregation, to create a godly public opinion, and to build up the communion of saints. Once congregations have heard good preaching of theological and biblical depth over a period of time, they find it very difficult to accept poor preaching, or to be enticed by actors or entertainers or moral exhorters or therapists in the pulpit.

There is great need for preaching with theological depth in our particular day. More people are going to college in our society than has been true of any other society. The number of lawyers, doctors, engineers has greatly increased over a century ago. The loss of a theological picture of reality or frame of reference in a society dominated by the secularity of television, education, and many popular magazines also calls for theological preaching which provides a Christian alternative. The centers of information and of political and social persuasion are increasingly secular. Hence theological preaching of the highest competence is essential today for persuasion and for the building up of the community of the saints.

A further reason why theological preaching should be emphasized is the abundant market for its wares. The theological preacher does not have many competitors. The approbation of the people is not always immediate, but it is lasting when it comes. This is the secular justification for theological preaching. There are, as I hope to indicate, more theological reasons to justify theological preaching. All preaching is by nature theological. The reference here is to preaching that is informed by the best theology of the tradition.

I

Jesus came preaching (Mark 1:14). His followers have preached ever since. Sometimes preaching occurs in great established churches, with marvelous music, with an established liturgy and with a budget that finances both preaching and the operation of the congregation. Much preaching, however, has taken place not in established churches, certainly not in great churches or in cathedrals, but along the highways, in empty stores, on the frontiers of life. Preachers have gone forth, not because they were offered a job or given financial security, but because they felt a compelling call by God to preach the gospel and to establish churches. The church in which I grew up was established by lay people in the 1760s, and for many years it was maintained by pastors who had to earn at least part of their living in nonecclesiastical endeavors. The roll of the great preachers has to include the Bonifaces, the Columbas, the Farels, the Wesleys, the Peter Cartwrights and the Sheldon Jacksons. There is finally only one justification for preaching, and that is the call of God. The support of an established church may make preaching more comfortable, but it cannot justify it.

Preaching is the announcement of the salvation that has come in Jesus Christ, calling people to repentance and seeking to build up the Christian community. Evangelism, according to Kittel's *Theological Dictionary of the New Testament,* is proclamation with authority and power. Signs and wonders accompany the evangelical message. They belong together, for the Word is powerful and effective.[3]

Many patterns of preaching are helpful. Yet there are good reasons to insist that the recovery of theological preaching, especially in the Reformed pattern, is crucial to the renewal of the church. This preaching responds to the crisis of a pluralistic secular society by providing a coherent vision of reality, rooted in the theological reflections of almost two millennia, and by enabling the Christian to find a theologically intelligible place in the world and in society.

This particular pattern of preaching has received three clear, precise formulations, from John Calvin, from the Puritans, and from Karl Barth.

Calvin's famous letter to the protector Somerset in 1548 concerning the reformation of the church in England contains a good introduction to Calvin's general understanding of the preacher's task.

> I speak thus, Monsignor, because it appears to me that there is very little preaching of a lively kind in the kingdom, but that the greater part deliver it by way of reading from a written discourse. I see very well the necessity which constrains you to that; for in the first place you have not, as I believe, such well-approved and competent pastors as you desire. Wherefore, you need forthwith to supply this want. Secondly, there may very likely be among them many flighty persons who would go beyond all bounds, sowing their own silly fancies, as often happens on occasion of a change. But all these considerations ought not to hinder the ordinance of Jesus Christ from having free course in the preaching of the gospel.
>
> Now, this preaching ought not to be lifeless but lively, to teach, to exalt, to reprove, as Saint Paul says in speaking thereof to Timothy (2 Timothy 3). So indeed, that if an unbeliever enter, he may be so effectively arrested and convinced as to give glory to God, as Paul says in another passage (1 Corinthians 14). You are also aware, Monsignor, how he speaks of the lively power and energy with which they ought to speak, who would approve themselves as good and faithful ministers of God, who must not make a parade of rhetoric, only to gain esteem for themselves; but that the Spirit

of God ought to sound forth by their voice, so as to work with mighty energy. Whatever may be the amount of danger to be feared, that ought not to hinder the Spirit of God from having liberty and free course in those to whom he has given grace for the edifying of the church.[4]

Calvin understood preaching to be the will of God for his church. The justification for preaching is not in its effectiveness for education or reform. It is not a practice for which other practices may be substituted should they prove to be more popular or useful. Preaching is rooted in the will and the intention of God. The preacher, Calvin dared to say, was the mouth of God. God does not wish to be heard but by the voice of his ministers.[5]

Calvin had no illusions about the impact of sermons. He knew, as he said in one sermon, that there were as many people in the tavern as at the sermon.[6] He knew that preaching would create problems and difficulties. It kills as well as makes alive; it hardens as well as renews.[7] The validity of preaching does not depend upon the response it elicits. It is a witness or a testimony that God wills to be made in his world even if all reject it.

This emphasis on the foundation of preaching in the will of God should not obscure Calvin's practical concern for edification. He preached to edify, to convince. Certainly on the human level he had confidence in its power. On a deeper level, however, he found justification for preaching not in its edification or in its power under the Holy Spirit to create the Christian person and a Christian society, but in the intention of God.

Calvin understood preaching to be a sacrament of the saving presence of God. Richard Stauffer suggests that preaching for Calvin was not only a moment of worship, not only a task of the church, but also something of a divine epiphany. "When the gospel is preached in the name of God, it is as if God himself spoke in person."[8] In the *Institutes,* Calvin quotes Augustine, who spoke of words as signs. In preaching, the Holy Spirit uses the words of the preacher as an occasion for the presence of God in grace and in mercy. In this sense, the actual words of the sermon are comparable to the elements of the sacraments.[9] The word in preaching accomplishes nothing apart from the work of the Holy Spirit, who illuminates the mind. (For Calvin, preaching is sacramental in the context of the order of salvation and as a means of grace, and not in the more general sense by which all creation may be sacramental. The distinction is important for Calvin, though he never explicated the meaning. The sense in which common grace may be saving is a modern question, not an issue in which Calvin was interested.)

The power of preaching as the Word of God does not reside in the sound of the words themselves, or even in their meaning. The power of preaching is the act of the Holy Spirit, which makes the words, the sound and their meaning, the occasion of the voice of God. "If the same sermon is preached, say, to a hundred people, twenty receive it with the ready obedience of faith, while the rest hold it valueless, or laugh, or hiss, or loathe it."[10] Yet the ultimate difference in the response does not reside in the sermon, the sound of the words, the rhetoric, or the meaning, but in the electing grace of God.

Calvin's sacramental doctrine of preaching enabled him, on the one hand, to understand preaching as a very human work and, on the other hand, as the work of God. The characteristic perspective that pervades all Calvin's theology, which on the one hand emphasizes the transcendence of God and refuses to identify the transcendent God with any finite or determinate object, and which on the other hand asserts the immanence of God in creation, and more particularly in the means of grace, has particular application to preaching. From one perspective, the human work of the sermon is critically important. The sermon's fidelity to scripture, the skill of the syntax and rhetoric, and the liveliness of the delivery are of fundamental importance and ought not to be minimized. From another perspective, a sermon is the work of the Spirit of God, which may make a poor sermon the occasion of God's presence and a brilliant sermon barren of power. Calvin unites the work of God and the work of man in the sacrament and in preaching without separation, without change, and without confusion. In practice he may have claimed too much for the minister and the words of the sermon. Yet in doctrine he knew that the words of the sermon are at best frail, human words, but words which can by the power of the Holy Spirit become the occasion of the presence of God.[11] For Calvin as for Luther, "the ears alone are the organ of the Christian man."[12] Hearing the Word of God makes one worthy of the name Christian.

John Calvin's preaching presupposes a biblical and theological framework. Sermons were part of a structured and clear vision of reality. Calvin's hearers knew that human life had its origin in the purposes of God and that God would determine its destiny. Human life was lived under the Lordship of God whose purposes would be accomplished in human history. The clarity of the biblical and theological framework made each sermon part of one clear vision of reality. Calvin had written the *Institutes* for this purpose—that is, to provide a coherent framework for his preaching and teaching.[13]

Calvin's theology may lack homogeneity, but not unity. For example, his understanding of the transcendence and immanence of God, the distinction between Creator and creature, gives a unity to his doctrines of the person of Christ, of the presence of Jesus Christ in the sacraments, of the church as a human work and a divine work. Or again, there is a unifying perspective relating and holding together Calvin's understanding of revelation in Jesus Christ and general revelation, of grace and nature, and gospel and law, of church and society. There is a unifying theme, preeminently expressed in the doctrine of predestination, and permeating everything Calvin said, emphasizing the immediacy of the divine activity and the initiative of divine grace. On a still deeper level, there is the unity created by Calvin's conviction that knowledge of God involves knowledge of man and knowledge of man involves knowledge of God, and that the whole of theology inheres in the explication of this relationship between God and man. In sum, Calvin had a vision of theological reality expressed in the *Institutes* very similar to Augustine's in the last twelve books of *The City of God*. It is this theological framework which informed all of Calvin's preaching and made of his preaching a unity and gave it a direction that otherwise would have been lacking.

Closely related to Calvin's theological vision of reality is the ground plan of scripture that was clearly in his mind. This ground plan, too, is explicated in the *Institutes*. The Bible as a whole, and Calvin's theology as a whole, impinged upon every sermon which he preached, and all of his sermons fit into one biblical and theological whole.

The importance of this unifying theological and biblical

context cannot be overestimated. It means that the homiletician must be a person knowledgeable in theology and in the Bible if the preacher is to stand in the Reformed tradition.

Calvin also had a vision of the holy community. This does not mean that Calvin had a blueprint which he was seeking to impose upon society. In the section on the Christian life in the *Institutes,* Calvin does not provide rules or regulations.[14] In fact, Calvin was something of a pragmatist, attempting to relate the Christian gospel to the complicated decisions and issues of human life. Yet Calvin could have answered the question, Who is a Christian person and what is a Christian society? with a clarity that gave direction to his preaching. He refers to the example of Jesus and he emphasizes the disposition of the self and the relationship of the self to God, to persons, and to things. He clearly regarded human life as a vocation from God, a calling that rendered the humblest task precious in the sight of God.

In sum, Calvin's preaching was a clear, unadorned proclamation of God's works in creation and redemption as set forth in scripture and in a framework established by the Christian community's reflection on scripture. It called people to decision, created them a community, and gave them an overarching vision of reality in which they could understand their own lives and their place in society.

This Calvinist preaching was powerful: Donald R. Kelley has commented:

> In all this ideological uproar arising from religious sentiment the most effective agent of transmission remained popular preaching. To this other forms of expression—psalm-singing and iconoclasm, public dialogue and disputation—were subordinate. The sermon elaborated and dramatized other forms of religious expression, including the catechism (which in Calvinist practice furnished material for a year of Sunday preaching) and confession; it gave emotional focus to the congregation and public thrust to its enthusiasm; it gave impetus to other kinds of demonstration, both musical and militant; and in general it represented a prime mover of public opinion. In the context of oral culture, certainly, no other kind of discourse better illustrates the transition from private conviction to public cause, from a profession of faith to concerted propaganda and even a platform of action. In the Refor-

mation as in earliest Christian times the ideological priority was clear—"And the gospel must first be published among all nations" [Mark 13:10]—and so the sermon now becomes the center of our attention.[15]

The second example of Reformed preaching is found in the Westminster Assembly's Directory for Worship.[16] The Puritans, like Calvin, believed that the only opportunity they needed was the freedom to preach the Word of God. They were convinced that, by preaching, the grace of God is mediated to human beings and that thereby society is changed. The history of Puritanism demonstrates the power of preaching to build up communities and to influence the shape of society.

Puritan preaching, like Calvin's preaching, took place within a unified theological vision of reality. This vision found classic expression in the Westminster Confession and catechisms. Furthermore, the Puritans had an even clearer vision than Calvin of who is a Christian person and what is a Christian society. This, too, had been delineated in the Westminster exposition of the Ten Commandments. Puritan preaching was in intention and in fact theological and biblical.

The Puritans, like Calvin, also gave attention to the style of preaching. They too emphasized that preaching must be plain style, free from rhetorical flourishes. From the beginning, the Reformers had emphasized simplicity and authenticity.[17] These virtues were closely related to their theology and their understanding of the Reformation of the church. Their intention was the evangelization of the church, that is, the removing of all human trifles and flourishes which impede the grace of God. God's grace is neither the extension of nor contrary to the wisdom of human psychology or public relations or drama. The church is free to use such wisdom so long as it does not intrude into the gospel or become a substitute for it. In worship and preaching human wisdom too easily becomes human trifles that obscure the gospel. Simplicity for Calvin was very close to sincerity. The simple uncovers reality and opens the way for the grace of God. The pretentious, the pompous, the contrived, the artificial, the too carefully polished cover up reality and obscure God's grace.

Plain-style preaching was also related to the Christian doctrine of what it is to be a human being.[18] The Augustinians had always insisted on the human being as a self, with the capacities of the human spirit to transcend the self, of the human mind to read off the facts of life, and of the human will to organize the energies of human existence. This psychology for Calvin was very simple, but in its simplicity he emphasized the spirit, the understanding, and the will. Hence the Christian faith has to be spoken to a responsible self, and from that human self there must be elicited a deliberate and conscious response.

The Puritans, as with Calvin, rejected magic, or to put it positively, they emphasized conscious choice and deliberate decision. Puritan preaching does not attempt to overpower human beings, or to deceive them. It attempts to engage them and to elicit from them a yes or a no.

The Puritan concern for language appropriate to the Word of God had very great theological and social significance. For a century and a half the Puritans struggled with the task of putting the Word of God in English, in the vernacular. William Haller has written:

> The authorized version of 1611 was the culmination of the effort of a long succession of English churchmen to put the word of God into the vernacular. Versed though they were in the learned tongues and reared in the tradition of letters, the translators did not do their work upon the level of academic Latinized English. Neither, on the other hand, did they English the Bible upon the everyday or vulgar plane. They turned their learning and skill to the task of developing out of the familiar common speech an English appropriate to the lofty matter they had in hand and yet moving and intelligible to the plain, unlearned reader. The result was the marvellous idiom of the English Bible.[19]

This language of the English Bible shaped American culture decisively until the Second World War. In its simplicity it opened reality and in its sensitivity to the majesty of its message it did and does deeply move people. Hence it was a manner of speaking very appropriate to the theological reality. Those who heard the Puritans had a sense of reality. The hearers felt the force and reality about which the preacher was speaking. As William Perkins put it, preaching must "observe an admirable plainness and an admirable powerfulness so that the ordinary person may understand and be powerfully moved."[20]

Puritan preaching in which the clarity and precision of the message is the medium and means of persuasion requires great personal gifts, concentration, and persistence. The temptation is always present to use gimmicks and tricks to persuade. Robert Baillie, the Scottish commissioner to the Westminster Assembly, protested in 1654 "the new guise of preaching" which "in a high, romancing, unscriptural style, tickling the ear for the present, and moving the affections in some, but leaving . . . little or nought to the memory or understanding. This we must misken, for we cannot help it."[21]

The Puritans had not only worked on language; they were also clear about the form of the sermon. Their homiletics received classical statements in William Perkins's *The Art of Prophesying*[22] and in the homiletical section of the Westminster *Directory for Worship*. The sermon contains the explication of the text, the doctrine, and finally the application. The Puritan preachers gave great attention to the doctrine, the general principles contained in the text, but they concentrated on the applications, on the ways this text transformed human life. The events of the soul were of cosmic significance, and the preachers charted in detail how the self moves from sin to victory.

A third explicit doctrine of preaching is to be found in the theology of Karl Barth. As is well known, Karl Barth intended his theology to be a preacher's theology. He was convinced that the problem in the life of the church is the corruption of the message, and that if we can get the message right and proclaim it with clarity, under the power of the Holy Spirit it will elicit a proper response.

Karl Barth's doctrine of preaching is summarized in his conviction that there has been committed to the church "the gospel, i.e., the good glad tidings of Jesus Christ, of the real act and true revelation of the goodness in which God has willed to make, and has in fact made himself the God of man and man His man. This great yes is its cause. It has no other task beside this."[23]

The church has the task of the "explicit proclamation of the gospel in the assembly of the community, in the midst of divine service, where it is also heard directly or indirectly by the world, that is, in what is denoted by the overburdened but unavoidable term 'preaching.' " Preaching differs both from the exposition of scripture and from theological study or lecturing. "Preaching does not reflect, reason, dispute, or academically instruct. It proclaims, summons, invites and commands."[24] Preaching is a work of human speech, but it is of decisive significance for the life of the church. Indeed, the church lives by hearing the Word of God in preaching. The chief task of theology is to examine the church's proclamation, primarily in preaching, in the light of the Word of God in Jesus Christ as attested in scripture. Preaching is the point where the whole theological task comes to focus. Barth himself argued that one reason for calling Schleiermacher a Christian theologian was his interest in preaching.[25] One cannot be a theologian in the Calvinist and Barthian sense without being a preacher. One real test of all theology for John Calvin was its preachableness.[26] A theology that cannot be preached, that is not persuasive, and that does not have preaching as its goal is not from the Reformed perspective a legitimate theology in the church.

These three doctrines of the sermon from Calvin, the Puritans, and Karl Barth have common emphases. (1) Preaching is proclamation of the gospel—what God has done for human beings in creation, judgment, and redemption. (2) Human life, especially in decisions of the will, has cosmic significance and the gospel must be applied to it. (3) All of this is done in the light of a biblical and theological vision of reality. The preacher proclaims the faith of the church. (4) Preaching is the means by which God's grace is mediated and the church as a community is established.

This preaching presupposes the highest levels of biblical and theological knowledge as well as the capacity to express it in clear, coherent English sentences, and to deliver it in a lively and effective way.

II

Preaching, especially as it has been practiced in the Reformed tradition, is at grave risk today. Several characteristics of our society which put preaching at risk need special mention.

The first is the development of the entertainment industry.

This development has two consequences. (1) It induces people to find the meaning of life in being entertained. Entertainment (soap operas, athletic events, even anchor news which turns great events into spectacles) relieves us of uniquely human responsibilities to think for ourselves, to set goals and to accomplish them. (2) Entertainment distracts our attention from the critical issues of life, and finally our heroes become not persons of substance and achievement so much as celebrities who attract our attention. Form takes priority over substance. In sum, entertainment, whether it is soap operas or political spectacles or athletic events, is not simply entertainment but also an escape from the hard realities of life and from the questions for which Christian faith is the answer.[27]

The emergence of the entertainment and communications industry presents another peril to preaching. The communications industry has developed skills and techniques which enable human beings of very limited greatness, education, and culture to have enormous power over other human beings. This was dramatically illustrated in the movie of a few years ago entitled *Marjoe*. Marjoe was a child evangelist, named after Mary and Joseph. As a child he grew up knowing the techniques and skills of the trade. The movie depicts him as an adult who has repudiated the faith and the tradition. He illustrates, however, the way in which the techniques, the procedures, the skills of the revivalist who himself no longer believes can elicit predicted responses, whether these responses are the giving of money or physical manifestations such as uncontrolled body motions. Speaking in tongues can be elicited by atheists who know the techniques, if they have a willing audience.

The movie *Marjoe* is offensive to Christian sensibilities. It is illustrative of human fraud at the worst. However, those in the ministry who have the strength to see it ought to see the movie. Religion is always a narrow razor's edge away from magic.[28] Magic in relationship to God is the attempt to get control of God and to fasten the infinite and indeterminate God to that which is finite and determinate, whether it be the bread and wine of the sacrament or the techniques of the revivalist. Magic in relationship to human beings is the effort to bypass conscious choice and decision. One of the greatest temptations for the minister is the practice of magic. On this point we should all be critically self-critical.

The modern communications industry reverses the traditional order of homiletical achievement. Classically, preaching has arisen out of the substance of what is proclaimed. The Christian message determined the pattern and form of preaching. The powerfulness of the message in determining the form was dramatically illustrated in the Puritan style and use of language. Today increasingly form and style take precedence over substance. Reinhold Niebuhr in his diary records his commitment that he would forsake the attempt to be a pretty preacher. The "pretty" preacher at least works at the task, and for this reason one hesitates to criticize in a day when much preaching is slovenly and careless. Nevertheless, Niebuhr was right. There is an incongruity between the gospel and a pretty sermon. This is especially true in the Reformed tradition. There must be something rough-hewn about the sermon. For Reformed preaching, the message is in a real sense the medium, and the worst heresy in preaching is for the medium to become the message.

The development of the communications industry, as well as the entertainment industry, jeopardizes good preaching by tempting persons to subordinate content to form and to practices which may be humanly effective but which are theologically destructive.

Great preaching depends on the integrity of the human heart and mind, on the part of both the preacher and the congregation. It is not through the practice of magic or the communication arts, but through the integrity of the proclamation itself which under God creates the Christian community.

Second, preaching is threatened today by the breakdown of a coherent understanding of human reality, of life in the world, in society, and in the church.

Until quite recently, a basically Christian construction of reality was implicit in the life of society. While the society itself may have given only tentative commitment, it at least declared its allegiance to a Christian vision of what it is to be a human being in the world. This Christian vision lived for many years in very attenuated forms, but nevertheless it lived.[29]

The constructive coherent vision of reality that was implicit in our society greatly strengthened the church in its proclamation. There was a time in American life when evangelism was little more than bringing persons who were basically Christian in their interpretation of reality into the organized life of the church. Today our society less and less has any legitimating understanding of what it is to be a human being and of the place of human beings in the world. There is no general agreement about the origin of human life or the destiny of human life or the meaning of human life between birth and death. This means that increasingly the preacher can no longer depend on a knowledge of the history of Israel or a general theistic consensus. The situation is more radical than that which faced Peter, or that which faced Paul at Mars' Hill. For the first time, we live in an increasingly secular culture with no pervasive natural theology as well as little biblical knowledge. In Calvin's day an atheist was one who denied that God was active in the world. Today atheism is denial of any cosmic purpose.

This breakdown of the overarching coherent view of the human reality in the world is true not only of society but also of the church. Most significantly, it is increasingly true in theological education. The ordination of ministers and the creation of theological seminaries to prepare pastors for the church is predicated upon the assumption that the minister is not free to express his or her idiosyncratic ideas about the meaning of human life. Ordination, however, means that the minister bears witness to the Christian faith as it has been understood and mediated through the centuries by the Christian community. This fact has both practical and theological significance. It has practical significance because the pastor is not always at an intense level of theological conviction when he or she is asked to perform a specifically Christian service. One may be asked to conduct a funeral service at the very moment when one's faith in eternal life is wavering. The minister must have the will to believe what the churches believe. The responsibility of the minister on that occasion is not to testify to the vagaries of his or her own soul but to bear witness in this crisis for the church community to the church's faith, a faith that has received the approbation of the people of God through the centuries.

Karl Barth, in his discussion of Christian freedom, holds

together the freedom and responsibility Christian baptism as well as ordination entails.

> The Christian is not free to adopt any current religious idea, to espouse his own private philosophy, and then to urge this upon the community. On the other hand, he is both free and yet also summoned and obliged to reflect on the Word which underlies the community and is to be declared by it, and to give responsible expression to his reflections. No one will do this obediently unless he is prepared to let himself be stimulated, advised and guided by others, including professional theologians. No one will do it obediently if he is not in dialogue not only with God but also with his fellow-men and fellow-Christians. The freedom at issue is freedom in the community and not a foolish freedom on inspirations.[30]

Ministers and theologians must first of all understand their role in the church as interpreters of the tradition, not as the creative inventors of new theologies. The theological community may, as all human communities, be dominated by the hubris to create the great new theology. The history of the past thirty years is strewn with the wreckage of such attempts. There have been great creative theological developments in the Christian community, but these have usually been wrought by persons who were very modest, who had not set out to be the great creative theologian, yet who in being faithful interpreters of the tradition had restated the tradition in a persuasive way in the idiom of a new time.

The first task of a pastor of a church or a theological seminary is faithfully and convincingly to tradition the Christian faith as it has been handed on to us in trust from those who built our churches and our seminaries.

The problem of the breakdown of a coherent worldview is complicated by the loss of Christian knowledge. In a former day, preachers could assume that the members of their congregations had certain biblical knowledge, that they understood theological terms, even if they were in other ways uneducated. Those who have been pastors of many old churches have stood in awe in the presence of the theological wisdom of persons with very little formal education. We now have churches in which there is no network of information that makes theological conversation possible.

The problem is even deeper, and involves theological competence, a problem that can be illustrated in changes in the theological curriculum since the Second World War. In 1940, in almost every Presbyterian seminary, theology was taught from a basic text. Whether this text was Hodge or Strong or Berkhof did not really matter;[31] they were all essentially the same working out of the theology of seventeenth-century Protestantism as modified in particular by the American evangelical experience. These theological textbooks were written in a pattern that is easy to learn. The Puritans sought to write theology so that its basic structure could be quickly memorized.[32] Each theological course covered the gamut of theology from a perspective that had been worked out in the Christian community. The student with average ability but with diligence could grasp a coherent statement of the faith. This enabled the pastor to become an effective theologian who could give an answer that had been formulated in the church's history to all the questions that members of congregations were likely to ask. This was a realizable goal, and as a result, persons of very limited ability went out and still proclaimed a coherent view of reality that enabled people to find their place in the world.

When one contrasts the situation of fifty years ago with the teaching of theology today, certain points become immediately clear. In few if any seminaries is one dogmatic text the basic form of instruction for young theologians, with the exception perhaps of the Lutheran and the Baptist churches. In most Presbyterian seminaries, graduates frequently leave the seminary having read a few pages of Niebuhr, a few pages of Barth, a few pages of Tillich, a few pages of the experimental theologies of the last thirty years, without having a clear grasp of any coherent pattern of theology which has received the approbation of the people of God through use in the church over a period of time. The result is all too frequently that a person is called to preach without having any coherent view of reality and without being able to say in simple outline to an inquirer what it is to be a member of the Christian community, that is, in a way which distinguishes the church from a civic club, from a political party, from a therapy group, or from many other good and useful human communities.

There cannot be a recovery of great preaching until there is the recovery of a theological framework for preaching, both on the part of the preacher and on the part of the congregation.

Third, preaching today has a new audience, especially outside the church, but also within the church. Willem A. Visser 't Hooft, in one of his last essays, pointed out that three faiths were battling for the soul of Europe: paganism, secular humanism, and Christian faith.[33]

Paganism finds the meaning of life in its vitalities and energies, particularly in the intensification of those vitalities and energies. It defines life primarily in terms of the physical realities of nature. Modern paganism does not necessarily endow these vitalities and energies with any divine power, but simply affirms that in the ecstasy and in the intoxication that comes from the intensification of these energies, the meaning of life is found.

The second faith that battles for the soul of human beings in Europe and, in particular, in American society, is secular humanism.[34] In many ways, secular humanism is a product of Christian faith. There has been no finer statement of secular humanism than that produced by John Dewey, a former theological student, entitled *A Common Faith*.[35] Dewey wanted to have religious values without religion, and without theology. Christians may argue that secular humanism is possible only in a society that is still living off of the theological capital of the Christian faith, which invested human life with the significance and dignity of the Creator, and which, on the basis of God's work in creation and redemption, affirmed that human life has abiding significance over against the overwhelming evidence in the world that it does not. Secular humanism is an especially enticing faith as long as it can assume the presence of those qualities of life which have historically been rooted not in secular humanism but in the living faith of the church.

Fourth, preaching can no longer presuppose a Christian society and more particularly a universal natural theology. A natural theology existed prior to the church and provided a point of contact for preachers of the ancient church, however kerygmatic their sermons may have been. A scientific, technological, secular society is bereft of this kind of reflection. Human nature, the structure of human existence, however, remains the same. Therefore, the absence of reflection on the questions of human existence and on the world itself may create a yearning for that which Christian faith declares to be the real nature of human existence and the world. This will mean that the language as well as the content of preaching must have the note of reality and must clearly, precisely, authentically declare the faith and relate it to concrete human experience.

Preaching that will be effective in the last of the twentieth century will have to have three dimensions: (1) it will have to provide a biblical and theological framework for understanding human existence; (2) it will have to give a specific Christian response both to resurgent paganism and to secular humanism; (3) it will finally have to do what Puritan preaching did—give to human beings guidance how they may understand the meaning of life and how to live the Christian life in a pluralistic, secular, mobile society.

III

The greatest threat to preaching in the great tradition is theological. The problem is twofold: the hiatus between academic theology in a secular setting and the church as a community of faith and worship and the issues that arise out of the pluralism of a secular culture.

The achievement of competence in explicating and proclaiming the faith requires the discipline of the rational analysis of the faith as well as the mastery of texts, of ideas and their relationship, of processes, and of the coherence and consistency of the ideas when put together.[36] It also includes the testing of the integrity of the faith as Barth insisted and the intelligibility of the faith for human experience as apologetic theologians demanded.[37] The movement from the academic study of theology to the confessional theology of the church and to preaching is not simple. A radical difference exists between assenting to a proposition and committing one's life in trust to Jesus Christ as Lord and Savior, between risking one's academic reputation and risking one's personal destiny or the destiny of a congregation of people.[38]

There is no convincing evidence that theologians today are more rational or intellectually brighter than theologians of earlier generations. There is evidence that the secular culture has an eroding effect on Christian faith. A recent study of biblical interpretation concludes that a secular culture has now achieved a "thoroughgoing nontheological study of Scripture."[39] Christian theology is also studied as one among many theologies or philosophies. The study of scripture and theology in a secular context has value for the Christian community. Paul Tillich once insisted that external criticism is necessary for the health of Protestantism.[40] The study of the faith by those who do not affirm the faith is an option for a secular university. Yet the church must assess the significance of such study for its own life. There is no evidence I know that indicates that the nontheological study of scripture or the secular study of theology can prepare persons to gather congregations and to build them up as the communion of saints. Even in the seminaries of the church the movement from academic theology to kerygmatic theology is not automatic or easy.

Theology for the past two centuries has also been preoccupied with a skepticism about the reality of what Christians perceive to be the revelation of God and about the adequacy of language to express such a revelation, or to put it another way, with the question of whether theology is possible.[41] This is a question a secular culture forces Christian theologians to ponder. For some the question may never be answered. But the quandary and anguish is not the gospel or the Christian message. The acceptance of the calling to preach and to teach the faith means that the question of the possibility of Christian faith has been resolved as far as human beings can answer such questions. All of us have to pray, "Lord, I believe; help thou mine unbelief" (Mark 9:24, KJV). None can boast. Yet the acceptance of the calling to preach and teach in the church presupposes that the pastor or teacher has with "fear and trembling" made this commitment as a responsible human act. Until this commitment is made, preaching as the New Testament and the church have conceived it is not possible. No other quality is as basic for Christian preaching as this commitment.

The contemporary discussion about the possibility of theology or the foundation of theology or the public character of theology is new only in idiom. New Testament Christians were aware that one comes to confess that Jesus is the Christ only by the power of the Holy Spirit. There is no evidence that their faith had any other foundation than Jesus Christ. They went forth to preach this good news publicly to all people. John Calvin was surely aware of doubt. Yet in the opening chapters of the *Institutes* he deliberately adopts the theological wisdom of Augustine as his own: "We believe in order to understand." For him the "proof" of Christian faith on the human level was rhetorical, the persuasive exposition of the faith in the language of the people.

In the present theological context the essential condition for preaching is the answer to the question, "But who do you say that I am?" (Mark 8:29; Matt. 16:15; Luke 9:20). The Christian community did not have its origin in the understanding that Jesus was a stoic wiseman, or a revolutionary or a prophet of Sophia, but in the passionate conviction that he was the Christ, the Word made flesh, and that in his life, death, and resurrection God wrought salvation for all people. It is possible to be a responsible human being without this commitment, but one cannot be a Christian without it, certainly not a Christian preacher.

Another threat to preaching with great practical significance is the pluralism of our society, the implicit assumption that there are many roads to God.

The unified communities of the past are now gone. John Calvin could not have imagined denominationalism, much less a secular society in which not only Christian groups but non-Christian groups have equal access and freedom.

Pluralism, however, is not a totally new phenomenon. The church in the second century, for example, lived in the midst of a highly pluralistic society, and on the human level it ran the risk of disappearing in the social mix of that society.

Today pluralism confronts us in at least three ways: practically, socially, theologically.[43]

1. There is the simple historical, practical fact of pluralism. Many of our neighbors share neither our faith nor our style of life nor our understanding of human responsibility. The media continually bombard us with varied styles of life and remind us of the living religions of the world. Finally, the history of the world in our time brings us into collision with living religions in new and dramatic ways, though no doubt it is possible to exaggerate

the newness. This is not the first time, for example, that the Christian community has confronted Islam.

2. Pluralism confronts us in our customs of niceness and politeness. Religion and politics are topics that are not appropriate in polite conversation. It is no longer proper to ask a person about his or her religion, nor is it proper culturally or aesthetically to question interfaith marriages. The acceptance of the existence of other faiths, even on the most basic level of a pluralistic society, constitutes a psychological problem. How can we, on the one hand, affirm, practically speaking, that all religions have their validity, and yet be serious about our own. This is the practical and psychological problem. It erodes preaching without our knowing it.[44]

3. Pluralism also confronts us in theology. Historians of religion are increasingly insisting that the theology of the future must be a theology of world religions.[45] The new theology of pluralism is being expressed with as much dogmatism, with as much intolerance, and with as many pejorative representations of opposing views as any Christian orthodoxy has ever been expressed, which as with Christian orthodoxy may indicate a basic uncertainty.[46] It is an issue with which the church has to deal, in particular, because the theologians who write about the myth of Christian uniqueness still find their audience and readers in the Christian community. The theological justification of a radical pluralism is finally a more serious challenge to traditional Christianity than the existence of pluralism itself.

One of the clearest statements of the radical modification of Christian faith which some theologians think pluralism demands has been given with clarity and vigor by Gordon Kaufman.

> From our modern historical vantage point, however, looking back at the many great and diverse cultural and religious traditions that have appeared in human history, all of these diverse conceptions and pictures seem best understood as the product of human imaginative creativity in the face of the great mystery that life is to all of us. Out of, and on the basis of such traditions of meaning, value, and truth, all men and women live. . . .
>
> Christian theology would understand itself in essentially the same terms that it understands other religious activity and reflection—namely, as human imaginative response to the necessity to

find orientation for life in a particular historical situation. It would thus keep itself open to insights, criticism, and correction from other points of view, including other religious and secular perspectives and worldviews. . . .

To acknowledge forthrightly and regularly that our theological statements and claims are simply ours—that they are the products of our own human study and reflection, and of the spontaneity and creativity of our human powers, imaginatively to envision a world and our human place within that world is to set us free from these all too easy but false moves toward authoritarianism, which has characterized Christian theology in the past.[47]

Kaufman's view would seem to undercut any basis for preaching. In the place of preaching there may be a theological lecture or conversation that has equal validity with other theological lectures and conversations. If theology is just conversation, just the imaginative construct of human creativity as Kaufman suggests or as Richard Rorty concludes about philosophy, one voice in the great conversation, then there is very little to preach.[48]

Congregations that gather to hear a preacher are called out by their conviction that the Bible is the Word of God and that Jesus Christ is God incarnate. This has been true from the first century to the twentieth century. These two views about the authority of scripture and about the significance of Jesus Christ are now openly challenged, sometimes with more rhetoric, but sometimes, as in the case of Gordon Kaufman, with great clarity by many theologians in the life of the church. The public persuasive power of the new theologies in calling forth worshiping communities is thus far minimal.

The advocates of a theology of world religions speak very vigorously against the triumphalism of the church, against the arrogance of the Christian claim of uniqueness, and even call the traditional views of the church idolatry.[49] This criticism has to be taken seriously.

How can we, on the one hand, affirm the authority of the Bible as the Word of God and Jesus Christ as God incarnate and avoid the obvious perils of triumphalism, arrogance, and idolatry? It is no doubt true that Christian theologians and Christians have been guilty of all of these, though I know of no reason to believe they have been any more guilty than are the advocates of a theology of world religions in their own proposals. Arrogance, triumphalism, idolatry are universal human problems. Modern secular universities, Harvard and Yale, for example, illustrate the human problem of arrogance and ruthless, even violent, intolerance of dissenting opinion quite as much as the church ever has.[50]

The solutions pluralism offers are all at the expense of the integrity of Christian faith. From the pluralist perspective, the claim that the Word became flesh is always foolishness or a scandal. Only within the community is Jesus Christ the power and wisdom of God for salvation. The theological language from the tradition and from the Bible still has great power. One evidence of this is use of the language as well as the resources of the community by scholars whose own theology is very different from that of the church.

The constructive facing of the problem of pluralism begins with the question of stance or method. John Knox, longtime professor of New Testament at Union Theological Seminary in New York, writing in 1967, declared:

> It [Christian inquiry] embraces every aspect of man's life, and indeed of the cosmos; but the base from which the inquiry proceeds is the Church's existence in its concrete reality and the recognition that certain truths about God and man are expressed in that existence. The Church will vigorously encourage this inquiry in order not only to identify these truths clearly and surely and thus inform, confirm, and enrich the Christian experience of its members, but also to be in position to interpret them as far as possible in terms which those outside the Church can understand.
>
> On the other hand, I do not see that the Church has any obligation, or that it belongs to its nature, to encourage theological inquiry which does not begin with what I have called this existential a priori. I do not mean that it will forbid (if it has the power) or impede inquiry conducted on the basis of other presuppositions, nor do I mean that the Church's own thinking may not often be corrected, enlarged, and quickened by the challenge of such thinking by others; but I cannot see that the Church itself could appropriately carry on such inquiry without denying itself. In a word, the Church's theological inquiry will be *its own,* just as any individual's theological inquiry will be his own, proceeding from premises established within its own life (and thus in a sense

"revealed"), however strongly supported by, because illuminative of, the world and human experience as a whole these premises may prove to be.[51]

Étienne Gilson, the Thomist scholar, in his autobiography confesses that for forty years he misread Thomas, refusing to see that he was a theologian, not a philosopher. As a theologian he began with revelation and as a man of faith was free to welcome all truth from whichever side it came. Augustine said, "Love God, and do what you will." A disciple of Thomas can say, "Believe, and think what you will. Like charity, faith is a liberator." The starting point is faith. "The church knows that refusing the temptations of vain philosophy she may suffer temporary losses but, by giving in, she would cease to exist."[52]

> The God whose existence we demonstrate is but part of the God whose existence we hold to be true on the strength of our faith in His words. In this sense the God of rational knowledge is, so to speak, included within the God of faith.[53]

The public and persuasive power of theology and preaching has not historically been based on theological argument that begins on some neutral ground, if there is such, certainly not on a secular ground. The great persuaders or preachers, such as Athanasius, Augustine, Thomas, Luther, Calvin, Wesley, always began with revelation and spoke from the perspective of faith. All theology is public, that is, spoken to human beings as human beings calling them to decision. Preaching that explicates the faith with clarity and seeks to understand the social, political, cultural, economic, and personal dimensions of life in the light of that faith has always persuaded people. Augustine and Calvin alike understood that rhetoric that is theologically responsible is a "proof" of Christian faith.[54] On the human level the church has lived by the persuasiveness of preaching. There is abundant evidence in the statistics of American church life today that this is still true, even when the preaching is theologically inept.[55] If we begin with pluralism, there is no possibility of maintaining the historical Christian faith. An inescapable tension and contradiction exist between pluralism and the profoundly different understandings of reality which exist among religions. If we begin, however, with our deepest Christian commitments about Jesus Christ, there are at least five affirmations we can make that help us to deal constructively with the truth wherever it may be found as well as the fact of pluralism.

1. The first response is pragmatic and prudential. A variety of religious groups exists in our society. The pragmatic and prudential question is how these religious communities who do in fact exist can operate in the same society. This is no simple question, and it may be revealed, as time goes on, that communities are not possible unless there is a greater consensus than seems to be true today.[56] In any case, one response is pragmatic and prudential, to work out ways that diverse groups can live together with decency and with dignity.

2. The second response is humility. Humility is implicit in the Christian doctrine of creation which affirms that we are creatures of a particular time and space and of limited intellectual powers. The very fact that we are creatures means that our perspective is parochial. Furthermore, Christian theology affirms that all human beings are sinners. As Reinhold Niebuhr liked to insist, it seems impossible for us not to affirm that our truth is the truth, to realize that we both have and do not have the truth.[57] Yet as H. Richard Niebuhr wrote, the relativity of our perception of the truth does not mean that that which we perceive is relative.[58]

Christian doctrine requires a humility that recognizes the human limitations of finite intelligence, of a particular human experience, of a location in a specific space, time, and social group, and the sinful limitation of self-interest. This humility applies to the advocates of the relativity of all human awareness, of the sociology of knowledge, as well as to others. This relativism and limitation of our knowing also applies to all the major decisions of life, to the experience of falling in love or choosing a career. Yet the fact that we cannot know absolutely that another person loves us does not prevent us from risking our lives that our conviction is true. The Christian must be aware of the limited, broken, and fragmentary character of his or her perceptions; but for centuries Christians who have known their own perception of God's presence in Jesus Christ is broken and flawed have affirmed in faith that it is also true.

The Enlightenment and contemporary pluralism encourage the belief that the final truth about the world is hidden from us.[59] Theologians may engage in theological conversation but there may be no one "out there." Hence there is the great temptation even in the community of faith to soften the question of truth. Theology is construed as a cultural linguistic activity, which it is;[60] or as the narrative of Jesus taken seriously because it is followable, which it surely is.[61] Yet if the doctrine of the Trinity does not attempt to say in a faltering way who God is, and if the life and teaching of Jesus is not only the way but also the truth, why should anyone bother either with the Trinity or with Jesus Christ or Christian discipleship? Christian faith and theology have their origin in the initiative of God or not at all.[62] Revelation as the origin of Christian experience as well as of understanding contradicts the basic assumptions of an Enlightenment culture.

Every human being must speak with the humility of a creature and a sinner. This is no more a problem for orthodox Christianity than it is for the secular exponent of the sociology of knowledge. Human life in every dimension of personal existence must be lived on the basis of reasonable certainty and tacit understanding.[63] On this basis believers with humility may say "the Word became flesh" is the truth.

3. We can respond with respect for human dignity. It is our Christian conviction that God created every human person as a self who must be responsible in the presence of God. There are depths of the human self which have to be respected, and no state and no society has the right to invade the privacy of the self.[64] Christians above all ought to insist upon not only the right but the responsibility of every human being to assume the dignity of a child of God and to answer for himself or herself in the presence of God. Christians, on the basis of their own theological convictions, respect and protect the privacy of a person. This is what it means in part to confess that a human being is the child of God.

4. We can respond to the coming of Jesus Christ in a manner congruent with the coming itself. The birth of Jesus is told with stark simplicity. Mary was a humble chambermaid to her Lord, and Joseph a carpenter. The birthplace was a stable. Jesus was born, not among the powerful or the rich, but among plain, genuine human beings who waited for the Lord. This distinctive

character has survived the temptation of artists and writers to portray it otherwise.[65] The Word of God came into our midst without the trappings of power. He did not seek to overwhelm. The reality itself was sufficient. Furthermore, Jesus came not for the righteous or for the powerful, but to the poor, in the biblical sense of those who want help and who know that God is their only salvation. John Murray Cuddihy speaks of the homely Protestant and the decorum of imperfection.[66] There is the decorum of sinners saved by grace. Yet we must remember the unostentatious, meek sinners of the New Testament dared to die for their faith and to witness for it before the rulers and the powerful people of the world.

God's grace in Jesus Christ "was not a unilateral decision of force or a dictatorial declaration of will or a sovereign overpowering." God's grace is not brutal. Barth continually insists that God's grace provides human beings time and space they do not deserve.

> What is the purpose of the space which is still given to man, of his actual existence in this new and further time after the reconciliation of the world with God as already seen and proclaimed in Jesus Christ? We can now give the positive answer. Its purpose is obviously this—that God will not allow His last Word to be fully spoken or the consummation determined and accomplished and proclaimed by Him to take place in its final form until He has first heard a human response to it, a human Yes; until His grace has found its correspondence in a voice of human thanks from the depths of the world reconciled with Himself; until here and now, before the dawning of His eternal Sabbath, He has received praise from the heart of His human creation.[67]

5. The final response must be theological. From the beginning, Christians have been shaped by the conviction that God had acted for the salvation of all people in Jesus Christ. Every page of the New Testament is written with this conviction. Jesus Christ is the one who brings to fulfillment the longings and yearnings of all human beings. "All things have been delivered to me by my Father; and no one knows the Son except the Father, and no one knows the Father except the Son and any one to whom the Son chooses to reveal him" (Matt. 11:27). What God had foretold by the mouth of the prophets he has now fulfilled

(Acts 3:18). Or the God who made the world and everything in it and who commands all people to repent has now judged the world by the man whom he appointed and raised from the dead (Acts 17). The Word, God in his self-expression, by whom all things were made, became flesh and dwelt among us (John 1). "In many and various ways God spoke of old to our fathers by the prophets; but in these last days he has spoken to us by a Son, whom he appointed the heir of all things, through whom also he created the world. He reflects the glory of God and bears the very stamp of his nature, upholding the universe by his word of power" (Heb. 1:1–3). The Christian community in every time and place has lived by this faith, which has received its classic theological statements at Nicaea and Chalcedon.

This faith is a confession, not a demonstration. No historian or theologian can show that Jesus is the Christ. Yet Christians have always confessed it as the truth as well as faith. The confession is not a manner of speaking or feeling, but the conviction that Jesus is in reality the incarnation of God, and that what is true for the Christian is true for all people. In the light of this conviction, they have sought to understand the world. The conviction about the uniqueness and significance of Jesus Christ arises out of faith perceptions, out of repentance and commitment, not out of a study of religions. Yet this faith illuminates and makes sense out of all human experience.

Augustine summarized the consequences of his rubric "We believe in order to understand," for a pluralistic society, in this way:

> This heavenly city, then, while it sojourns on earth, calls citizens out of all nations, and gathers together a society of pilgrims of all languages, not scrupling about diversities in the manners, laws, and institutions whereby earthly peace is secured and maintained, but recognising that, however various these are, they all tend to one and the same end of earthly peace. It therefore is so far from rescinding and abolishing these diversities, that it even preserves and adapts them, so long only as no hindrance to the worship of the one supreme and true God is thus introduced.[68]

Calvin refused to speculate whether God would have become incarnate if human beings had not sinned and needed redemption.[69] Yet there was never any doubt that the God who redeems is also the God who creates. Hence all truth is consonant with what has happened in Jesus Christ, and can be included within the Christian faith.[70] The theological basis for the persuasive interpretation of all creation in the light of the revelation of God in Jesus Christ has always been affirmed by Reformed theology. Today this persuasive proclaiming of the faith is crucial.

The Augustinian way of dealing with this problem can be abused. As Gilson warns, "Second rate thinkers will use Revelation as a substitute for rational knowledge. . . . Thus confronted with a wisdom of Christians elaborated by Christians and for the exclusive benefit of Christians, unbelievers find themselves in a rather awkward position."[71] The danger is very clear, but in fact the theology of Reinhold Niebuhr in our time demonstrates the powerfulness of this approach in getting the attention of secular intellectuals.[72]

Contemporary theologians of the Reformed way have dealt with this problem in various ways. Karl Barth's attention was fixed on Jesus Christ to the exclusion of world religions. Yet, having made this point, Barth was free to hear true words spoken in the secular world.[73] Jesus Christ was the abolition of religion. Revelation defines religion. Religion as a general human activity is unbelief. Barth's attention is on the divine acts that make Christianity as a religion possible.

Emil Brunner was more aware of world religions. For him, all religion is rooted in revelation, and complicated by sinful human responses to that revelation. The critical point is not religion, but Jesus Christ, who stands in judgment on all religions, including the Christian religion.

> Jesus Christ is both the Fulfillment of all religion and the Judgment on all religion. As the Fulfiller, He is the Truth which these religions seek in vain. There is no phenomenon in the history of religion that does not point toward Him. . . .
> He is also the Judgment on all religion. Viewed in His light, all religious systems appear untrue, unbelieving, and indeed godless.[74]

Hendrik Kraemer came to the problem with a great knowledge of world religions. On the one hand, this knowledge gave him an appreciation of world religions which he understood as a human response to God's universal revelation of himself. At the same time, it made him more aware of the differences between religions and of religions as closed systems. Christianity can never be the simple fulfillment of other religions.

> The Christian revelation, as the record of God's self-disclosing revelation in Jesus Christ, is absolutely sui generis. It is the story of God's sovereign acts having become decisively and finally manifest in Jesus Christ, the Son of the Living God, in whom God became flesh and revealed his grace and truth. . . . Religious experiences or ideas are, of course, not absent from the Bible, and they are by no means unimportant, but in no sense are they central. What is central and fundamental in the Bible is the registering, describing and witnessing to God's creative and redemptive dealing with man and the world.[75]

Insofar as Jesus fulfills persistent yearnings and apprehensions, he also recasts them. Furthermore, God as he is revealed in Jesus Christ is "contrary" to the sublimest pictures we made of him before we knew him in Jesus Christ.[76] In his final writing, he concludes, "If we are ever to know what true and divinely willed religion is, we can do this only through God's revelation in Jesus Christ and through nothing else."[77]

The positions of Barth, Brunner, and Kraemer may not be persuasive to many who are impressed by the fact of world religions, but their theological reasoning can be convincing for those who begin with the revelation of God in Jesus Christ and with the New Testament. A critic may say that it is not true that Jesus is God incarnate, but the integrity of the theological arguments of Augustine, Calvin, Barth, Brunner, and Kraemer cannot be denied, given the fact of "the Word made flesh." In a variety of ways in their theology, this faith seeks understanding, that is the intelligibility of world religions and of pluralism.

The critical decisiveness of what happened in Jesus Christ is the foundation for Christian preaching. Without the intensity of this conviction, preaching will languish, however much it may be maintained by the structures of the church, and however much it may serve as entertainment, moral exhortation, political advice, or therapy. In recent years we have heard a great deal about burn-out, even in the ministry. *Fortune* magazine once declared that

burnout meant one had a job for which he or she was not qualified.[78] It may also be that we are engaged in a work for which we
have lost our enthusiasm. For example, there is the English professor who has to teach English but who no longer loves English
literature, or the historian who has to teach history but who is no
longer excited by the drama and meaningfulness of human life
on this planet. Without the passionate conviction of faith, there
cannot be Christian preaching, any more than there can be great
teaching of literature and history without an enthusiasm for literature and history. Hence the recovery of preaching first of all is
rooted in the living faith and the conviction of the preacher.

Pluralism undercuts not only the necessity for preaching but
enthusiasm for preaching. It certainly undercuts any justification
for the enormous expense that preaching entails on the part of the
gifts of the worshiping, believing community. It constitutes a challenge for the preacher to proclaim Jesus Christ through whom all
things were created, in whom all things are held together (Col.
1:16–17).

IV

The need for the recovery of preaching in our time is plain
enough. The health of the Christian community has always been
reflected in great preaching. It is difficult to find a period of vital
Christian growth in the entire two millennia of Christian history
without great preaching. The need for great preaching today in
an increasingly pluralistic and pagan society is clear enough.

The recovery of great preaching is more complex. In any
case, it is not simply a matter of courses in homiletics. Preaching
requires personal commitments, scholarly competences, and technical skills.

1. The recovery of great preaching involves the renewal of
faith. The origin of preaching is in the heart, not in the head, not
in reasoned argument but in the passionate conviction of the
human heart. Hence preaching is a gift of the Holy Spirit for
which we must hope and pray.

2. The recovery of great preaching calls for the revival of the
Christian community as a disciplined, knowledgeable, worshiping community of people. The recovery of preaching and the

recovery of the community will have to take place together, because there can be no recovery of a vital Christian community, well informed, apart from the recovery of great preaching. And on the other hand, a great congregation makes a great preacher.

3. The recovery of great preaching involves the recovery of the Bible, which has been assimilated into one's thinking, and the recovery of theological competence that likewise has become part of the structure of one's personal existence.

4. The recovery of great preaching depends on a recovery of a framework of theological reality that holds life together in a coherent way and in which we can see our place in the church and in the world. Preaching has to do with the ultimate issues of human origin and destiny and not with the occasional facts of politics or organization. Ideally, the preacher should recapitulate in his or her own life the history of doctrine, what the church through the centuries has believed, confessed, preached, and taught.

5. The recovery of great preaching requires the acquisition of a language that is precise and clear, that has the quality of reality, and that is appropriate to communicate the Christian gospel. As long as English is spoken, this must build upon the remarkable literary and theological achievement of the Puritans. Language appropriate to the faith cannot be finally learned in academic communities but only as those learned in the tradition engage a broad range of people, learned and unlearned, in theological conversation. The scientific, technological, secular character of our culture makes the problem of language all the more important. As Calvin put the traditional theology of the church in the language of ordinary discourse, so that is our task today.

Preaching has always been powerful to move people, to shape personalities and communities in many times and places. It is not likely that its power is diminished today. All people who seek to shape human history, politicians, ideologues, advocates, would give anything to have what is available to the church in the gathering of people. The great crowds on Saturdays at college football games are impressive, but within a few miles' radius of football stadiums, more people gather to worship God and hear a sermon on Sunday.[79] This gathering of the people is a phenomenon that cannot be duplicated in our society, and it is a challenge and opportunity for those called to preach.

CHAPTER FOUR

Teaching

John Calvin found the apostolic succession, or the continuity of the church today with the church of the apostles, in the teaching of the faith, which hands on the apostolic witness from generation to generation. On the deepest level, the apostolicity of the church is found in obedience to the living Lord of the church and in the presence of the Holy Spirit. The human work which maintains the continuity is not ordination, not an office, but the preaching and the teaching of the gospel. The church was founded "not upon men's judgments, not upon priesthoods, but upon the teaching of the apostles and prophets."[1]

I

The teaching task of the church has its warrant in the practice of Jesus. He was called teacher by his disciples (Mark 4:38), by the people (Matt. 19:16), and by his enemies (Matt. 22:24). He referred to himself as teacher at least four times. The Gospels refer more than forty times to him as teaching. The message which he proclaimed was called teaching (Matt. 7:28).

C. H. Dodd popularized the distinction between preaching and teaching.[2] This distinction is important in its emphasis that our salvation is found in what happened in Jesus Christ and is not simply information. Neither is it simply insight which illuminates life. It is what God has done to forgive sin and to call us to repentance, what God has done to heal and transform our lives.

Preaching is a summons, a proclamation. Teaching is the explication of preaching. Yet the two cannot be separated, for preaching, even the preaching of Peter and Paul in Acts, involves teaching, and teaching, at least teaching in the Christian community, is always preaching. In fact, it may be argued that more teaching is done in the eleven o'clock worship hour than at any other time in the life of the church.

Jesus himself was born into a community that traditioned the faith by teaching. The words of Moses in Deuteronomy are still as moving a charter of a community of faith as can be found anywhere.

> Hear, O Israel: The LORD our God is one LORD; and you shall love the LORD your God with all your heart, and with all your soul, and with all your might. And these words which I command you this day shall be upon your heart; and you shall teach them diligently to your children, and shall talk of them when you sit in your house, and when you walk by the way, and when you lie down, and when you rise. And you shall bind them as a sign upon your hand, and they shall be as frontlets between your eyes. And you shall write them on the doorposts of your house and on your gates.
>
> Deuteronomy 6:4–9

The commands of Deuteronomy and the practice of Jesus are not unique. All human communities live by teaching. Edward Hirsch of the University of Virginia, in his best-selling book *Cultural Literacy,* writes:

> The weight of human tradition across many cultures supports the view that basic acculturation should largely be completed by age thirteen. At that age Catholics are confirmed, Jews bar or bat mitzvahed, and tribal boys and girls undergo the rites of passage into the tribe. According to the anthropological record, all cultures whose educational methods have been reported in the *Human Relations Area Files* (the standard source for anthropological data) have used memorization to carry on their tradition.[3]

Hirsch supports this point by noting that our distaste for memorization is "more pious than realistic." Children have "an almost instinctive urge to learn specific tribal traditions."[4] They are fascinated with catalogs of information and exhibit an amazing capacity to memorize complete baseball, football, and basketball statistics.

Hirsch's chief point is the knowledge-bound character of all cognitive skills, a point he elaborately documents. Reading and writing cannot be effectively taught simply as skills, "as empty skills independent of specific knowledge."[5]

His concern is that American high school graduates do not share much knowledge, or rather that the knowledge they do share is "ephemeral and narrowly confined to their generation." Yet real literacy depends upon the breadth of one's acquaintance with a national culture. Literacy depends on the background information, "a network of information that all competent readers possess."[6] The tragedy of contemporary culture is that one can no longer assume that people know what in the past was known by every literate person.

Hirsch's *Cultural Literacy* and Allan Bloom's *Closing of the American Mind* have received the approbation of the reading public, as their phenomenal sales indicate. Best-seller lists do not establish the argument of the book so honored, but they are an accurate indication of the state of the market and the judgment of the public. Each book indicates that the heritage which has been entrusted in our culture is at risk.

The same problem exists in the church as is evident not only in polls of religious knowledge but also in the ineffectiveness of programs that seek to teach theological and ethical skills before acquiring the specific knowledge of the biblical and theological traditions.[7] In the church as well as in society, all cognitive skills require specific knowledge.

The Presbyterian Church until mid-century gave medals for church attendance, awards for memory work, and the Bible was learned as it is written. All these practices can be criticized, but in retrospect the question must be raised whether they were not discarded too quickly, whether they were not more effective in establishing the Christian community than the practices that followed after them. These earlier practices did contribute effectively to the maintenance of the Christian community, and they provided data for theological and moral discourse. It is no more possible in the church than in society to develop cognitive skills without specific data. We can teach people to read instructions and directions, as many Communist countries have done, but without the mastery of great literature, significant thought about the great issues of life and death is seriously limited. Growth to Christian maturity requires knowledge of the scriptures and of the church's reflection on its life and faith.

The situation in the church is complicated by our society. The church no longer exists in Christendom or in Protestantdom. In the quite recent past in many American communities, Christian knowledge was transmitted not only by the church but also by the society. Many public schools were, in fact, Protestant schools in which the Bible was read, Bible stories were told, and prayers were offered to God. These schools persisted into the 1960s. In earlier periods spelling books and reading books contained a vast amount of data from the Bible and Christian theology.[8]

Abraham Lincoln was not a member of the organized church, and in the nineteenth century, the organized church itself was weak. Yet Abraham Lincoln's second inaugural address is one of the finest theological writings of the nineteenth century. Lincoln had assimilated biblical knowledge, biblical language, and biblical ideas from the culture as well as from the church.[9] Today, an Abraham Lincoln is no longer a possibility. In the twentieth century, all the Presidents have been members of the organized church, but only Woodrow Wilson and Jimmy Carter, and possibly Harry Truman, have been biblically literate.

In 1950, more than 50 percent of the college students in America were in church colleges or in private institutions, most of which had been established by the church, and some of which at that time had the symbols of the church at the center of the school's life. The Protestant chapel was on the campus of elite universities and the presidents of those universities participated in the service of Christian worship, even at Harvard, Yale, and Princeton. Today universities are increasingly secular and secularizing. Almost 80 percent of the college students in America are in state institutions.[10]

As late as 1950, if the church did not teach people the Bible and the faith, the society in various ways did. This is now no longer true, though, as Allan Bloom has pointed out, the Bible is the one book American people generally have in common, the book that has shaped American life more than any other book.[11] Here it is also worth noting Sydney Ahlstrom's judgment that the Puritan and Reformed communities were a major influence in shaping the life and institutions of colonial America, an influence that was articulated in the Westminster Confession and catechisms.[12] The result of the deterioration of biblical and classical literacy is, as Bloom notes, that American young people today know quite well what a beautiful body is, and they spend enormous sums of money and time in acquiring a beautiful body, but they do not know what a beautiful soul is. In fact, they are not sure there is any such thing as a soul or a self.[13]

The secularization of education from the kindergarten to the graduate school is a most serious problem, but it is aggravated by the secular or pagan perspective of the media. Surveys, as noted in chapter 1, indicate an exceedingly low sympathy or empathy for Christian faith on the part of the media.[14] This is true of newscasters and, in particular, of the soap operas that consume so much television time. The impact of television which brings alien theological, philosophical, and moral ideas into the bedrooms and the living rooms of church people is difficult to calculate.

The condition in the culture and the condition in the church emphasize the importance of the church's recovering the capacity to hand on the traditional Christian faith in our society. Lionel Trilling was once asked about his responsibility to students as human beings. He responded that his first responsibility to all students as human beings, regardless of their particular situation, was to represent to them as best he could the tradition of English literature. If he did not do this, he argued, no one else would. Hence this was the greatest service that he could render the student, no matter what the student's personal condition may have been.[15]

The great task of the church today is to preach and to teach the faith in a secular and pluralistic society, to hand it on in the Christian community. If the church does not do this, no one else in a secular and pluralistic society will do so. If the Presbyterian Church does not tradition, does not hand on, does not teach the Presbyterian way, no one else will do so.

II

Teaching in the church is different from teaching generally in that it begins with an awareness of the holy, a sense of the numinous. The church is not a club, not a therapy group, not an educational institution, not an agency for social change. It is the people of God who live in the awareness of the mystery that encompasses human existence, and who believe that that mystery has been transmuted into meaning in Jesus Christ. No one ever stated this better than John Calvin did in the *Institutes of the Christian Religion,* and no one has ever put more emphasis upon this perspective for the life and work of the church, for its teaching and pastoral ministry. Teaching in the church is above all the explication of what God has done for human salvation.

This perspective is apparent in Calvin's understanding of theology as the explication of the dialectical relation of God and man. As he put it in the opening words of the *Institutes,* "Nearly all the wisdom we possess, that is to say, true and sound wisdom, consists of two parts: the knowledge of God and of ourselves. But, while joined by many bonds, which one precedes and brings forth the other is not easy to discern." He then goes on to say that "it is certain that man never achieves a clear knowledge of himself unless he has first looked upon God's face."[16] In life and in theology everything has to do with God and with God's relationship to us.

Calvin makes the same point in his explication of the Christian life.

> We are consecrated and dedicated to God in order that we may thereafter think, speak, meditate, and do, nothing except to his glory. For a sacred thing may not be applied to profane uses without marked injury to him. . . .
>
> We are God's: let us therefore live for him and die for him. We are God's: let his wisdom and will therefore rule all our actions. We are God's: let all the parts of our life accordingly strive toward him as our only lawful goal.[17]

Calvin knew, with a clarity few have in the history of the church, that the chief business of human life is having to do with the living God. All of the Christian life has to be lived in this awareness. This is especially true of teaching. This is the difference between the church school or the Sunday school and the public school. In the church school we have to do with the issues of life and death, with the ultimate meaning of our human existence, with issues of ultimate concern.[18]

Karl Barth in our time has made this point about the holiness of the church with typical clarity and vigor.

> Holy means set apart, marked off, and therefore differentiated, singled out, and taken (and set) on one side as a being which has its own origin and nature and meaning and direction—and all this with a final definitiveness, decisively, inviolably, and unalterably, because it is God who does it. The term indicates the contradistinction of the Christian community to the surrounding world, and in particular to the other gatherings and societies which exist in the world. It is not a natural society after the manner of the nations, nor is it based on social contracts, or agreements, or temporary or permanent understandings and arrangements. It is not a society of necessity and compulsion like the state, nor is it a free society for a particular purpose like an order or a club or an economic or cultural union. It has its own basis and its own goal. It cannot, therefore, understand itself in the light of the basis of other societies or follow their goals.[19]

Without the awareness of the holy, or, to put it another way, without the presence and the gifts of the Holy Spirit, the whole character of the church and the teaching in the church are changed. Teaching in the church must always be in the context of the holy, which only the Holy Spirit can give. Without this gift of the Holy Spirit,

> even the most holy work is profane; its [Christian community] preaching is simply a kind of explanation and instruction, or enthusiastic protestation; its baptism and the Lord's supper are religious rites like others; its theology is a kind of philosophy, its mission a species of propaganda, etc. They all have their interest and importance and practical value from other standpoints—intellectual, moral, psychological, sociological—but they cannot be holy without the work of the living Lord of the community. No institutions within which its activity is done, no good will on the part of men who act, no old or new technique which is used, can make them holy or prevent them from again becoming secular.

> The community is entirely in the hands of its Lord, and that means that it is thrown back on his having mercy upon it and making its unholy activity holy and acknowledging it as such.[20]

The awareness of the holy is no human achievement, and certainly cannot be programmed or contrived. It is always a gift. Teaching must be done in a way that claims the promise of God's presence in a manner appropriate to the expectation of the gift of the Holy Spirit. The holy must not be construed in moralistic terms, and most emphatically not in a sense of obedience to rules and laws. All ministers, as Calvin surely knew, are creatures, limited by time and space, and more than that they are sinners. Yet in his lofty doctrine of the ministry, he believed that ministers by their persons, by the manner in which they carried out their responsibilities, were a means by which the congregation knew that they had to do in the life of the church, not with another human endeavor, however good, but with the Lord God, creator of heaven and earth. We cannot command the sense of the holy. But if we do certain things, we are more likely to be aware that we have to do with the living God, more aware of the presence of the Creator and the Redeemer, at once both frightening and fascinating.

Calvin made two decisions which helped to ensure that teaching would take place in the context of holiness. He insisted that teaching was an integral part of the work of a pastor.[21] Not every teacher is a pastor, but every pastor is a teacher. In particular, the pastor is the teacher in the congregation. The ordinances for the church in Geneva combined preaching and catechetical instruction. Calvin also combined teaching with discipline. Admonition and warnings are in part the work of the pastor as a teacher.[22] Teaching as the maintenance of Christian doctrine is also the work of the pastor as well as the doctor. "In the preaching of his Word and sacred mysteries; he [God] has bidden that a common doctrine be there set forth for all. . . . Indeed, those in authority in the church turned over to idols the office of teaching for no other reason than that they themselves were mute."[23] Teaching is always a dimension of the pastoral ministry.

Calvin likewise made teaching an integral part of the life of the church. He joined it to worship, making mastery of the catechism a condition for admission to the mature life of the church and to the Lord's Table.

> How I wish that we might have kept the custom [of] . . . a catechizing, in which children or those near adolescence would give an account of their faith before the church. But the best method of catechizing would be to have a manual drafted for this exercise, containing and summarizing in simple manner most of the articles of our religion, on which the whole believers' church ought to agree without controversy. A child of ten would present himself to the church to declare his confession of faith, would be examined in each article, and answer to each; if he were ignorant of anything or insufficiently understood it, he would be taught. Thus, while the church looks on as a witness, he would profess the one true and sincere faith, in which the believing folk with one mind worship the one God.
>
> If this discipline were in effect today, it would certainly rouse some slothful parents, who carelessly neglect the instruction of their children as a matter of no concern to them; for then they could not overlook it without public disgrace. There would be greater agreement in faith among Christian people, and not so many would go untaught and ignorant; some would not be so rashly carried away with new and strange doctrines; in short, all would have some methodical instruction, so to speak, in Christian doctrine.[24]

Calvin and later Calvinists always assumed a theologically literate congregation to support their preaching. In Geneva, catechetical instruction was supplemented by lectures on the scripture, some of which would later be published as Calvin's commentaries. Preaching itself was instructive not only in doctrine but in the nature of sustained discourse for many congregations before the widespread development of public education. Calvin also advocated Bible reading as a means to theological literacy and above all, to mature Christian growth.

III

Teaching in the church gives instruction (1) in the scriptures, (2) in theology, (3) in the interpretation of human existence in the world in the light of Christian faith, and (4) in the duties and practices of the Christian life. This instruction is on the human level essential for the life of the community of faith; it is also the primary teaching obligation of the church. Furthermore, if it is not done by the church it will not be done by anyone else.

Many of the older manuals of Christian instruction were based on the creed, the commandments, the prayer, the sacraments, and the general duties and practices of Christians.[25] The early Protestant catechisms also followed this pattern. Any contemporary instruction must begin with this basic instruction. A secular culture and the present lack of a consensus about a catechism point to the need to teach the Bible as the Word of God and the theology of the tradition as the condition for any possible teaching about contemporary issues and problems.[26]

The first task of Christian education is the handing on of the Bible as the language and the story of faith. In teaching the Christian faith, the church must give priority to the Bible. Calvin put this very clearly.

> Let this be a firm principle: No other word is to be held as the Word of God, and given place as such in the church, than what is contained first in the Law and the Prophets, then in the writings of the apostles; and the only authorized way of teaching in the church is by the prescription and standard of his Word.[27]

The young Calvin, in a remarkable introduction to Olivétan's French Bible (1535), declared:

> But I desire only this, that the faithful people be permitted to hear their God speaking and to learn from [His] teaching. Seeing that He wills to be known by the least to the greatest; since all are promised to be God-taught (Is. 29:9); since He confesses as yet always to be working among His own, whom He calls "weaned from milk, torn from the breasts" (Is. 28:9); since He gives wisdom to children (Matt. 11:5). When, therefore, we see that there are people from all classes who are making progress in God's school, we acknowledge His truth which promised a pouring forth of His spirit on all flesh (Joel 2:28; Acts 2:17).[28]

For those who grow up in the Christian community, the Bible is not a strange book from nineteen centuries ago. The Bible, its language, its stories, and its worldview are the earliest memories by which those in the church live. The Bible—not simply the printed book, but primarily the language, the teachings, the narratives, the promises—has been handed on from generation to generation as God's Word, our priceless treasure.

Teaching about the Bible is secondary to teaching the Bible. The conviction that the Bible is sufficiently plain, "that not only the learned but the unlearned, in a due use of the ordinary means, may attain unto a sufficient understanding of them," is a classic Protestant doctrine which has been established through the centuries.[29]

Northrop Frye has observed that in order to understand English literature, one must first know the Bible, not on the top of one's mind but in the depths of one's person.[30] A knowledge of the Bible, which comes so early in life and is so pervasive of one's thinking that it settles to the bottom of one's mind and becomes the filter through which all our thinking develops, is important for understanding literature, but it is critically important for understanding the Christian faith. Hence the first task of Christian teaching is to hand on the Bible simply as it is written, so that its stories, its narratives, its images and metaphors, its teaching, become the warp and weft of our life.

It is possible to state Christian theology in abstract, nonhistorical terms, that is, to state it in a language other than that of the Bible. In some measure, this is true of the Westminster Confession of Faith, whose writers wanted to be precisely correct. It was true in some measure of both medieval Catholic and Protestant scholastics. In our own time, Karl Rahner has made a remarkable statement of Christian faith in nonbiblical language.[31] It can be legitimately argued, however, that these more abstract statements of Christian faith are viable only so long as the history out of which the faith developed is known; Christian faith must finally be stated in the language of history.

Today the knowledge of the narratives, the history, the language, the metaphors and images of the Bible is at great risk. A secular society has effectively eliminated them from school textbooks and from much of culture. Hence a first step in the renewal of the church is the teaching of the Bible as it is written. The content of the Bible, the structure of the biblical story, has a priority over any other knowledge of the Bible.

The Christian community reads the Bible as the narrative of the deeds of the triune God, of the God and Father of our Lord Jesus Christ, in creation and redemption, and the narrative of human beings "taking a hand in their fates and fortunes, pulling at the story in the direction they want to carry it, making decisions of their own" in response to God.[32] The Bible as the church reads it, is not simply the re-presentation of a kerygma or the disclosure of a way of being human in the world. It is primarily the narrative of the concrete, personal acts of God in the world and the authentic acts of human beings in response. Therefore the first task in the church is to read the Bible as the Word of God with attention focused on the narrative of what God has done, culminating in the life, death, and resurrection of Jesus Christ. This narative is the source of the church's life and is the context in which the parables, the exhortations, the wisdom, and the theological reasoning of the Bible must be understood. This "common sense" reading of the scriptures in the context of the church's faith is crucial for the church's life and also for its theology. Culture and social contexts have changed. The readers of the Bible need modern wisdom. Yet the basic decisions of human life today are easily identified with those of the first century. Moreover, it is our faith that the God of Jesus Christ is the same. Hence the truth of the Protestant rubic that ordinary Christians can read the scriptures for themselves is a primary basis of the church's life.

There are other ways to read the Bible. It is also a historical document and an influential Near Eastern writing. In the church, however, the Bible is first read as the Word of God. This Word discloses who God is and what God has done for our salvation. Moreover, this Word is addressed to us and calls for our response. The Christian community reads the scriptures as God's gracious message and summons to each of us.

The Bible is a human work and it can be studied as any other book. Its role as an influential book in ancient history would justify study, but could not possibly account for the tremendous company of historical critics who spend their lives studying it. Apart from the community of faith, biblical scholarship could only be maintained in radically reduced form. The critical study of scripture, on the other hand, does not sustain the community of faith. Few if any persons have moved from the critical study of scripture to Christian commitment. The Bible must first be read and taught as the Word of God. Teaching about the Bible must follow after teaching the Bible as it is written, that is, as the narrative of the acts of God for our salvation.

The church has always read the Bible critically and with an awareness that critics outside the community of faith could doubt its truth as the Word of God. Tertullian, Origen, Augustine, among others in the ancient church, took notice of the criticisms.[33] John Calvin, along with other Protestant Reformers, made use of the best humanist skills of his day.[34]

Augustine, whose theology was guided by the rubric "We believe in order to understand," likewise insisted that reason must be used to distinguish faith from credulity. This means that Christians must read the Bible not simply as the believing community but also as persons of reason under the command to love God with all the mind as well as the heart. Christian faith does depend upon the historical reliability of the scriptures and in particular of the portrait of Jesus Christ in the New Testament. In this sense, Christian faith is at the mercy of history. This does not mean, however, that the Christian community is simply at the mercy of highly trained historical critics. Historical study is notably subjective and the final judgment about the historicity of the narratives must be made not simply by scholars in their study but also by the commonsense wisdom of persons who in their own lives have experienced the passage of history. Judgments about the scriptures must be made finally in the worshiping church, not in scholars' studies. Historical criticism cannot establish that the Bible is or is not the Word of God. This conviction is always a personal decision that may be helped or hindered by critical study.

Christians read the Bible as the Word of God with an openness to critical study, but without slavish dependence upon such study, which may be directed by an alien faith.

The second task of Christian education is to teach the theology of the church—the church's message as it has been put together in rational, coherent statements. This is the theology of the ancient creeds: the Apostles' Creed, the Nicene Creed, the Chalcedonian Definition. It is the theology of the Reformation confessions. It is the theology of the great creative theologians such as Augustine, Luther, and Calvin. The great task of teaching is to make this theology available to members of the Christian community.

The classical Protestant theologians were preachers who wrote their theology for the Christian community. Yet even so, the second generation of Protestant theologians contained persons such as Wollebius and later the Puritans who endeavored to summarize further the Christian faith in forms that could be easily memorized and in terms of structure committed quickly to memory.[35] Until the Second World War, the mainstream of Protestant theology, particularly in the Reformed tradition, was written for the Christian community and was intelligible not only to theologians but also to literate lay people. One of the disturbing trends in the theology of the past thirty years has been the increasing tendency of theologians to write for other theologians, not for the Christian community.[36]

The great responsibility of a church theologian is, on the one hand, to be a faithful interpreter of the tradition and, on the other hand, to make this tradition available to any literate person. This is one of the basic meanings of Protestantism. It is also significant to observe that in the history of doctrine, the great creative theologies have not been written so much by persons who intended to write the new theology, but by theologians who were attempting in their particular time to be faithful interpreters of the tradition to the people of the church. John Calvin liked to insist that one test of theology is its preachableness and its capacity for edification.[37] A similar test, very useful in our time, is the test of readability. Any great Christian theology ought to be accessible to the Christian community, and persuasive in the church and to the world.

Next to teaching the Bible, the great responsibility of the Christian teacher is to make the resource of the Christian tradition available to people in the congregation, to represent faithfully the church's theology to the people. Ordination means that the minister of the church, the teacher of the church, has the responsibility to forgo his own idiosyncratic understanding of the faith and to be a faithful interpreter of the tradition.[38] The great task of Christian education is to make this tradition available to young people who are growing up and to older people whose faith is being buffeted and challenged by the crises of life.

Catechetical instruction has been important in all Christian traditions, and in particular in the Reformed tradition.[39] The early Reformed theologians were great writers of catechisms. Calvin regretted that he was not able to revise sufficiently the second edition of his catechism.[40] The Puritans were prolific writers of catechisms.[41] The writing of catechisms in the contemporary world and the practice of catechetical instruction are greatly diminished. In part this is due to the rejection of the catechetical method on educational grounds, and it is even more due to a lack of consensus among the leadership of the church as to the meaning of Christian faith.[42] The catechism had the great advantage of raising the right questions, as well as phrasing brief, concise, and relatively complete answers to those questions.[43] The memorization of the catechism gave the Christians theological resources upon which they could depend in moments of crisis.

The third task of Christian education is to help people interpret the world in the light of Christian faith. The Christian revelation does not provide us with facts so much as with insight and clues in the light of which we can understand the world about us.[44] The revelation in Jesus Christ enables us to recognize the revelation of God in the whole creation as well as in Christian history. A foremost task of Christian education is to develop the capacity of people to think in the light of the revelation of God in Jesus Christ about politics, about economics, about the crises and challenges of life. This responsibility of the educator was put remarkably well in those two classic rubrics of theological work, Augustine's claim that we believe in order to understand and Anselm's insistence that faith seeks understanding, that is, intelligibility.[45] The great Christian claim is that the Christian revelation does more justice to the facts, enables people to understand better what is happening in the world, and gives more meaning to life than any other faith whatsoever.

The negative side of this responsibility to teach persons to think in the light of the revelation of God in Jesus Christ is the exposure of the alien faiths by which many people in our society live. Reinhold Niebuhr carried on a twofold apologetic.[46] The task of the Christian apologist is to uncover the faiths by which people live and to expose the inadequacy of the concepts that govern their thinking. The positive task of the apologist is to show how Christian concepts do more justice to the economic, social, and political facts than do the concepts of a secular society. Niebuhr knew that there is nothing more irrelevant than an answer to an unasked question. Therefore an important aspect of Christian thinking is the exposure of the alien faiths and the uncovering of the basic questions of human life to which Christian faith responds.

The fourth task of Christian education is, as some ancient manuals indicated, instruction in household duties.[47] The Reformed community has always been skeptical of religious exercises. Calvin knew that exercises easily become substitutes for authentic piety. Furthermore, they lead to introspection and remoteness from life. For Calvin, the Christian life is lived amid the ordinary experience of life in the family and in the world. Therefore the exercises of Christian piety were very few and very simple.[48] They were preeminently the worship of God on Sunday and the keeping of the Lord's Day holy, daily Bible reading, daily prayer, table blessings, and the stewardship of money and time. These are all routine activities of church members. Calvin and subsequent Reformed church people apparently believed they were sufficient. In a secular and pluralistic society, the practice of these simple exercises of the faith cannot be taken for granted. Hence the educational ministry of the church must teach and encourage these practices as a basis for the Christian life in our time. The practices do not guarantee Christian living, but it is more likely that those who worship God on Sunday, who read their Bibles, who engage in daily prayer and who offer a blessing when they gather for a meal, and who give of their money and time shall effectively meet the crises and challenges of life in our time than those Christians whose lives do not have this basic discipline.

The teaching of the practices of the Christian life is a theological task. In sacraments, in liturgy, in Christian piety, much teaching in the church today conflicts with the Reformed tradition and with the theology of the creeds.[49] A church theology that emphasizes the transcendence of God cannot with integrity be united with devotional practices drawn from mystics or from the general religiosity of this and every age which minimized the distinction between creator and creature. The popular substitution of spirituality for what Calvin and later Calvinists called piety is sufficient evidence of confusion as to Christian practice and of the need for theological instruction. The task of education in Reformed churches is to teach a piety and church practices that are congruent with Reformed theology.

IV

The educational task is basic and simple. It is also realizable. Any congregation can decide that every child who reaches twelve years of age will have basic Christian knowledge which will enable that child to participate effectively in the life of the Christian community. This is a realizable goal that can be achieved through the cooperation of the church school, the pastor, the session, and the home.

The realizable goals will include memory work. (No list can be complete and final, but the following suggestions are adequate as a foundation for Christian communication and participation in the life of the church.)

The books of the Bible in order
The Apostles' Creed
The Lord's Prayer
The Ten Commandments

Psalm 23
Matthew 5:3-11
Matthew 6:25-34
Luke 2:1-14
John 3:16
John 14:1-7
Romans 8:28-39
1 Corinthians 13
2 Corinthians 5:17-21

Hymns (at least two of the following)
"Now Thank We All Our God"
"All People That on Earth Do Dwell"
"How Firm a Foundation"
"A Mighty Fortress Is Our God"

Prayers:
The general prayer of confession
The general prayer of thanksgiving
At least two table blessings

This *memory* work, which is a realizable goal, will give young people the biblical resources not only for the living of the Christian life, but also for participation in the common life of the Christian community in a meaningful way.

Any thirteen-year-old young person ought to be familiar also with biblical stories and parables. The following list again is a realizable goal.

Narratives:
The story of Adam and Eve
The story of Noah
The story of the Tower of Babel
The story of Abraham
The story of Isaac and Jacob
The story of Joseph
The story of Moses and the Exodus
The story of the giving of the Law at Sinai
The story of Samuel
The story of David
The story of one of the prophets

Crucial to participation in the Christian community as well as the Christian life is the historical material of the New Testament:

The story of the life of Jesus
The story of Peter
The story of Paul, including his missionary journeys

The parables of Jesus provide much of the teaching of Jesus in non-metaphysical story form, as well as many of the images of the Christian life. Some are very important for the language of faith. For example:

The parable of the prodigal son
The parable of the good Samaritan
The parable of the lost coin

The knowledge of this biblical material does not necessarily make one a Christian. Yet it is difficult to understand how one can be a Protestant Christian, effectively participating in the life of the community, and living in the world as a Protestant Christian, without this basic information. This knowledge is not an end in itself, but a means to Christian living today. It provides the universal vocabulary of the Christian life. The church, at such great risk today in a secular and pluralistic society, must give priority to teaching the basic, specific data which are necessary for participation in the life of the Christian community.

A basic knowledge of the history of the church and the practice of church life is also essential for meaningful participation in the life of the church. Again the church can ensure a basic knowledge. A basic list for identification would include the following:

Ancient Catholic Church
Orthodox Churches
Roman Catholic Church
Protestantism
Younger churches or Third World churches
Pentecostalism
Apostles' Creed
Nicene Creed
Augustine
Thomas Aquinas
Martin Luther
John Calvin
John Knox
Life of a missionary: Boniface or David Livingstone
Karl Barth
Reinhold Niebuhr
Presbyterian, Congregational, Episcopal
Francis Makemie
John Witherspoon
Charles Hodge
Session, presbytery, synod, General Assembly
Sacrament
Brief chart of Presbyterian history
Westminster Confession of Faith and catechisms

The distinctive characteristics of the Reformed and Presbyterian theology and ethos.
The one, holy, catholic, apostolic church.

This list is open-ended and it is prepared for Presbyterians. Any church can prepare such a list of basics and by teaching it enable church members to participate meaningfully in the life of the church.

V

In addition to the teaching of the faith in the immediate context of the church's life, Protestant churches have through the centuries developed schools, colleges, and seminaries which are attached to the church. They are not integral to the church's life as a believing community, but they may be essential to the well-being of the church's life.

The Protestant emphasis upon the supreme authority of the Holy Spirit speaking through the words of Scripture and upon the priesthood of all believers meant that the Bible should be translated into the vernacular and that the people should be taught to read the Bible for themselves. William Tyndale believed that this would make the boy behind the plow the equal of any king or archbishop. The reading of the Bible by common people had significance both for the commonwealth and for the church.[50]

Therefore Protestants from the beginning established schools to teach people how to read—not how to read instructions and directions, not to make them more efficient and more effective—but to read the Word of God, which would enable them to think more deeply and more critically about the fundamental issues of life.

In America, Protestants were at the forefront of the movement to establish public education.[51] In many instances, church schools became public schools. Yet the public school, until after the Second World War, was in many instances still a Protestant school. In the last three decades, American education has become radically secularized. The fundamental issue is not prayer in the public school, but rather the exclusion of religious content from public school instruction. On a still deeper level, the question arises as to the manner in which young people are educated. There is no such thing as Christian mathematics or Christian history or Christian literature, but it makes a very great deal of difference whether mathematics, science, literature are taught in such a way that Christian faith is an open possibility. The battle over creationism in the public school is never as simple as it seems, especially to the liberal wing of society. It is a paradox that many devout Christians radically oppose Jerry Falwell with his creationism but have no complaint about the mystical atheism or agnosticism of Carl Sagan that is in all our public schools.[52]

The recent developments in American education raise the question of whether the church can tradition itself in a highly secular and pluralistic society without once again establishing church schools.[53] This is a very difficult decision for many Protestants who have, in some measure, identified public education with the kingdom of God. The secularization of public education, however, the teaching of courses in such a manner as not to leave open the possibility of faith, or to make faith in God an unnecessary hypothesis, endangers the faith at its very fundamental roots. Therefore Protestant churches, if they are to survive, will have to face with all seriousness the question of church schools in a way that has never been raised in American education until now. It is significant to note that the Protestant churches which are growing most rapidly in our society are precisely those which have established their own school system.[54]

The churches have also carried on their educational program in church colleges. Most of the colleges established before the middle of the nineteenth century were brought into being by Presbyterians and their Congregational allies, that is, by the Reformed community. The church college was an agency of the church. Most church colleges required courses in the Old Testament and the New Testament taught from the perspective of those who believed the Bible was the Word of God.

The church college served the church by providing an opportunity for Christian people to engage in the academic discipline in the context of the church's faith, worship, and life. Calvin believed that education in the liberal arts was a form of Christian discipleship. Piety and learning belong together.[55] The Calvinists who settled America always built colleges as well as churches to prepare young people for service in the church and state.[56]

J. R. McCain (1881–1965), who was president of Agnes Scott College and one of the most influential educators in America, always said that a church college was a very simple idea. If you want a church college, you invite church people to teach and to administer it. In selecting the faculty at Agnes Scott College, as well as the administrators, McCain declared that he gave more attention to prospective teachers' records of participation in the church than he did to any verbal statement about belief. In retrospect, one has to say that McCain was very wise and very profound in what he had to say. The secularization of a college begins of necessity with the secularization of the faculty and the admissions staff. Yet this cannot happen without the complicity or direction of the president and the board.

Today there is very little difference between many church colleges and state institutions, either in instruction or in manner of life on the campus. John Knox, who for many years was professor of New Testament at Union Theological Seminary in New York, wrote in an article on the identifiability of the church, published as a part of an Episcopal symposium on theological freedom and social responsibility, this perceptive comment:

> What seems to me an intolerable anomaly is the church's maintaining at great cost schools and colleges which are indistinguishable in every important respect from secular institutions. In doing this it finds itself often actually supporting and maintaining cultural forces hostile to both the thought and ethos of the church, at the cost of resources with which it might be equipping its children better to understand and resist these destructive pressures.[57]

The churches have carried on their educational ministry by establishing seminaries to train persons to be pastors in local congregations. Today seminaries are in crisis, for there is no convincing evidence that seminaries are adequately training persons for the responsibility of gathering a congregation and giving leadership in the coming into being of the church as the communion of the saints.[58]

At least three contemporary trends in theological education undercut the effective training of pastors.

1. Seminaries have a built-in tendency to become institutes for the advanced study of religion. Increasingly faculty members are trained in graduate schools of secular universities and sometimes without any seminary education in the church tradition in which they teach or without seminary education at all. The advanced study of religion is a proper function of a university, but it is not the first task of a seminary.

2. Seminary faculties increasingly place emphasis on what is called the academy or guild. Professional organizations and magazines have proliferated in the last three decades.[59] Teachers in seminaries frequently write for professionals, not for the church.[60] This emphasis on the academy has increased the technical competence of faculty, but there is no evidence that it has produced as effective pastors as the older seminary tradition.

The tendency to become an institute for the advanced study of religion and the emphasis on the academy or guild influence the ethos of seminary life. Concern for Christian identity is undercut.[61] Preaching becomes a lecture. The bias of the intellectual specialists, writes Stephen Sykes, is "inherently towards discovery and intellectual novelty."[62] The seminary's purpose to educate pastors to preach a message of salvation and to build up the congregation as the communion of saints is undercut by the concerns of the academy which has little or no concern with maintaining Christian identity or with preaching the Christian gospel to call people to faith and repentance.

3. The influence of pastor-scholars in seminary faculties has declined. In the résumés of seminary faculties, at least at the institutions with which I am familiar, there are always references to pastorates, but when the fine print is read, this usually means one or two years in relatively small churches, and not infrequently, while a dissertation is being finished or while waiting for a teaching position. The movement of persons from the pastorate to the theological seminary faculty and from the seminary faculty back to the pastorate was once characteristic of much of theological education. The fact that it is no longer the case, and increasingly less so since the Second World War, is due not simply to the theological seminary but to the decline of the pastor who is also a scholar as well as to the highly specified definition of scholarship in the seminary community.

The renewal of the church will have to begin with the renewal of theological education. Theological education must give students a clarity as to their identity as Christians, and more particularly, to their identity as Christians in a particular way. The renewal of theological education must once again emphasize the pastorate as the high calling in the church. To achieve these ends seminaries must insist on a level of competence that matches the competence of the best lawyers, the best physicians, and the best business leaders in the community.

It is not likely that the renewal of the seminaries will come about through the action of seminary faculties themselves. In some way those who are pastors and elders must be more intimately involved, along with professors, in setting the policies and programs of theological education.

VI

The education that will contribute to the renewal of the church is basic and fundamental. Its aim is to provide, in our pluralistic and secular society, the language, the narratives, the metaphors, the prayers, the hymns, the basic practices of the Christian life which provide the background, the network of information essential for the Protestant and Reformed way of being Christian. This is the foundation, and on this foundation many other programs can be built.

In this development we have much to learn from learning theory, from research into the stages of religious development, from education theory. In the church we ought to have all the wisdom of secular schools of education. In education we ought to spoil the Egyptians.[63] Our educational task, however, must be determined basically by theological considerations, and it must begin with foundational knowledge upon which not only all cognitive skills but all the practices and insights of the Christian life rest.

Education that will serve the church will set modest goals. It will hand on the content of the faith, provide the network of information, biblical, theological, and ecclesiological, that is necessary for participation in the life of the church. It will presuppose the worship of the congregation and the pastoral ministry of

the church. Education is not the church. It is on the congregational level a dimension of the pastoral ministry. Unless the
teacher passes on the material of the tradition, nothing else the
teacher may do really matters. The renewal of the church begins
with modest but realizable goals in handing on the faith from
generation to generation.

VII

Finally, education cannot be expected to accomplish more
than is possible. One of the illusions of our time is that education
can solve personal problems as well as social problems. Quite
recently, a graduate school of political management was char-
tered by the State of New York. It is highly improbable that a
school for political consultants will make politics either more
moral or more effective.[64] Consider the case of the stockbrokers
who engaged in insider trading. They did not do so because they
had not had a course in business ethics. They knew what they did
violated civil law and human decency. It is more likely that they
used insider information not out of ignorance but out of human
sin, and more particularly, because the community in which they
really lived did not clearly and specifically forbid this activity. The
problem, in short, with the brokers is more likely that they did
not participate in a serious worshiping, believing community
which gathered to acknowledge the transcendent judgment of
God each Lord's Day, not that they lacked education in ethics.

Willard Sperry, a dean of Harvard Divinity School, once
declared that contrary to the counsels of pedagogy, "we go on
teaching our children by rote if need be, a good many counsels of
truth which they cannot fully understand and to which they often
find no immediate parallel."[65] Personality is shaped by the liturgy, by the bowed heads of family and friends acknowledging
the transcendence of God, by hymns expressing the prayers of the
heart, and the hearing of the Word of God.

None of this is to say that education is unimportant. It is to
say that we ought not to expect it to do more than it can. It has
to be placed in the context of the life of the worshiping, believing, obeying congregation of Christian people. Education can
provide the foundation and the background information that en-

able us more effectively to participate in the life of the believing community. This is no inconsiderable service. Indeed, it is a service without which the Christian community cannot thrive.

Good teachers in the church as well as outside the church are "committed to teaching what they have learned to love."[66] Teaching, as does every other church ministry, grows out of the life and faith commitments of the community.

CHAPTER FIVE

Pastoral Care

Pastoral care, as well as preaching and teaching, arises out of the theological commitments of the church and is determined in its nature and in its practice by those commitments. The ministries of the church are established by the Word of God, which proclaims the gospel, calls to repentance and faith, teaches, and exercises pastoral care. The service of the Word of God includes not only the call to repent and believe the gospel but teaching and pastoral care. The pastor, because of the nature of the Word, must combine pastoral care with preaching and teaching.

John Calvin was a pastor. He was a theologian in order to be a pastor, not a pastor in order to be a theologian. Pastor was his preferred definition for the minister. He himself, in an exceedingly busy life, exercised pastoral duties to individuals as well as through his membership on the consistory. His letters, filling almost ten volumes and numbering over four thousand, are frequently pastoral in substance.[1] He was, through his letters, a pastor of the Reformed congregations as well as individuals throughout Europe.

For Karl Barth, a quintessential theologian, being a pastor is also a theological task. "The cure of souls thus means in general concern for the individual in the light of God's purpose for him, of the divine promise and claim addressed to him, of the witness specially demanded of him. God is the One who is primarily and properly concerned about souls. They are always in his hand."[2] In *Church Dogmatics,* volume IV, Barth has written as part of his own theology some of the finest writings available anywhere on practical theology and on pastoral care.

I

For Calvin and for Barth, as for the Reformed tradition historically, pastoral care is determined theologically. The Christian understanding of what it is to be a human being, of the church, and of grace gives content to pastoral care.

Four theological doctrines emphasized in Reformed theology are fundamental for determining pastoral care today. They define what it means to be a person and the nature of the church. They distinguish pastoral care from secular therapies.

First, every human being is created in the image of God, and the purpose of human life is to glorify God and to enjoy him forever. Creation means that we are creatures, whose lives are the expression of the purposes of God. Human beings do not just happen. They are because God thought of them before they were, called them into being, gave to them their individuality, their identity, and their name.

Herbert Butterfield has observed that one distinctive contribution of Christian faith to Western culture was a sense of the preciousness of human life.[3] Human beings are valuable not because of any inherent characteristics but because God, the creator of heaven and earth, willed that they should exist and knows them by name, numbering the hairs on their heads. This is surely no easy doctrine in the light of the observable facts about the origin of human life. Nevertheless, it is basic to a Christian understanding of human existence, and it is fundamental for pastoral care. Nicolas Berdyaev, in a very telling observation, declared that where there is no God, there is no man.[4] By this he meant that when God is left out, a human being has value only as he or she is a member of the right family, the right class, the right political party, the right culture. Christian faith has affirmed that every human being is a child of God, and indeed the dwelling place of the living God. "Truly, I say to you, as you did it to one of the least of these my brethren, you did it to me" (Matt. 25:40).

Creation also means that we are limited by space and time,

by intelligence, by energy. There are limits to what we can know and do. We can live in only one space and we see everything from our parochial setting. We cannot escape from time. Our lives are therefore irreversible. We go this way but once. Finally we die.

Creation means that we are creatures of flesh and blood, of instinct and impulse. Augustine, according to Peter Brown, was distraught by the powerful impulse of sex, not because sex in itself is evil, but because of the power of sex over the human will.[5] In paradise, Augustine imagined not life without sex, but life in which there was a harmony of sexual desire and will.[6]

The fact is that human life, from personal disorientation to depression, anger, and sex, can be overwhelmed by human vitalities and energies.[7] The biochemical inheritance that is part of the givenness of human life means that for many persons life is a very uphill battle, and indeed an impossible task. What may appear to be a Christian personality may reflect in reality little more than a good biochemical inheritance. Only God knows what individuals have done with the givenness of their creaturely existence. Some who appear strong and Christian persons may have done less with what they were given than some who struggle through life.

Our society is very much aware of the power of the social matrix over human life. It has been less willing to admit the power of genetical inheritance, the power of one's biochemical makeup in determining human personality. Indeed, one Nobel laureate, David Baltimore, has declared that Americans are not prepared to come to grips with understanding the human diversity that is written into life at the genetic level.[8]

We are not only creatures with the limitations of creaturely existence, but we are unique creatures made in the image of God. The human self has the remarkable capacity to objectify and to observe its creaturely existence, its social matrix, its history. This very remarkable capacity for self-objectification and for self-reflection is the uniqueness of human life.[9] To be human is to be free, answerable, responsible. The freedom we have may be very little in some instances, but to be human is in some measure to be free, with the capacity to organize and control the energies and vitalities of life, to overcome the social matrix and even our own past history.

To be made in the image of God, with the power of the

human spirit to transcend every human achievement, means that human life is fulfilled by no human achievement but by God. Every human achievement always opens up new possibilities of achievement; every act of love opens up new possibilities of love.[10] Our highest achievements are transcended by our freedom and we know that there is something further. As Augustine put it, "Thou hast made us for thyself, and restless are our hearts until they find rest in thee."[11]

Human beings are finally defined by the fact that they hear the Word of God. The distinctiveness of human existence is not the ability to touch thumb and forefinger or to make tools, not the power of the human mind to read off the facts of the universe and even to think the universe, not the capacity for language or the transcendence over time in memory and anticipation. It is not even the power of the human spirit to objectify life and go beyond every human achievement. The uniqueness of human existence is that God addresses us, summons us, and elicits our response.[12]

Second, the doctrine of sin bears on pastoral care. Human beings, made good by a good God, are broken by sin. This theological conviction tells us something not only about human beings but also about the nature of the church. Peter Brown, in his remarkable biography of Augustine, Bishop of Hippo, contends that the Pelagian-Augustinian controversy was, in the final analysis, a debate about the nature of the church, and therefore about pastoral care.[13]

Roman society at the turn of the fifth century was chaotic and confused. In that situation the old Romans as well as the Christians were concerned to bring order out of chaos and discipline to life. Into that situation there came from Britain a great hulk of a man with a powerful personality by the name of Pelagius.

Pelagius wanted Christians without spot or wrinkle.[14] As Brown put it, Pelagius thought of the church as a small group in a pagan world.[15] It was an elite community that had achieved a clear understanding of who they were in contrast to the mediocrity of society in general. The church was composed of superior people who stood in judgment upon society. Pelagius wanted not only the perfect individual but also the perfect community.

He imposed perfection not only on individuals but on the church.

Pelagius also wanted to reform society. He and his followers were outspoken in their criticism of Roman society. Under his influence, rich young nobility gave up their wealth and renounced self-seeking. The Pelagians were committed, for example, to the redistribution of wealth. Perhaps nowhere is the heart of Pelagianism and its optimism more clearly revealed than in the conviction of some Pelagian groups that accumulated wealth was just another bad habit that could be shrugged off by Christians on baptism.[16]

This vision of the Christian life and of a society transformed by human willpower and discipline is very compelling. Here is the triumph of the human spirit over passion, weakness, temptation, over every obstacle. Here is the superiority of the human person over the heritage of the past, over fate, over corruptions of the social order. The Pelagians were determined to triumph over the disordered, undisciplined society. They would maintain a different life from the conventional, mediocre lives of their neighbors.

There is something very Christian in Pelagius's concern. Certainly every Calvinist should know this. Like Calvin, Pelagius wanted every Christian to be a monk.[17] The councils of perfection rest upon all.[18] Unlike Calvin, he believed a sinless life was a simple possibility. He exulted in the grace of God in creation and in the power of the human will. Whenever this vision of the possibilities of human existence is lost, and whenever zeal to be perfect as our Father in heaven is perfect dies, the Christian community will be the loser.

Pelagius's position challenged Augustine's fundamental understanding of Christian faith, especially of the church and the Christian life. Pelagius, from Augustine's perspective, obscured the difference between the church and a community of good pagans.[19] Augustine thought of the church as an inn for convalescents, not as an aristocratic elite, certainly not as an elite corps for social reform. Augustine knew, as few in the history of the human race have ever known, the significance of the human will. He defined a person in terms of the human will. A person is not as he or she thinks, but as he or she wills. More specifically, a person is as the person loves. But Augustine knew that many achievements in life are beyond the power of the human will. Augustine made the case not so much for the power of the human will but for the power of grace.[20] "No subject gives me greater pleasure. For what ought to be more attractive to us sick men, than grace, grace by which we are healed; for us lazy men, than grace, grace by which we are stirred up; for us men longing to act, than grace, grace by which we are helped."[21] For such declarations as this, the church called Augustine the Doctor of Grace.

Augustine's case is far more difficult to make than is the case of Pelagius. The ordinary Christian saw in Pelagius only a sincere believer who wanted Christians to take faith seriously. Pelagius had popular Christianity on his side, and he also could and did appeal to the theological tradition of the East that had exulted in human freedom and capacity for communion with God. In a sense, it was Augustine, in a provincial church in North Africa, against the world.

Augustine based his case on the complexity of the human situation which he believed Pelagius had greatly oversimplified. Augustine admired Pelagius's zeal for righteousness, but he believed his zeal was without knowledge. Original sin was an important factor in Augustine's case. He knew that no baby is born into a situation of innocence. The sin of Adam and all of Adam's descendants infects the life of every newborn person. Original sin has always been an offensive idea, and Augustine sometimes clumsily related it too much to sex, to conception, or gave the impression it is an infection in the bloodstream or defect in the genes. But surely few articles of Christian faith are so empirically verifiable. Once human beings sinned, sin became the heritage of the whole human race and a part of the structure of society. It penetrates the life of every newborn person in those mysterious ways which persons penetrate and influence other persons before the child's first conscious moral decision.

Augustine knew that the corruption of human existence is not superficial. It was not a recent habit that could be easily excised. It reached into the depths of the human person, even beyond conscious awareness. He also knew that the corruption was so pervasive in society that the only options open on public issues involved one in evil. Augustine knew that sin is not simply a matter of perversity, of contempt for God. In a very remarkable sentence in the essay on nature and grace, Augustine says, "Many sins are committed through pride, but not all happen proudly . . . they happen so often by ignorance, by human weakness; many are committed by men weeping and groaning in their distress."[22] Augustine also knew that we frequently conquer one sin only to fall victim to another. He once wrote a rich widow, "I have, however, often observed this fact of human behavior, that, with certain people, when sexuality is repressed, avarice seems to grow in its place."[23] Peter Brown comments that the Pelagians, in their shrill denunciation of the way of the world, never said anything as profound as that.

Augustine knew that the Christian life is never simple. The good are never as good as they think they are, and the bad are never as bad as they are thought to be. The good is never a simple possibility. Augustine's favorite word for sin was concupiscence, but he meant by it not sensuality as such, but self-assertiveness, and he knew that it infects our best deeds as well as our worst.[24] As Reinhold Niebuhr has put it, for contemporary Pelagians, our causes are never as righteous as we think they are, and our participation in them is never as devoid of self-interest as we think.[25] T. S. Eliot was truly Augustinian when he declared that the third gift reserved for age was "the rending pain of re-enactment." By this gift, a person sees vividly all that he or she has done and been, uncovers motives long hidden and, more especially, comes to an awareness "of things ill done, and done to others' harm" that had once been taken as virtuous but now are seen to be corrupted by self-interest.[26]

Augustine's case was more difficult to present than Pelagius's, but far truer to the facts. The difficulty of Augustine's case can be easily demonstrated. Sermons that denounce evil and sermons that emphasize the general religious quality of life are easily understood by American congregations. Sermons that proclaim God's forgiveness and mercy are more difficult for audiences that do not know they need forgiveness.[27] Yet a sermon that emphasizes the gospel, that we are all sinners saved by grace, that our security is not in our own achievements but in the grace of God, always touches a few hearts very deeply in any congregation.

The Pelagian controversy may teach us something about preaching, but it also teaches us something very significant about the church. For the Pelagians, the church is an aristocratic elite, a community of moral heroes. The church is a disciplined army of the Lord in conquest of the world, the flesh, and the devil. Augustine preferred to think of the church as an inn for convalescents.[28] He acknowledged that the Pelagians had a zeal for God, but they were not realistic about who human beings are. The Pelagians thought human beings needed illumination; Augustine thought they needed healing.[29] A sinner needs a true confession of weakness, not a false sense of capacity. The sinner is not quickly healed but must look forward to long and precarious convalescence in the inn of the church. As Augustine put it, "Our present inquiry is about the man among thieves, left half dead on the road, who, being disabled and pierced through with heavy wounds, is quite incapable of mounting up to the heights of holiness with the facility wherewith he was able to descend therefrom; who moreover, is still in the process of cure, even though he is already in the inn. God does not therefore enjoin impossibilities; but in his injunction he counsels you both to do what you can for yourself, and to ask his aid in what you cannot do."[30]

Augustine had faced the same question in his controversy with the Donatists. They too wanted a church without spot or wrinkle, though they concentrated their demand upon the priesthood.[31] Augustine was attempting to hold together the holiness and the catholicity of the church. The Pelagians and the Donatists were denying the catholicity of the church for the sake of the holiness of the church, which the Pelagians defined in moralistic terms and which the Donatists defined in sacramental as well as moralistic terms. Augustine had a concern for morals and for sacraments, but he knew that the holiness of the church inheres not in the holiness of its members, not in the holiness of its priests, but in the holiness of God, in the action of God through his Word and Spirit, by which sinners are healed and made whole again.

God's grace is God's freedom to act without means or with means. We cannot program God's grace. God's grace is God's action in creation, in judgment, and in redemption. It is God's action in the sermon, in the fellowship of the Christian community, in the sacraments. God's grace became incarnate in Jesus Christ, and it abides in the church through the work of the Holy Spirit. The church is the context of the appointed means of God's healing grace.

The church is composed of sinners, and it lives by the forgiveness of sins. Whenever the church forgets this fact, and whenever the church is tempted to believe that it is the righteous, then the very existence of the church is at great risk.

It is very interesting to observe that the church has always been tempted to Pelagianism. This is a human perversity rather than first of all a theological perversity. The evidence is that today the Pelagians are found on both the left and the right wing of the church. The right wing and the left wing alike define the church in terms of human righteousness and achievement, though their definitions of righteousness are obviously different. It is difficult for the crusader and the advocate of a cause or an orthodoxy to show mercy. Sinners need an Augustinian, not a Pelagian of the right or left, for a pastor.

Third, pastoral care is also determined by the doctrine of salvation. This doctrine can be stated in terms of gospel and law and also in terms of justification and sanctification.

For Calvin, the law is the gospel.[32] God's grace is prior to the law, and the law is itself gracious. It is God's gracious will for human life. It is a burden only for those who reject it. The gospel includes the law. It abrogates not the law but the rigor of the law. The theological task, theoretically in doctrine and practically in the church, is holding together gospel and law, knowing that the law is gospel and that the gospel includes the law. This is not simple, but it can be done perhaps more easily in the life of the congregation than in theological statements. It is implicit in the Gospels themselves. For example, Jesus declares, "Think not that I have come to abolish the law and the prophets; I have come not to abolish them but to fulfil them. For truly, I say to you, till heaven and earth pass away, not an iota, not a dot, will pass from the law until all is accomplished. Whoever then relaxes one of the least of these commandments and teaches men so, shall be called least in the kingdom of heaven; but he who does them and teaches them shall be called great in the kingdom of heaven. For I tell you, unless your righteousness exceeds that of the scribes and Pharisees, you will never enter the kingdom of heaven" (Matt. 5:17–20).

On the other hand, Jesus ate with tax collectors and sinners. When the Pharisees criticized him, he declared, "Those who are well have no need of a physician, but those who are sick. Go and learn what this means, 'I desire mercy, and not sacrifice.' For I came not to call the righteous, but sinners" (Matt. 9:12–13). Jesus helped rich and poor, tax collectors and the elite of Israel, the weak and the powerful. The only people whom he could not help were those who thought they were already righteous.

It may be easier in the actual life of the church to hold together the law as gospel with the gospel which includes law than it is in the theoretical propositions of theology. The law is the enemy when it becomes the way we achieve salvation without the grace of God. The law is an evil when it becomes a way for us to fulfill our own lives. It may be the biblical law or natural law or any scheme or cause by which we "save" ourselves and fulfill our lives. Life is fulfilled by response not to a demand but to love.[33]

The Christian doctrine of salvation can also be stated in terms of justification by grace through faith and sanctification, God's grace as mercy which forgives our sins and God's grace as power which transforms us into the image of Christ. In the Christian life we hold together in one experience these two dimensions of the Christian life. Justification by grace through faith, the forgiveness of sins, is the presupposition of everything else. It is the fountain from which everything flows, the base from which everything is built in Christian living. The experience of having been and of being forgiven not in terms of a general disposition of things but by a mighty act of God is the presupposition of everything else in Christian life and experience.

Yet forgiveness of sins is not the end of the Christian life.[34] The end of the Christian life is a human person transformed into the image of Christ.

When we look at the historical reality of the church, we are compelled to emphasize justification by faith, the forgiveness of sins. Yet the strength of the Wesleyan revival in the eighteenth century, a time of great declension in the church, was the emphasis upon the possibilities which are implicit throughout the New

Testament, an emphasis on what has been called an optimism of grace.[35] The writers of the New Testament exhort as well as preach, teach, and comfort (2 Cor. 5:20; Rom. 12:1; Heb. 13:22).

There is the human possibility of growth in grace, but when this becomes self-conscious, especially when it becomes a source of righteousness and superiority, it becomes self-destructive. To be a Christian is to know that one lives on the one hand by forgiveness of sins and on the other hand by the power of the Holy Spirit to transform life. To be a Christian is to know that growth in grace is possible, but it is also to know that one sins in one's best deeds as well as one's worst, and that when evil is conquered on one level, it always emerges in a new form on a higher level of spiritual growth.

Every person in Christ is a new creation, growing to Christian maturity. Sanctification or transformation into the image of Christ defies quantification and even description. It cannot be contained in rules and regulations. It is a discipline of grace and a disposition of the self. It surely includes such qualities as trust in God, gratitude for the gift of life, humility and repentance, humaneness and openness to the neighbor, a readiness to forgive, a capacity to detach oneself from things, a sense of accountability, or answerability to God for our use of life's time and energy.

Reformed Christians have always believed that progress in the Christian life is possible.[36] Character may be formed. Consistency in dispositions and actions grows as the actions and thoughts of a person become who a person is. Christians also grow in knowledge, in the power of imagination, in the capacity to see the world in the light of Jesus Christ. In Reformed Protestantism there has always been an emphasis on the embodiment of the purposes of God in family life, in business, in society, at least in a broken and fragmentary way.

In the pastoral life of the church forgiveness is promised to sinners and forgiven sinners are encouraged in personal growth and sanctification. Pastoral care provides the context in which forgiveness is known and in which sanctification is nurtured according to the New Testament.

Fourth, the doctrine of the church as the mother of the faithful influences pastoral care. In a very remarkable paragraph,

Calvin declares, "I shall start, then, with the church, into whose bosom God is pleased to gather his sons, not only that they may be nourished by her help and ministry as long as they are infants and children, but also that they may be guided by her motherly care until they mature and at last reach the goal of faith. 'For what God has joined together, it is not lawful to put asunder' (Mark 10:9), so that, for those to whom he is Father the church may also be Mother."[37] The church is the fellowship in which God has placed the means of grace, and which therefore nurtures, sustains, supports Christian people in their earthly pilgrimage.

This doctrine of the church is of theological and practical significance. For the church is not an aggregation of individuals but a communion of saints who share in a common life in the power of the Holy Spirit, in a common understanding of life, a common way of living, a common hope. The spiritual gifts of the members mutually strengthen the fellowship. To be a Christian is to be in the fellowship of the church.

This doctrine is of practical significance, since human life is so made that faith, manners and styles of living, hopes and commitments can only be sustained in community. As stated in previous lectures, the community of faith in which we participate has a great deal to do with whether or not we experience the Bible as the Word of God, or whether we experience events in the world as the acts of God. Every style of life is sustained by some community. The significance of the community is greatest when it involves active, consistent participation.

The role of the church as the nurturing, sustaining institution becomes increasingly important in a secular, pluralistic, mobile, scientific-technological society. The old communities, which were established and maintained by homeplace, by family traditions, by the settlement of a family in a particular community over many years, are increasingly a thing of the past. Furthermore, in older and simpler communities, the society itself provided the kind of supports the church gives. The community today supports people only in very feeble ways in life's crises. It does not nurture them at all in the faith and commitments of the Christian life. Participation in a community of worship, of fellowship, of faith is critically important simply because of the diversity and secularity of the society.

II

What, then, is pastoral care in the light of these convictions? The classical Protestant definitions are still helpful.

Zwingli defined pastoral care in terms of the contrast of the true shepherd and the false shepherd. The true shepherd is one who preaches and teaches the gospel and who cares for the people.[38]

Martin Bucer gave as adequate a definition of pastoral care as can be found anywhere: "To draw to Christ those who are alienated; to lead back those who have been drawn away; to secure amendment of life in those who fall into sin; to strengthen weak and sickly Christians; to preserve Christians who are whole and strong, and urge them forward in all good."[39]

Calvin defined pastoral care in terms of aids to beget an increased faith in us and advance it to its goal. Pastoral care is the work of the church.[40]

Pastoral care is the responsibility of the church to nurture, sustain, and support Christian people in the living of the Christian life and in fulfillment of God's purpose for their lives. It can be thought of in our time preeminently as the incorporation of people into the life of the church, into the context of the means of grace. The really great task of pastoral care is to encourage people to gather with the people of God, to worship, to hear the sermon, to receive the sacrament. It is bringing people into the fellowship, the communion of saints, into the context of the fellowship meal or church supper, into the context of Christian conversation.[41]

Neither the church nor the pastor is the Redeemer. God alone is the Redeemer.[42] The definition of the church as the redemptive community can be very misleading. Redemption is God's work. Pastoral care is the bringing of people into the context of the means of grace, which have been appointed in the New Testament and through which we have the promise that the Holy Spirit works. Human communities admittedly can be sustaining and can ease the pain and struggle of life. Pastoral care, however, is more than human empathy, more than human love. Yet in the context of the appointed means of grace (preaching, sacrament, prayer), the human activities of pastoral care become means of grace. Luther listed Christian conversation as a means of grace alongside preaching and the sacraments.[43]

III

How, then, does pastoral care accomplish its purpose? In recent years it has become popular to belittle hints and suggestions about how pastoral care is actually carried out.[44] Yet hints and suggestions are critically important. No theory and no scientific competence can ever replace the actual experience of pastors who have gathered congregations and built up the communion of saints. Apart from such wisdom, no significant pastoral care and no church growth is likely to occur. The plethora of books by professors and therapists on pastoral care and the paucity of books by pastors of long experience reflect a radical change in pastoral care from its practice in the tradition of the church.[45]

1. Pastoral care, just as is the case with education, takes place as the people gather for worship. If it does not take place here, it is not likely to take place anywhere. For Protestants, the sermon became the chief means of grace, assuming the task that the medieval church had given to seven sacraments.[46] The sermon for Protestants traditionally is the primary means by which God's grace is mediated to troubled human souls.

Preaching is always an exercise in pastoral care, for the gospel has to do with faith, hope, and love, with the sustenance and the transformation of the human soul. In this sense pastoral care occurs when the gospel is preached.[47] It ought not therefore to be necessary to emphasize that sermons ought to be pastoral. When this becomes self-conscious, it may become self-defeating. The preacher needs to be aware that the sermon is an exercise of pastoral care, but not too aware, that is, not so aware that the gospel is distorted in attempting to exercise pastoral care. The sermon becomes a means of pastoral care preeminently as it proclaims the forgiveness of God, God's providential care of life, the grace of God which transforms human life, the promises of God which give us hope in the presence not only of death but of the frustrations and disappointments of human life and experience. Great preaching is always pastoral.

Preaching, particularly in a generation that is self-conscious about being "prophetic," is tempted to become legalism, the proclamation of the law. Some sermons are little more than moral exhortations. Yet moral exhortations are not very helpful. They may incite anger or paralyze the will. They are generally negative, proclaiming what is wrong, but are not positive, indicating concretely how life can be improved. Most people are for justice but few know what justice is in a particular situation or how it can be achieved. On the theological level the Christian life is not a response to a demand. Pastoral preaching always proclaims the grace and mercy of God and helps struggling people work out the meaning of human mercy and justice amid the complexities of our times. Only those who have known mercy can show mercy.

2. Pastoral care brings the resources of Christian faith to bear on the crises and passages of life. All cultures have given attention to the quite obvious events that shape and determine human existence. These are common for persons inside and outside the church: birth, marriage, maturation, or the transition from childhood to adult life, and death. The great and specific responsibility of the church is to deal with these events not as simple human happenings but as human happenings illuminated by Christian faith.

In addition to the crises and passages of life that are part of the structure of human existence, other crises are more personal. All human beings sooner or later look into the abyss, and all sooner or later face failure. No one ought to underestimate the vicissitudes of life. Life is an uphill battle and in the end we all lose. Pastoral care means that the church must be alive to these possibilities, and bring to bear upon them the support and the resources of the Christian community, as well as the assurance of God's grace.

There are also the crises of faith and doubt. Doubt is a universal human problem. In the church there is always the will to believe, and there is always the resource of a believing community which can be brought to bear upon doubt. The church is a community that understands doubt, accepts it as one of the crises of human existence, and seeks to overcome it in a worshiping, believing community.[48]

There are the crises that grow out of the disparity between

what we as human beings are and what we know we ought to be, crises of spiritual and moral failure. Here too the church must be sensitive to need and bring to bear upon these crises the optimism of grace.

Pastoral care is always concrete, bringing the gospel to bear upon the actual needs of the congregation as these needs arise. It offers prayer and the reading of the scripture. It is the presence of the church. It brings the resources of the world to the assistance of those who have difficulty living in the world. It cares for people in the concreteness of their lives.

3. Pastoral care must also involve quite specific actions.

The first is the visitation of the people in their homes. This is a very ancient practice, especially in Protestantism. It was encouraged at the time of the Reformation.[49] Richard Baxter, in his great book *The Reformed Pastor*, in the seventeenth century insisted upon it. It became the characteristic pastoral action in the life of the church in the nineteenth and twentieth centuries. Few aspects of pastoral care are so easily documented as the constructive consequences of simple pastoral visitation. It may not be so much what the pastor does or says when entering the home, but simply his or her presence as the pastor of the church. This becomes symbolic of the church's concern. "A house-going pastor makes a churchgoing people." The truth of this rubric can be validated in almost every pastor's experience. There is no activity so productive of good for the pastor in the new church than the resolution to visit in as short a time as possible every home in the congregation. As Baxter knew, there is no substitute for the pastor's knowing the members of the congregation by name and having been physically present in their homes.[50]

The second traditional activity of pastoral care is the visitation of the sick. Again, it is not so much what the pastor does or what the pastor knows, but his or her simple presence in the room of illness. A glass of water awkwardly but lovingly given is far more significant than the giving of a glass of water with clinical precision but without love.[51] In the pastoral care of the sick, it is useful to know many things, such as the simple advice not to shake the bed, as well as the dynamics of illness. But the task of pastors is not to do what nurses and doctors may do better, but simply to be the presence of the church and to witness to the concern of the Christian community and to the Christian hope in the presence of illness.[52]

The third task of the pastor is the visitation of those who face unusual crises and trouble. In our time, many people are bereft of the support of families. Therefore, the loss of a job, the breakup of a marriage, the difficulty of rearing children are serious and pervasive problems. The visitation of such people and the offering to them the resources the church has to help them are part of pastoral care.

The fourth form of visitation is calling on prospective members. There are various ways in which evangelism can be carried out. The means of evangelism most appropriate to pastoral care is the bringing of people into the context of the means of grace. Pastors cannot save people and churches cannot save people. God saves people. Therefore evangelism is bringing people into the life of the church as the context of God's appointed means of grace.

Others think of evangelism in more theological ways, that is, in theological conversations about becoming a Christian. Some of these are stylized and printed in manuals similar to those provided insurance salespersons.[53] They may have their place. Certainly evangelism may involve long conversations with people about many theological issues. The commonest form of evangelism, however, is inviting people into the life of the church, into the context of the means of grace. Again the power of visitation is very great. The number of members a church takes in is, all other things being equal, directly in proportion to the number of visits to people in their homes or in their workplaces. Visitation by members of the church may be very effective, but there is not now nor is there likely to be any substitute for visitation by the pastor. There is considerable evidence that one reason church growth has slowed is the decline in visitation by the pastor upon those outside the church.

Pastoral care is an expression of the church's ministry of compassion for those in and out of the church. There is no substitute for this. The ministry of compassion, Calvin argued on the basis of Acts 2:42, is a sign of the church's existence.

The church's ministry of compassion is necessarily varied. It gives bread to the hungry, finds employment for those out of work, advises and helps those in financial difficulty. The church does what needs to be done. Yet it serves human needs not as a welfare agency but as a community of faith in which members share their wisdom of the world as well as their human graces and their faith. The church has always built hospitals and provided relief for the poor, services rendered for those in and out of the church. Today the church may need once again to provide institutional care for the sick, hospitals for the restoration of those who are chemically dependent, homes for orphans and troubled youth, care for older people. The church needs to provide for the poor and develop programs for affordable housing. The church must visit, according to our Lord's command, those in prison, and give pastoral care to those released from prison. Yet in these works the church must be clear about its own existence. The pastor is not a psychiatrist, not a medical doctor, not a social worker. In these extensions of pastoral care the church must use the wisdom of the world with integrity, never compromising the competence of secular wisdom in the churches. Above all, the pastor must work as a minister of the Word of God, never forgetting that the church is a community of worship and faith. Within the church the effectiveness of the wisdom of the world may be enhanced and humanized.[54]

The illustrations of the way in which the church must give real help to real people cannot be exhausted. In every congregation there are persons who are broken by the challenges and frustrations of life, and they no longer have the support of a general community where they are known and in which they are supported. The task of the church is to work out ways in which to minister to these people. In pastoral care Christians must develop an imagination that opens up new ways to give real help to troubled human beings.

IV

Pastoral care is finally the work of the entire community. The pastoral care that is exercised when the community gathers to worship God must be supplemented by other communal gatherings.

Christians from the beginning have been people who ate

together.[55] The communal meal on an evening in the middle of the week, for example, is a remarkable opportunity for the communion of saints to be realized, for pastoral care to be exercised. Pastoral care is exercised when the congregation gathers for a marriage. Marriages are held in the church because marriage is a responsibility of the community, and the community has an interest and concern in the marriage that takes place. The Westminster Confession insists that marriage ought to take place only in the Lord.[56] This has now fallen into disuse and even sounds quaint. However, the hazards of marriage in a highly pluralistic and mobile society are very great, and it may be that the church will have to recover an insistence that it is proper for Christians to marry only in the Lord. The church's concern is not simply with the decision of two persons to get married but with the affirmation that a marriage, which establishes a family, has social significance, and is not simply a private concern of those who are getting married. Marriage is preeminently the concern of the church, therefore the congregation gathers when marriage takes place.

The funeral has an ambiguous history in early Protestantism.[57] The first Protestants were uncertain about religious services at the funeral in reaction against the corruption of funeral practices. Death is one of those occasions when we are aware of the limitations of existence, and in the presence of the mystery that encompasses us. Therefore it is a fruitful soil for magic and for human fantasy. Some of the early Reformers corrected this simply by reducing or eliminating the funeral service. In our kind of society, in which death symbolizes the insignificance of human life considered in and of itself, it is critically important for death to be the occasion for the community to gather. In a city in which persons live anonymous lives, and with cremation, which leaves no visible symbol of a human life, death becomes the moment of transition from personal existence to virtual nothingness. When a person dies in a city, it frequently appears to be as if the person never was.

Death challenges the Christian community as to the meaning of life, as to the significance and endurability of community, as to the fate of human personality. There is no act of the church more fraught with seriousness than the committal when a human person, not only all that person is but also all that person has done, is committed to the care of God. In the presence of death the community gathers, on the one hand to give support to those who have been bereaved, and on the other hand to declare for themselves and for their world their conviction that life has meaning, that the church is a community composed of the living and the dead, and that in Jesus Christ we still have communion one with another, that God raises the dead and the human life is fulfilled, not annulled, in God's eternal kingdom.

Death, according to Karl Rahner, ought not to be an event that happens to us and overwhelms us.[58] It is not simply a natural event or a fate. It is the supreme act of human freedom as the Christian brings this episode of human existence to end and anticipates the life to come. When the congregation gathers at death it participates with those who die in bringing their historical existence to its conclusion and in affirming their passage to eternal life.

Pastoral care, therefore, is the work of the Christian community as a community, and not simply the work of members of the community, the pastor, or of committees, or of individuals with special assignments. There are certain exercises of pastoral care which can be rendered only by the community itself.

The God who calls us into existence and who calls us to be his chosen people has placed us in a community. Pastoral care is finally the church being what it says it is, the people of God, the communion of saints, members sharing in a common life, that is, a common faith, a common hope, a common commitment.

Contemporary studies have enlarged our knowledge of the person and also our knowledge of how personhood is shaped by biochemical factors as well as the social matrix. We also know much more about the dynamics of human societies. Pastoral care must utilize this knowledge in the context of the community of faith. The primary base and criteria of pastoral care that will renew the church are, however, scripture, theology, and the tradition of Christian practice.

A recent review of books on pastoral care concluded that the most influential books of the nineteenth century were based upon the tradition in the church. In the last fifty years they have been based overwhelmingly on empirical sciences.[59] There is no evidence that the empirically determined methods have been as effective in gathering, upbuilding, and sending forth the church as the older pastoral care. While they have gained dominance, the churches have declined. Pastoral care in the church must use secular, empirically derived wisdom, but must not be determined by it.

Pastoral care in the church must always seek the integrity of being the Christian community at work. It will use the best wisdom of the world and support physicians, nurses, psychiatrists, lawyers, social workers, experts in construction, manufacturing, and business who wish to work in the context of the church's ministry. Yet the pastors of the church must not confuse their work with work of professionals. The pastor has a calling to be a servant of the Word of God. Pastoral care in the church is a unique ministry that cannot be duplicated anywhere else in society. It is the building up of the community of saints.

CHAPTER SIX

The Christian Witness in the World

The Christian witness in the world is integrally related to the very existence of the local congregation, as well as to the church's responsibilities for preaching, teaching, and pastoral care. Every congregation is the church of Jesus Christ in the whole world, or it is not the Christian church at all. Every minister must declare, as John Wesley did, "The world is my parish."[1] When the apostle Paul proclaimed over against abundant evidence to the contrary that the weak and fragile congregation in Corinth was the church of the living God, he also affirmed that that congregation was the church of Jesus Christ in the whole world (1 Cor. 1:1–2; 2 Cor. 1:1).

The New Testament always presupposes the fact that the church is the church for the whole world. In Matthew, the risen Christ is recorded as saying, "All authority in heaven and on earth has been given to me. Go therefore and make disciples of all nations, baptizing them in the name of the Father and of the Son and of the Holy Spirit, teaching them to observe all that I have commanded you; and lo, I am with you always, to the close of the age" (Matt. 28:18–20). In Acts, the risen Christ sends forth his disciples, saying, "But you shall receive power when the Holy Spirit has come upon you; and you shall be my witnesses in Jerusalem and in all Judea and Samaria and to the end of the earth" (Acts 1:8). In the great prayer for unity in John's Gospel, Jesus prayed "that the world may believe" (John 17:21). In Revelation, there is the vision of "another angel flying in midheaven, with an eternal gospel to proclaim to those who dwell on earth, to every nation and tribe and tongue and people" (Rev. 14:6). To be the church is to be the church of Jesus Christ in the whole world.

The writer of First Peter puts the reality of the church very well. On the one hand, the church is "a chosen race, a royal priesthood, a holy nation, God's own people." Unless the church is this, it does not exist. On the other hand, the church exists to "declare the wonderful deeds of him who called you out of darkness into his marvelous light" (1 Peter 2:9). The church is not simply mission. It is first of all a living, worshiping, believing community, which is gathered, built up in the communion of saints, and sent forth into the world.

Karl Barth in our time has written:

> The community has to speak apostolically in the more specific sense . . . of mission in the narrower sense which is also the true and original sense, in which sending or sending out to the nations to attest the Gospel is the very root of the existence and therefore of the whole ministry of the community. In mission the Church sets off and goes (*poreuthentes,* Mt. 28:19), taking the essentially and most profoundly necessary step beyond itself, and beyond the dubiously Christian world in which it is more immediately set, to the world of men to which, entangled as it is in so many false and arbitrary and impotent beliefs in so many false gods of ancient or most recent invention and authority and reflecting its own glory and misery, the Word which God has pronounced in Jesus Christ concerning the covenant of grace which He has concluded with it is still alien and must therefore be taken as a new message. The vocation which constitutes the community is directly the command to take this message to this world, to the nations or the "heathen." As it is obedient to this command, it engages in foreign missions.[2]

The witness to the world was continually alive in the ancient church. Justin Martyr (c. 100–c. 165) wrote, "The first Apostles, twelve in number, in the power of God went out and proclaimed Christ to every race of men"; and "There is not one single race of men, whether barbarians, or Greeks, or whatever they may be called, nomads, or vagrants, or herdsmen dwelling in tents, among whom prayers and giving of thanks are not offered through the name of the Crucified Jesus."[3] Tertullian (c.

160–c. 230) declared, "Christ commanded them to go and teach all nations. . . . Immediately, therefore, so did the apostles." Origen (c. 185–254) continued the theme: "The gospel of Jesus Christ has been preached in all creation under heaven, to Greeks and barbarians, to wise and foolish. . . . It is impossible to see any race of men which has avoided accepting the teaching of Jesus"; "The divine goodness of Our Lord and Savior is equally diffused among the Britons, the Africans, and other nations of the world," but also "Many people, not only barbarians, but even in the Empire, have not yet heard the word of Christ"; and "The gospel has not yet been preached to all nations, since it has not reached the Chinese or the Ethiopians beyond the river, and only small parts of the more remote and barbarous tribes." John Chrysostom, who founded a training school for evangelists to Goths, wrote, " 'Go and make disciples of all nations' was not said for the Apostles only, but for us also."[4]

Preaching, teaching, and exercising pastoral care are not separate parts of the church's work. They are mutually related dimensions of the one vocation of being the Christian community. None stands alone. The Christian witness in all the world is not an added or an optional task. It is the way the Christian community expresses its essential life. The Holy Spirit gathers the church, upbuilds the communion of saints, and sends the church forth in the world. The gathering, upbuilding, and sending are the work of the same Holy Spirit in the one church.[5]

I

There are at least five reasons why any consideration of the renewal of the church must include the witness to Jesus Christ in all the world. Four of these reasons have to do with the existential reality of the church and with the responsibility for preaching, teaching, and pastoral care in the local congregation. The fifth reason is the claim of the world upon the church.

1. The call to universal Christian witness delivers the congregation from too much introspection and too much preoccupation with its own existence. Evil always lives parasitically upon the good, and this is especially true in the life of the church. The church's fellowship, preaching, teaching, and pas-

toral care may become self-serving, particularly in a society that is narcissistic in disposition and inordinately preoccupied with its own potential.

The desire to witness to Jesus Christ in all the world arises out of the revelation that creates the church. Jesus Christ—his life, his death on the cross, his resurrection—is the greatest event in the history of the world. Christians measure time by "before Christ" and "in the year of our Lord" because Jesus Christ, for the Christian community, is the dividing point of time. Hence, so great an event, which creates, transforms, and shapes the Christian community, must be shared with all the world. Those who have received good news want to tell it on the mountains, in the valleys, and in every place. What happened in Jesus Christ is the greatest good news that ever came to human beings.

Christians from the beginning knew that the greatest gift they had to share with people in the world was the news of Jesus Christ. Having told the good news of Jesus Christ, Christians then gave bread, medical care, and service to every human need. However, there has never been any doubt about the logical priority of giving the gospel to all the world. Bread is crucially important to those who are starving, but it must not be forgotten that when one has given bread to a starving person and when that person is revived, all the basic problems of human existence still remain. We do not live by bread or by medical care or by political planning. Sooner or later, we die by these things. Therefore, unless Christians have something greater than bread or medical care or political planning to give, we are all in the end undone. "In doing good," Richard Baxter wrote in *The Christian Directory,* "prefer the souls of men before the body" unless the man is drowning or famishing.

The very nature of the church's own existence and the gospel it proclaims mean that the church's attention must be focused not only on its own life but on its mission in all the world to share the good news which creates the church.

2. The witness to all the world maintains the catholicity of the church. The church exists not for some people, not for a peculiar type of people. The church exists for all people. In fact, the church is the existence for which God made human beings. The church is the true human life. Hence the obligation to share

the faith with all the world serves to establish the catholicity of the church itself.

The remarkable *Letter to Diognetus,* dating from the first part of the second century, thought of Christians as a "new race or way of life" which was for all people.

> For Christians cannot be distinguished from the rest of the human race by country or language or customs. They do not live in cities of their own; they do not use a peculiar form of speech; they do not follow an eccentric manner of life. This doctrine of theirs has not been discovered by the ingenuity or deep thought of inquisitive men, nor do they put forward a merely human teaching, as some people do. Yet, although they live in Greek and barbarian cities alike, as each man's lot has been cast, and follow the customs of the country in clothing and food and other matters of daily living, at the same time they give proof of the remarkable and admittedly extraordinary constitution of their own commonwealth.[6]

There is no finer statement of the catholicity of the church than that found in Cyril of Jerusalem's catechetical lectures.

> The Church, then, is called Catholic because it is spread through the whole world, from one end of the earth to the other, and because it never stops teaching in all of its fullness every doctrine that men ought to be brought to know: and that regarding things visible and invisible, in heaven and on earth. It is called Catholic also because it brings into religious obedience every sort of men, rulers and ruled, learned and simple, and because it is a universal treatment and cure for every kind of sin, whether perpetrated by soul or body, and possesses within it every form of virtue that is named, whether it expresses itself in deeds or words or in spiritual graces of every description.[7]

Augustine also thought of the Christian community as the universal human community.

> While this Heavenly City, therefore, is on pilgrimage in this world, she calls out citizens from all nations and so collects a society of aliens, speaking all languages. She takes no account of any difference in customs, laws, and institutions, by which earthly peace is achieved and preserved—not that she annuls or abolishes any of those, rather, she maintains them and follows them (for whatever divergences there are among the diverse nations, those institutions

have one single aim—earthly peace), provided that no hindrance is presented thereby to the religion which teaches that the one supreme and true God is to be worshipped.[8]

Missions is a catholic task. It is to all people, to persons in the ghettos, to Communists, to affluent secular Westerners, and to Muslims. Missions is by people to people simply as human beings. Moreover, the missionary task is amazingly catholic. There are an estimated 262,000 full-time Christian missionaries, and of these 177,000 are Roman Catholic, 54,000 are Protestant, 1,200 Orthodox. There are 35,000 Third World missionaries, some of whom are included in the Protestant and Roman Catholic numbers.[9] The great missionary movement of the nineteenth century contributed significantly to the developing ecumenical awareness of the twentieth-century church.

3. The witness to all the world brings to focus for the Christian congregation the existential reality of the church itself. The congregation which gives sustained attention each year to its obligation to witness to Jesus Christ in all the world is compelled to concentrate its attention upon the nature of its own existence. The exhortation to missions and the study of missions focus upon that to which Christians witness, and that which is at the heart of the Christian community's existence. Christian mission raises the theological question, Why should the gospel be preached to Jews, Muslims, Buddhists, animists, secular humanists who have religions of their own? What is the theological justification of missions to convert and to build churches? The answer to this question has always been the conviction that is the foundation of the church's existence. Jesus Christ is the Word made flesh who has wrought salvation for all people. There is no possibility of a revival of the church in America until there is a revival of the faith by which the church lives and which compels it to tell the story of Jesus Christ everywhere.

The Christian witness has to be undergirded by the contribution of funds as well as the sacrificial service of persons who are willing to leave their homelands, their families, their friends, and commit themselves to service in very difficult places in the world. The Christian witness in all the world makes concrete and specific the verbal confession and calls for sacrifice.

The Christian witness to all the world is what distinguishes Christian people from all other people. Every other service the church can render is in some way duplicated by the state, by philanthropic organizations, by people of good will. The witness to Jesus Christ is the unique and decisive work of the church. In doing this work and in reflecting upon it, the witness itself becomes a means of grace to the local congregation. For this reason, Martin Kähler (1835–1912) shrewdly observed that the Christian world witness or mission is the "mother of theology."[10]

4. The Christian witness in all the world brings the problems that have tortured the life of the church in the last three decades into sharp focus. It is significant that the decline in mainline churches, in particular the Presbyterian Church, has paralleled a greater decline in the missionary enterprise of the church.[11]

The vitality of the Christian witness to the world is integrally related to the vitality of the Christian faith of the community. When the church is most alive as a worshiping, believing community, it is most vigorous in the Christian witness to the world. Mission is the expression of the faith that Jesus, the "Word made flesh," is my Savior and Lord.[12]

Many factors put this witness at risk in every age. It is dependent on a living faith for which we pray and hope but which we cannot guarantee. It requires great courage and sacrifice on the part of the missionary and it requires financial support from those who send the missionaries. Hence the witness is fragile, sustained finally by faith. Christian missions is subject to the same hazards that erode Christian faith in our society.

This witness to the world is put at risk by a secular and pluralistic society. This culture on the one hand sees no reason for conversion and on the other hand regards the Christian witness an uncivil intrusion into another person's life or culture.[13]

The Christian witness is justified by some in the church on the basis of culture, education, and medical help.[14] Missions improves life. Ernst Troeltsch, whose work called in question the uniqueness of Christian faith and therefore the theological validity of mission, concentrated his attention on the cultural influence of Christian faith.[15] "Mission today is the expansion of the

European and American world of religious ideas, closely linked to the expansion of the European sphere of influence."[16]

Christian theology provides no basis for missions conceived primarily in terms of culture, education, or medicine, and evidence does not indicate that Christians will support missions when conceived in cultural categories. Furthermore, missions have been criticized for cultural imperialism as well as for evangelization.[17]

The malaise of the church is also revealed in the efforts to modify the Christian witness as proclamation by an emphasis upon presence, dialogue, and mission in the general sense of human good.[18] The problems here are obscured by the fact that Christian missions *is* presence. The simple testimony of the Christian community's existence was a form of evangelism in the ancient world and it continues to be so today. Some of the most notable missionaries in our time, such as Samuel Zwemer and William McElree Miller in the Islamic world, carried on their work under great restrictions, but they were absolutely clear about the priority of witnessing to the decisive work of Jesus Christ for human salvation. Christian missions locally and worldwide is presence, if presence is possible.

Dialogue has always and without exception been part of the Christians' witness.[19] There have, of course, been persons in every era who have not wished to dialogue, who simply proclaimed. No one can underestimate the effectiveness of simple proclamation, but it is also true that dialogue has likewise borne witness to Jesus Christ. The problems arise when dialogue becomes an end in itself and undermines commitment to the decisiveness of what God has done in Jesus Christ. This is the open possibility of every dialogue. The integrity of this possibility must be respected. But when this happens the Christian witness is lost. Dialogue cannot be substituted for witness.

The witness to Jesus Christ is also a mission that includes every good work. Those who preach the gospel to evangelize and establish churches have led the way in reducing languages to writing, in ministering to the sick, in relieving hunger, and in teaching better methods of agriculture. Yet in the New Testament, Paul always preached the gospel before he asked for an offering to relieve hunger. This order is not only good theology, it is also a practical necessity. Faith in Jesus as the Christ, the Son of the living God, is the motivation for works of charity and mercy, as the history of the church demonstrates.

Presence, dialogue, and compassion have always been mission activities. Yet none is essential to the Christian mission. Indeed presence, dialogue, and compassion are not possible in many areas of the world where the gospel must be proclaimed today. The Christian witness to the world takes place in at least a hundred ways. No one way is essential. The only essential is the Word of God and the conviction that what God has done in Jesus Christ is for the salvation of all people. A close connection exists between the command of Christ to witness in all the world and the renewal of the church, as these four reasons indicate. The witness to the world compels us to acknowledge what has always been the existential reality of the church and the commitment without which the church is no longer the Christian community.

II

5. The fifth reason why a renewal of the church is served by the Christian world witness is the need for Christian witness in our time. The past fifty years have been characterized by radical political, social, and economic changes. New nations have come into existence; economic systems have developed and then passed away; mass transportation and especially communication have radically changed the life-styles and the nature of human communities. Possibly the most significant change has been the drastic explosion in population, a development that has been greatly assisted by modern medicine.

These changes have brought new opportunities for the Christian community. There has been massive global growth of electronic Christianity. David Barrett reports fifty-six global ministry networks with forty-two million computers which are rapidly increasing. There is a new mushrooming of literature on evangelization and a proliferation of conferences (four hundred) on evangelization each year. There are now fifty new global plans for world evangelization each year and twenty-five hundred mass campaigns a year. Another very significant fact is the emergence of one thousand Third World mission agencies. There has emerged what Barrett calls the East Asian colossus, with eighty million Christians.[20]

On the other hand, there are disturbing factors. Seventy countries are now closed to Christian missions, and these are increasing by four a year. Six hundred cities of one hundred thousand population in the world have little or no Christian witness. One hundred forty megacities of one million or more are hostile to Christianity. The martyrdom of people for their Christian faith is increasing and is now in the vicinity of three hundred thousand persons a year.

Twenty-five and a half percent of the world, or 1.3 billion people, are unaware of Christianity, Christ, or the gospel. No Christian broadcasting exists in thirty major languages, with from five to eighty-five million native speakers. Today roughly one third of the world is Christian, one third of the world has heard about Jesus Christ, but one third of the world has yet to hear the witness. The tremendous increase in Asian Christianity enabled the percentage of Christians to rise to 34.1 percent of the world's population, thus reversing an eighty-year decline of Christians as a percentage of the world population.[21]

The large number of people in the world who have not heard of Christian faith constitutes a great challenge to the church. The challenge is all the more acute because they live in areas where it is difficult to enter, much more to make a Christian witness.

In the nineteenth century the Christian community, as a result of the great missionary activities of that time, became the first worldwide Christian community. The truly worldwide character of the church has enriched the life of provincial and local churches, but it also creates many new hazards and risks as Christian people experience the cultural, political, economic, and social crises of this era.

The history of the world at the turn of the twenty-first century confronts the Christian church with a crisis, challenge, and opportunity similar to that of barbarian invasions of the fifth century and the discoveries of the fifteenth and sixteenth centuries. Augustine's counsel for those who suffered the brutalities of the sack of Rome is Christian wisdom for today. The most important fact is not what happens to a person but what a person does with what happens to him or her. Christians differ from other people not in what happens to them but in the fact that they respond with faith, hope, and love (*City of God,* Book I). Crisis is always an opportunity.

III

The story of the Christian witness to the world is one of the most thrilling and exciting in all of human history. In our age it is popular to debunk this history and to point to its foibles.[22] Every human enterprise is conducted by sinners and is subject to all the fragileness and limitations of human existence. Yet relatively speaking, the missionary enterprise of the church is a story of remarkable faith, heroism, and self-sacrifice which may not be matched by any other human story.

The story begins in the New Testament, when Paul walks across the Mediterranean world proclaiming the gospel of Jesus Christ to Jews and to Gentiles, making converts and establishing churches. Human history would be radically different from what it has been if Paul had gone east rather than west. Many of the qualities that are most precious in Western civilization are the consequence of the powerful Christian witness in the Mediterranean world. A struggling community of believing people, always at risk, maintained its existence, and from the middle of the third century to the beginning of the fourth, experienced a massive growth, becoming a very significant community in the Roman Empire, so that Constantine aligned himself with the Christian community, as sooner or later any Roman emperor would have had to have done. By A.D. 500, according to David Barrett's estimate, 20 percent of the world's population was Christian, and the Christian community had reached out in the east to India, to China, to Ethiopia and northern Africa, and in the north even to Britain. The great missionaries of the medieval period, Augustine, Columba, Boniface, are representative of a host of persons who gave up comforts and risked life for the sake of the proclaiming of the gospel.

With the opening of transportation around the world, the Roman Catholics quickly sent missionaries to the far corners of the earth. Matteo Ricci to China, Francis Xavier to India and Japan, Bartolomé de Las Casas to South America. Later Protestants would likewise send missionaries around the earth.

The great century, according to Kenneth Scott Latourette, was the nineteenth. William Carey, the Baptist cobbler-pastor, preached in 1792 his very remarkable sermon, "An Inquiry Into the Obligation of Christians to Use Means for the Conversion of Heathens." Carey himself went to India, and his sermon marks the beginning of the greatest century in the history of missions.

In the nineteenth century missions became the concern of every church member. Missions were no longer the task of religious elites, the monks, or the clergy; no longer the responsibility of the government. Missions became the responsibility of every member of the church. Children gave their pennies. Women baked cakes and sewed for mission. The missionaries became a part of the local congregation, known by name and honored for their service. By 1900, 34.4 percent of the world's population could be classified as Christian, a figured that after some decline now holds again.[23]

The historical witness to Jesus Christ in all the world for twenty centuries opens up the existential reality of the church and therefore uncovers the malaise of the church today. It also serves to give the church its proper identity and to invigorate and even exhilarate it for service today. One of the most influential books in early Protestant history was John Foxe's (1516–1587) *Book of Martyrs*.[24] This book mightily shaped not only the Christian community, but also the ethos that played a significant part in the shaping of the American nation. It is easy, of course, to criticize Foxe's work as hagiography, but the fact is, it told the story of persons who, in a relatively remarkable way, lived the life of Christian faith and were willing to seal their testimony with their death. The witness of the martyrs served to shape the character and the life of those to whom the stories were told. One of the weaknesses of the church today is the loss of any sense of heroes of the faith and any knowledge of the martyrs. The story of the missionaries has likewise served a very useful purpose in the education of the church and in the development of Christian character.

The stories of the missionaries, such as those of Boniface and Columba, John Eliot, William Carey, the haystack prayer meeting, Shepherd and Lapsley, David Livingstone, the vision of the evangelization of the world in this generation, tell us what it is to be Christian and excite us with the possibilities of embodying the purposes of the living God in a human life that is lived for something more than personal comfort and happiness. There are persons of living memory in all three Presbyterian Churches that make up the Presbyterian Church (U.S.A.) today who recall the high status that missionaries had in the church and the familiarity of local congregations with their names, their families, and their work. In the Presbyterian Church, the names of missionaries were once very much alive. They were among the ablest persons in the leadership of the church. They and their work were known in local congregations, which they truly represented. They significantly shaped the form and character of local congregations while proclaiming the gospel in distant parts of the world.

The mission work of the nineteenth and first half of the twentieth century established the churches of the Third World. Singapore is now a center of Christian leadership and publications. The church in Korea is a marvelous illustration of the power of the gospel. This growth of the church has occurred in spite of overwhelming obstacles. Today the Christian community in China is estimated as high as 52 million persons.[25] It is a vivid testimony that the Word does not return void.

The deliberate effort to remember the heroic work of Christian witnesses around the world in bearing witness to Jesus Christ, and then in their work to establish schools and universities, to provide medical care, and to teach a humaneness of life is of vast importance for the renewal of the church today. The discrediting of the missionary serves the useful purpose of reminding us that all of us are sinners, but it obscures the fact that among sinners there are very great differences. Among sinners, some live willingly in comfort and affluence, and others have heard the call to serve God in places requiring both personal and financial sacrifice. The American church that did so much in missions in the century and a half before 1950 was far less affluent than the church today.

IV

The church lives by the power of the Christian witness. The witness by the power of the Holy Spirit becomes the faith of people. Hence to be the church is to be concerned to witness to Jesus Christ throughout the whole world, and to maintain the catholicity of the church as the true and proper destiny for every human being.

None of us knows what the future holds. Yet in the past, those occasions when cultures have broken up, when human communities have been disrupted, have also been the occasions when the church has grown most rapidly. It may well be that these are the times when the church is becoming more and more a worldwide community, with the emergence of strong Christian communities in the southern hemisphere and in particular with the powerful Christian communities in the East, such as Korea and Singapore, which are now among the chief centers of Christian faith. Kenneth Scott Latourette, in his seven-volume *History of the Expansion of Christianity,* developed the thesis that the church moved forward in great pulsations. Each advance is followed by a recession, which is in turn followed by another advance. In the periods of recession, the groundwork is laid for the next advance. When Professor Latourette completed his seven-volume history, he did not know whether we were still in the period of advance which began, he believed, with William Carey, and in particular with the conclusion of the Napoleonic wars in 1815, or whether we were in a period of decline. He was, however, convinced that if we were in a period of decline, the groundwork was being laid for another advance and for the establishment of Christian communities in new places and in new forms.[26]

None of us dares to boast. In the New Testament there is the warning that God is not dependent upon our hands or our feet or our voices. God can from rocks raise up children to Abraham. We therefore dare not presume. But today there is the invitation that we realize the nature of the church in the community in which we are by receiving there graciously and thankfully the witness of faith which has been handed on with devotion and care now for sixty-five generations. There is also the call to be witnesses to this apostolic faith in all the world. In this way, we not only serve the world but we also realize our own existence in a new and powerful way as the church of the living God.

The command of Christ to preach the gospel in all the world and the obligation Paul felt to preach the gospel throughout the Mediterranean world uncover the reality of the Christian faith and of the Christian community. There is an integral relation between the general malaise of the church and the decline in the church's concern to evangelize the world. The heart of the crisis in the church is revealed in the unease of many church officials and of individual Christians to speak of missions as preaching the gospel to convert people and to establish churches. In recent years many have found it more comfortable to speak of mission in cultural, medical, political, and social terms than in terms of evangelization. The Christian witness to the world leads to the question which is at the heart of the church's life, "Who do you say that I am?" Those who preach the gospel in the world answer with Peter, "You are the Christ, the Son of the living God" (Matt. 16:16).

Epilogue

The argument of this book has been simple because it builds on the tested wisdom of the church tradition. It has attempted to relate the tradition to life in our times without seeking novelty in language or content. The summary can therefore be brief and concise.

The church is the mystery of God's grace, a gift for which we have to wait. Its origin is God's election and covenant, not a program, a technique, a scheme of action. The promise, which Christians claim from Jeremiah, declared, "I will put my law within them, and I will write it upon their hearts; and I will be their God, and they shall be my people" (Jer. 31:33).

The church is chosen by God, but Christians have been commissioned by the crucified and risen Christ to preach, teach, baptize, and make disciples of all nations. Preaching, teaching, pastoral care, prayer, Christian fellowship and conversation, and deeds of compassion are the ordinary means of God's grace. They are therefore the primary means that the Holy Spirit uses for the renewal of the church. When churches take seriously preaching, teaching, and pastoral care, congregations generally thrive, even in a secular society.

The primary guides for the renewal of the church are the New Testament and the church's reflection upon New Testament teaching and practice. Church theology and church practice are never final in form or content, but they do represent the tested wisdom of the Christian community. Church renewal and growth today and in the future are not likely to be in any essential matters different from church growth and renewal in the past. The church must make use of the wisdom of the world. The social scientists, the psychologists, the historians have wisdom that may be very useful in describing the symptoms, but they cannot by their wisdom either make the diagnosis or prescribe the cure. Gertrude Himmelfarb, in her penetrating analysis of contemporary historians *The New History and the Old: Critical Essays and Reappraisals,* pinpoints the resistance of history generally to objective analysis. She describes the inadequacy of psycho-history,

> which denies to the past an integrity and will of its own, in which people acted out of a variety of motives, and in which events had a multiplicity of causes. It imposes upon the past the same determinism that it imposes upon the present, thus robbing people of their individuality and events of their complexity. Instead of respecting the actions and professed beliefs of contemporaries, it presumes to expose the real impulses that lay behind those actions and the real feelings that conditioned those beliefs.[1]

Concerning quanto-historians, she writes:

> The subjects to which quantifiers have tried to apply their techniques are not homogeneous. They can be added up, measured, charted, only by violating the particularity of each episode, . . . by ignoring the dissimilarities and attending only to the superficial similarities, by arbitrarily focusing on some one characteristic that is specifiable and measurable—and for which, moreover, we happen to have quantitative evidence. The medium, Barzun suggests, has become the message. A mechanistic approach to history implies a mechanistic view of man.[2]

Theologians such as Augustine, Calvin, and Barth have always emphasized that the essential reality of the church is invisible. The church, which is the mystery of God's grace, shares with all history the mysteries of the human self and of divine providence.

Moreover, most studies of the church are very selective in their quantifications. An easily quantifiable statistic that is directly related both to church attendance and to church growth is pastoral visitation, especially visitation in the homes of people, but such a statistic is seldom if ever mentioned in sociological studies. Along with pastoral visitation, the church, humanly speaking, depends upon the persuasiveness of preaching in the hour of worship on Sunday morning, yet few social studies point to the quality of preaching. In analyzing the church's loss of students on college campuses or the decline of youth organizations in the life of the church, social studies point to statistics, but they seldom raise the question of church decisions that mightily affected those declines. The church must be as wise as the world and accept with gratitude what is true in objective studies of the church. Yet these studies, as has been frequently indicated in this book, while useful, often obscure the real reasons for decline.

The church practice as advocated in this book is not meant to be exclusive of other patterns of church life. In addition, it does not claim to be the middle ground between right-wing and left-wing proposals. The middle ground has become a cliché that all advocates assert. The only claim that is made here is that the pattern of church life advocated has been tested in the actual experience of the pastorate and is quantifiably effective. It is also claimed that it is in agreement with the theological tradition of the church.

The theological renewal of the church depends not simply on sound theology and effective practice but also on personal commitment, especially in the leadership of the church. The renewal of the church is finally a question of faith: "Who do you say that I am?" and a question of vocation appropriate to the answer which Peter gave, "You are the Christ, the Son of the living God" (Matt. 16:16). "Do your best to present yourself to God as one approved, a workman who has no need to be ashamed, rightly handling the word of truth" (1 Tim. 2:15).

> Walk about Zion, go round about her,
>   number her towers,
> consider well her ramparts,
>   go through her citadels;
> that you may tell the next generation
>   that this is God,
> our God for ever and ever.
> He will be our guide for ever.
>   Psalm 48:12–14

Notes

Preface

1. Wade Clark Roof and William McKinney, *American Mainline Religion: Its Changing Shape and Future* (New Brunswick, N.J.: Rutgers University Press, 1987); Robert Wuthnow, *The Restructuring of American Religion* (Princeton, N.J.: Princeton University Press, 1988); Andrew M. Greeley, *Religious Change in America* (Cambridge, Mass.: Harvard University Press, 1989); James Davison Hunter, *American Evangelicalism: Conservative Religion and the Quandary of Modernity* (New Brunswick, N.J.: Rutgers University Press, 1983), a perceptive analysis of the "evangelical" wing of American Christianity; James Davison Hunter, *Evangelicalism: The Coming Generation* (Chicago: University of Chicago Press, 1987); and Jeffrey K. Hadden, *The Gathering Storm in the Churches* (Garden City, N.Y.: Doubleday & Co., 1969), a perceptive analysis that the passing of twenty years has proved to be correct.

2. Robert Wuthnow's "The Restructuring of American Presbyterianism" (*Reformed Journal* [Aug. 8, 1989]: 14–21) is a good example of a church analysis that is unaware of the nuances of the church's life. Wuthnow has command of much data, but even when the facts are correct, the melody is missing. For example, he uses the words "liberal" and "conservative" indiscrimi-

nately, never defining what he means. Liberal and conservative are terms of dubious value in the life of the church today, but whatever they mean, liberal and conservative have far different connotations in the present situation than they do when applied to Presbyterian divisions in the eighteenth century or in the nineteenth century. Moreover, Wuthnow's discussion of college students and youth may be correct on facts, but it shows little sensitivity to the decisions that were made in the life of the church affecting youth work and campus ministries or to the changed content of what remained of campus ministries and youth work in the 1960s and 1970s. Whatever may be the problems in American Presbyterianism, they cannot be described simply as a clash between liberals and conservatives. Actually, 68–75 percent of Presbyterians voted for Ronald Reagan. The real division is not between those who believe in social action and those who believe in evangelism. The church lived with this controversy during decades of growth. The issue today has to do with the faith itself. Wuthnow points to the problem of "each side attempting to impute blame to the other side." But there are many sides in the Presbyterian Church. This is not to depreciate Wuthnow's article; it is simply to say that its usefulness is limited in guiding Presbyterians out of the present crisis. See "Mainstream Protestantism in the Twentieth Century, Its Problems and Prospects," addresses by Dorothy C. Bass, Benton Johnson, and Wade Clark Roof, published by the Council on Theological Education, Presbyterian Church (U.S.A.). See also Dorothy C. Bass, "Reflections on the Reports of Decline in Mainstream Protestantism," *Chicago Theological Seminary Register* 80 (Summer 1969), which nowhere mentions pastoral visitation, quality of sermons, or the crisis of faith. This author sees the problem very much from the perspective of the leadership that presided over theological education as the problem developed.

3. See Peter Berger, "Different Gospels, the Social Sources of Apostasy," *This World* (Spring 1987), p. 6.

4. Karl Barth, *Church Dogmatics,* ed. G. W. Bromiley and T. F. Torrance (Edinburgh: T. & T. Clark, 1936–1962), IV/1, pp. 654–655. "The emphasis in the present context must be upon the fact that the community called into being by the Holy Spirit, although it does not exist and must not be sought ab-

stractly in the invisible, also does not exist and must not be sought abstractly in the visible. It does exist openly in a very concrete form, a historical phenomenon like any other. But what it is, the character, the truth of its existence in time and space, is not a matter of a general but a very special visibility. Without this it is invisible. What is visible to all is the event of the *congregatio* and *communio* of certain men, its characteristic activities and achievements, its peculiarities by which it is distinguished from other historical structures, its deficiencies which it has with them in common, its relative advantages. But what actually takes place, what this is in truth, is not visible to all; it is visible to Christians only in this particular way or not at all. Without this special visibility all that can be seen is the men united in it and their common activity, and this will be explained in terms of the categories which are regarded as the most appropriate for the understanding and appraisal of common human activities, with an attempt to subordinate it to some picture of the world and of history. On this view it can be understood as a religious society within human society generally and side by side with other organisations."

5. Richard John Neuhaus, ed., *Unsecular America* (Grand Rapids: Wm. B. Eerdmans Publishing Co., 1986), pp. 116ff. Religious News Service reported (Dec. 20, 1989) that 5 percent of Lutherans and 25 percent of Catholics attend church services regularly in West Germany.

6. Robert Morgan and John Barton, *Biblical Interpretation* (New York: Oxford University Press, 1988), pp. 136–137. This passage was called to my attention by my colleague James L. Mays.

7. William Temple, *Christian Life and Faith* (London: SCM Press, 1931), pp. 100ff.

8. Czeslaw Milosz, *Nobel Lecture* (New York: Farrar, Straus & Giroux, 1981), pp. 14–15.

9. William C. Placher, *Unapologetic Theology: A Christian Voice in a Pluralistic Conversation* (Philadelphia: Westminster Press, 1989).

10. Augustine, *The Usefulness of Belief, Augustine: Earlier Writings,* ed. J. H. S. Burleigh, Library of Christian Classics, vol. 6 (Philadelphia: Westminster Press, 1953), pp. 291ff.

11. Anselm, *Proslogion,* Preface, in *A Scholastic Miscellany: Anselm to Ockham,* ed. Eugene R. Fairweather, Library of Christian Classics, vol. 10 (Philadelphia: Westminster Press, 1956), p. 69. See John E. Smith, *The Analogy of Experience: An Approach to Understanding Religious Truth* (New York: Harper & Row, 1973), an excellent discussion for preachers. See also John McIntyre, *St. Anselm and His Critics* (Edinburgh: Oliver & Boyd, 1934); G. R. Evans, *Anselm and Talking About God* (Oxford: Clarendon Press, 1978); Karl Barth, *Anselm: Fides Quaerens Intellectum* (London: SCM Press, 1960).

12. Barth, *Church Dogmatics* I/1, pp. 71ff.

13. H. E. W. Turner, *The Pattern of Christian Truth* (London: A. R. Mowbray, 1954), Lecture III, pp. 97ff.

14. John E. Smith, "Faith, Belief, and the Problem of Rationality in Religion," in *Rationality and Religious Belief,* ed. C. F. Delaney (Notre Dame, Ind.: University of Notre Dame Press, 1979), pp. 42–64; Smith, *The Analogy of Experience,* pp. 44–62.

15. Augustine, among others, spoke of "spoiling the Egyptians," taking the best wisdom available for the service of the gospel. As Paul advised, "Take every thought captive to obey Christ" (2 Cor. 10:5). See Frederick W. Norris, "Of Thorns and Roses: The Logic of Belief in Gregory of Nazianzen," *Church History* 52/4, pp. 455–464.

Chapter 1: Heritage and Trust

1. Kenneth Scott Latourette, *A History of the Expansion of Christianity,* vols. 4–6, *The Great Century* (New York: Harper & Brothers, 1941–45).

2. Andrew M. Greeley, *Religious Change in America* (Cambridge, Mass.: Harvard University Press, 1989); Wade Clark Roof and William McKinney, *American Mainline Religion: Its Changing Shape and Future* (New Brunswick, N.J.: Rutgers University Press, 1987); Robert Wuthnow, *The Restructuring of American Religion* (Princeton, N.J.: Princeton University Press, 1988); James Davison Hunter, *Evangelicalism: The Coming Generation* (Chicago: University of Chicago Press, 1987). These books, along with *Emerging Trends* (published by the Princeton Religion Research Center since 1980), provide elaborate data

about church trends. The most perceptive study, in my judgment, of the situation in the mainline churches appeared in 1969: Jeffrey K. Hadden, *The Gathering Storm in the Churches* (Garden City, N.Y.: Doubleday & Co., 1969). Hadden's analysis has proved to be almost clinically exact. Hadden emphasized the problems created by (1) the crisis of faith, (2) confusion about the mission of the church, and (3) a new type of church bureaucrat with little experience in or understanding of the local congregation.

3. There are many reasons for the inadequacy of these studies. First, the church as a community of faith is beyond human observation. Second, most studies are occasional and cover a vast array of materials that cannot be mastered in a short period or, possibly, without living in the community. External researchers are frequently dependent on persons in staff positions who may represent a particular bias which is a factor in the loss of members. Furthermore, social and psychological studies are not likely to uncover data that call in question their own commitments concerning the church.

The church needs objective studies, but I cannot think of instances in which they have been decisive factors in church renewal.

4. John Steinbeck, *The Grapes of Wrath* (New York: Viking Press, 1939), p. 120: "How can we live without our lives? How will we know it's us without our past?" Consider also Joseph Stein, *Fiddler on the Roof* (New York: Crown Publishers, 1964), p. 1. In Stein's play the fiddler on the roof had a hard time trying to scratch out a pleasant, simple tune without breaking his neck. His predicament was a parable of life for us all. "You may ask, why do we stay here if it is so dangerous? We stay because Anatevka is our home. And how do we keep our balance? That I tell you in a word—'tradition.' . . . Because of our tradition, we've kept our balance for many, many years. . . . Because of our tradition everyone knows who he is and what God expects him to do."

5. H. Richard Niebuhr, *The Meaning of Revelation* (New York: Macmillan Co., 1946), especially the chapter entitled "The Story of Our Life."

6. Ibid. In this day of revisionist history, history as "remem-

bered" is no more likely to need revision than histories "objectively" studied.

7. Sydney E. Ahlstrom, *A Religious History of the American People* (New Haven, Conn.: Yale University Press, 1972). On the Reformed influence of the Westminster Confession of Faith, see Louis B. Wright, *Religion and Empire: The Alliance Between Piety and Commerce in English Expansion, 1558-1625* (Chapel Hill, N.C.: University of North Carolina Press, 1943). Consider these words of Ralph Barton Perry: "It is safe to assume . . . that the influence of puritanism, in the broad Calvinistic sense, was a major force in the late colonial period, and that it contributed uniquely and profoundly to the making of the American mind when the American mind was in the making" (Ralph Barton Perry, *Puritanism and Democracy* [New York: Vanguard Press, 1944], p. 81). See also Michael Novak, *The Spirit of Democratic Capitalism* (New York: Simon & Schuster, 1982); Robert T. Handy, *A Christian America: Protestant Hopes and Historical Realities* (New York: Oxford University Press, 1971); Sidney Mead, *The Old Religion in the Brave New World* (Berkeley, Calif.: University of California Press, 1977); Edward C. Banfield, *The Moral Basis of a Backward Society* (New York: Macmillan Co., 1958), and David C. McClelland, *The Achieving Society* (New York: Irvington Publishers, 1976).

8. Charles Norris Cochrane, *Christianity and Classical Culture: A Study of Thought and Action from Augustus to Augustine* (New York: Oxford University Press, 1957); see Paul Tillich, *A History of Christian Thought: From Its Judaic and Hellenistic Origins to Existentialism*, 2nd ed., rev. and ed. Carl E. Braaten (New York: Harper & Row, 1968), pp. 1-16.

9. Herbert Butterfield, *Christianity in European History* (London: William Collins Sons & Co., 1952), pp. 14-15.

10. Augustine, *The City of God,* trans. Marcus Dods (New York: Modern Library, 1950), bk. 19; Peter Brown, *Augustine of Hippo: A Biography* (London: Faber & Faber, 1967), esp. pp. 299-312. R. A. Markus, *Saeculum: History and Society in the Theology of St. Augustine* (Cambridge: Cambridge University Press, 1970), ch. 7.

11. Tillich, *A History of Christian Thought,* p. 72; Rowan Williams, *Arius: Heresy and Tradition* (London: Darton, Long-

man & Todd, 1987), especially the Postscript; R. P. C. Hanson, *The Search for the Christian Doctrine of God: The Arian Controversy* (318–381) (Edinburgh: T. & T. Clark, 1988).
Wolfhart Pannenberg has written: "Especially some representatives of the young churches from the Third World consider the early ecumenical councils and the Nicene Creed simply as an expression of Hellenistic culture, a particular culture among others, which they do not want to dominate their own culture. Such a concern for cultural distinctiveness and for the inculturation of the Gospel into a plurality of human cultures is certainly legitimate. But on the other hand, cultural autonomy should not be absolutized at the expense of Christian unity. In the past the celtic, Germanic and Slavonic peoples of Northern Europe received the Christian faith from the Greeks and Romans. They received it in the form it had assumed in those cultures, and only in connexion with this process of reception has there emerged what today is known as European culture. There can be no Christian unity without reception of the Christian past as a common heritage, and it is a contingent fact of history that this heritage took its definitive form in the Hellenistic world, after the Greek and Roman Christians themselves had received the Gospel from Palestine and withstood the temptation of abolishing the OT as something foreign to Hellenistic culture. In this way, the Christians everywhere have become heirs of some of the great cultures of humanity. New cultural elements can always enter into this process of recapitulation within the unity of the church, but the church's continuity with its origins must not be disrupted by such dynamics. As the different traditions in Christianity appropriated the ancient creeds in different situations, so it may continue in the present world. Mutual recognition of such diversities of cultural context and application need not prevent agreement in recognizing the common heritage and its authority" (Cyril Rodd, ed., *Foundation Documents of the Faith* [Edinburgh: T. & T. Clark, 1988], p. 151).
12. James Atlas, "The Battle of the Books," *New York Times Magazine* (June 5, 1988): 26. See Virginia Stem Owens, "Giving Ourselves Airs," *Reformed Journal* 39 (Sept. 9, 1989).
13. John Headley, "The Reformation as Crisis in the Un-

derstanding of Tradition," *Archive for Reformation History* 78 (1987): 6.

14. Ibid., 16.

15. Albert Cook Outler, *The Christian Tradition and the Unity We Seek* (New York: Oxford University Press, 1957), pp. 110–111. See Rom. 8:31–32.

16. Karl Barth, *Church Dogmatics,* ed. G. W. Bromiley and T. F. Torrance (Edinburgh: T. & T. Clark, 1936–62), 1/2, pp. 473ff.

17. William Temple, "Revelation," in *Revelation,* ed. John Baillie and Hugh Martin (London: Faber & Faber, 1937), pp. 103–108.

18. Emil Brunner, *Revelation and Reason: The Christian Doctrine of Faith and Knowledge* (Philadelphia: Westminster Press, 1946), p. 12.

19. Ignatius, *Letter to the Trallians* 8–10, and Irenaeus, *Against Heresies* 3.1–11, *Early Christian Fathers,* ed. and trans. Cyril C. Richardson, Library of Christian Classics, vol. 1 (Philadelphia: Westminster Press, 1953); Origen, *On First Principles* 1.1, in *Origen: On First Principles,* ed. and trans. G. W. Butterworth (New York: Harper & Row, 1966), p. 1.

Consider these words of Augustine on the reading of the gospel: "So let us listen to the Gospel as though the Lord himself were present. And do not let us say: 'How fortunate were those who could see him!' For many of those who saw him also killed him, while many of us who have not seen him have also believed in him. The precious things that came from the mouth of the Lord were written down for us and kept for us and read aloud for us, and will be read by our children too, until the end of the world. The Lord is above, but the Lord of truth is here. The Lord's body in which he rose from the dead can be in one place only; but his truth is everywhere" (quoted by Aelred Squire, *Asking the Fathers,* p. 121; London: SPCK, 1973).

Compare the perceptive statement of a contemporary theologian, John McIntyre: "When the christological subject-matter is approached, it has to be borne in mind that we are dealing with a person towards whom the proper attitude is not one of scientific curiosity, or detached inquisitiveness, but ultimately one of worship and adoration, trust and obedience. . . . We shall not be satisfied with any christological analysis which eliminates from its conception of who he is all valid basis for an attitude of worship to him. It is on this very score that humanistic interpretations of the person of Jesus Christ fail, that they present to us someone who cannot sustain human *worship;* admiration, perhaps, even a sense of wonder at the courage he had in the face of danger and death, but never worship. That is given only to God. The questions with which the liturgical interest will always tax any christological analysis will, therefore, be: How easily does the analysis integrate with a living situation in which the believer trusts, loves and obeys Jesus Christ?" (John McIntyre, *The Shape of Christology* [London: SCM Press, 1966], p. 45).

20. See Lucien Febvre, *A New Kind of History and Other Essays,* ed. Peter Burke and trans. K. Folca (New York: Harper & Row, 1973); Steven Ozment, *The Age of Reform, 1250–1550* (New Haven, Conn.: Yale University Press, 1980), pp. 200–204.

21. Barth, *Church Dogmatics* IV/1, p. 758.

22. Karl Rahner, "The Development of Dogma," *Theological Investigations,* vol. 1, *God, Christ, Mary and Grace,* trans. Cornelius Ernst (Baltimore: Helicon Press, 1961), pp. 63–77.

23. Calvin on prayer, *Institutes* 3.20.50; on worship, 2.8.28–34; on stewardship, 3.20.39; on Bible reading, Commentary on Acts 8:28–31; Sermon on Deuteronomy 17:16–20.

24. *Calvin: Institutes of the Christian Religion,* ed. John T. McNeill and trans. Ford Lewis Battles (Philadelphia: Westminster Press, 1960), 3.3.16. See Karl Barth, *Church Dogmatics* IV/3.2, p. 506, on the problems of any psychological or biographical description of the Christian life.

25. John Calvin, *Opera Selecta,* ed. Petrus Barth, Guilielmus Baum, and Dora Scheuner (Munich: Chr. Kaiser, 1952), 2:15; Émile Doumergue, "Music in the Work of Calvin," *Princeton Theological Review* 7/4 (October 1909): 529–552. See Émile Doumergue, *L'art et le sentiment dans l'oeuvre de Calvin* (Geneva: Slatkine Reprints, 1970, reprint of the Geneva edition of 1902). See also W. Stanford Reid, "The Battle Hymns of the Lord, Calvinist Psalmody of the Sixteenth Century," *Sixteenth Century Essays and Studies,* vol. 2, ed. Carl S. Meyer (St. Louis: Foundation for Reformation Research, 1971).

26. Calvin, *Institutes* 2.8.34.

27. Karl Barth, *Church Dogmatics,* III/4, p. 50.
28. John H. Primus, *Holy Time: Moderate Puritanism and the Sabbath* (Macon, Ga.: Mercer University Press, 1989).
29. Augustine wrote: "But the Catholic Faith is made known to the faithful in the Creed, and is committed to memory, in as short a form as so great a matter permits. In this way for beginners and sucklings, who have been reborn in Christ but have not yet been strengthened by diligent and spiritual study and understanding of the divine Scriptures, there has been drawn up in few words a formula they must accept in faith, setting forth what would have to be expounded in many words to those who are making progress and are raising themselves up to attain the divine doctrine in the assured strength of humility and charity" (Augustine, *Faith and the Creed* 1.1, in *Augustine: Earlier Writings,* ed. and trans. John H. S. Burleigh, Library of Christian Classics, vol. 6 [Philadelphia: Westminster Press, 1953], p. 353). Also see Calvin, *Institutes* 4.1.3.
30. Outler, *The Christian Tradition,* p. 111.
31. William Temple, *The Hope of a New World* (London: SCM Press, 1940), p. 105; Adolf von Harnack, *The Mission and Expansion of Christianity in the First Three Centuries,* trans. James Moffatt (New York: G. P. Putnam's Sons, 1908), vol. 1, bk. 3, chs. 4 and 5; see p. 368. "A living faith requires no special 'methods' for its propagation" (p. 398). Harnack notes that the witness of the community is crucial in attracting people. They saw in the church a life they wished to share.
32. Raymond E. Brown, *The Birth of the Messiah: A Commentary on the Infancy Narratives in Matthew and Luke* (Garden City, N.Y.: Doubleday & Co., 1977), p. 65.
33. Wuthnow, *The Restructuring of American Religion,* chs. 7 and 8, pp. 133–214.
34. Latourette, *A History of the Expansion of Christianity,* 4:95–98; Ahlstrom, *A Religious History of the American People,* pp. 864–866.
35. Edward Albert Shils, *Tradition* (Chicago: University of Chicago Press, 1981), ch. 1.
36. R. P. C. Hanson, *The Continuity of Christian Doctrine* (New York: Seabury Press, 1981), p. 85; Jaroslav Pelikan, *The Christian Tradition,* vol. 1, *The Emergence of the Catholic Tradi-*

tion (100–600) (Chicago: University of Chicago Press, 1971), p. 15; idem, *The Vindication of Tradition* (New Haven, Conn.: Yale University Press, 1984), esp. chs. 2 and 3; R. P. C. Hanson, *Tradition in the Early Church* (London: SCM Press, 1962), esp. chs. 1 and 6.

37. Shils, *Tradition*, p. 183.

38. Karl Raimund Popper, *Objective Knowledge: An Evolutionary Approach,* rev. ed. (New York: Oxford University Press, 1979), p. 122; see Popper's comments on the consequences of the loss of libraries, p. 108.

39. "We do not usually call inertia to mind when we seek the great molding forces of history. And yet this humble characteristic is responsible for more of 'history' than all the campaigns, the movements, the revolutions we readily call to mind. The simple but quintessential fact that human beings persist in living their lives in familiar ways, which are the only ways they know how, is the very lifeline of social continuity itself.

"This inertia which exerts so powerful a drag on history undoubtedly has its biological and psychological roots. But it is more than just an 'innate' human characteristic. It is also the outcome of the historic social condition of man. For the persistence of habit acts as a protective reflex for the overwhelming majority of men who know very little except that life is a fragile possession, and that tried and true ways, however onerous, have at least proved capable of sustaining it" (Robert L. Heilbroner, *The Future as History: The Historic Currents of Our Time and the Direction in Which They Are Taking America* [New York: Harper & Row, 1959], pp. 193–194).

40. John T. McNeill, *Modern Christian Movements* (Philadelphia: Westminster Press, 1954), pp. 20–21.

41. Augustine, *Confessions,* bk. 11, *Augustine: Confessions and Enchiridion,* ed. and trans. Albert C. Outler, Library of Christian Classics, vol. 7 (Philadelphia: Westminster Press, 1955), p. 31.

42. Edwin E. Aubrey, *Secularism a Myth: An Examination of the Current Attack on Secularism* (New York: Harper & Brothers, 1954); Martin E. Marty, *The Modern Schism: Three Paths to the Secular* (New York: Harper & Row, 1969); Albert T. Mollegen, *Christianity and the Crisis of Secularism* (Washington, D.C.: Hen-

derson Services, 1951); Franklin Baumer, *Religion and the Rise of Scepticism* (New York: Harcourt, Brace & Co., 1960); David Martin, *A General Theory of Secularization* (New York: Harper & Row, 1978); E. L. Mascall, *The Secularisation of Christianity: An Analysis and a Critique* (London: Darton, Longman & Todd, 1965).

43. D. L. Munby, *The Idea of a Secular Society and Its Significance for Christians* (London: Oxford University Press, 1963).

44. Harvey Cox, *The Secular City: Secularization and Urbanization in Theological Perspective* (New York: Macmillan Co., 1965).

45. Greeley, *Religious Change in America*, p. 128. Data for the religious convictions of Protestants are numerous and confirmed in many surveys. According to a Gallup survey in 1981, 50 percent of Americans belonged to a religious organization and 43 percent of Americans attended religious services once a week or more. These figures for church participation were far greater than for any other nation in the industrialized West. The comparable figures for weekly church attendance were 21 percent for West Germany, 14 percent for Great Britain, 12 percent for France, and 5 percent for Sweden (Richard John Neuhaus, ed., *Unsecular America* [Grand Rapids: Wm. B. Eerdmans Publishing Co., 1986], pp. 115–116). See also the surveys of data in *Unsecular America*, pp. 115–126. Theodore Caplow concludes: "We have a fair amount of information . . . that religiosity has very significantly increased since the 1920s. . . . One concedes too much when one says, we're just about as religious as we used to be. We may be a great deal more religious than we used to be" (*Unsecular America*, p. 68). See Theodore Caplow, Howard M. Bahr, and Bruce A. Chadwick, *All Faithful People: Change and Continuity in Middletown's Religion* (Minneapolis: University of Minnesota Press, 1983).

46. S. Robert Lichter, Stanley Rothman, and Linda S. Lichter, *The Media Elite* (Bethesda, Md.: Adler & Adler, 1986), pp. 21, 22, 47; S. Robert Lichter and Stanley Rothman, *The Media Elite and American Values* (Washington, D.C.: Ethics and Public Policy Center, 1982).

47. See the perceptive analysis of Walter Moberly, *The Crisis in the University* (London: SCM Press, 1951).

48. Robert Morgan and John Barton, *Biblical Interpretation* (New York: Oxford University Press, 1988), p. 169; see pp. 171, 277.

49. Analyzing the hostile coverage of *The New York Times* of the Bolshevik regime in the 1920s, Walter Lippmann wrote: "The news as a whole is dominated by the hopes of men who composed the news organization. . . . In the large, news about Russia is a case of seeing not what was, but what men wished to see. . . . The chief censor and the chief propagandist were hope and fear in the minds of reporters and editors" (quoted by Lichter, Rothman, and Lichter, *The Media Elite*, p. 6).

50. Richard Hutcheson, Jr., *Wheel Within the Wheel: Confronting the Management Crisis of the Pluralistic Church* (Atlanta: John Knox Press, 1979), pp. 262–269. The instruction given to ministers with their Personal Information Forms encourages aggressive salesmanship of oneself and indicates no familiarity with the old Protestant doctrine of call.

51. James Turner, *Without God, Without Creed: The Origins of Unbelief in America* (Baltimore, Md.: Johns Hopkins University Press, 1985), pp. 262–269.

52. W. K. Jordan, *The Development of Religious Toleration in England* (Cambridge, Mass.: Harvard University Press, 1932–40); Roland Bainton, *The Travail of Religious Liberty: Nine Biographical Studies* (Philadelphia: Westminster Press, 1951).

53. Luther's doctrine of the priesthood of believers and the supreme authority of the Holy Spirit speaking in scripture are a basis for a Protestant doctrine of religious freedom.

54. John Murray Cuddihy, *No Offense: Civil Religion and Protestant Taste* (New York: Seabury Press, 1978); Robert N. Bellah and Frederick E. Greenspahn, eds., *Uncivil Religion: Interreligious Hostility in America* (New York: Crossroad Publishing Co., 1987).

55. Lichter, Rothman, and Lichter, *The Media Elite*, p. 8.

56. Richard M. Merelman, *Making Something of Ourselves: On Culture and Politics in the United States* (Berkeley, Calif.: University of California Press, 1984), pp. 30–32, 109–110, 240.

57. More than any other theologian, Thomas F. Torrance has studied this problem. Compare his address at the dedication of the Center of Theological Inquiry at Princeton with *The*

Ground and Grammar of Theology (Charlottesville, Va.: University Press of Virginia, 1980); *Christian Theology and Scientific Culture* (Belfast: Christian Journals, 1980); *Transformation and Convergence in the Frame of Knowledge* (Grand Rapids: Wm. B. Eerdmans Publishing Co., 1984); and *The Christian Frame of Mind* (Edinburgh: Handsel Press, 1985), esp. ch. 2.

58. Harry Emerson Fosdick, "Will Science Displace God?," *Adventurous Religion and Other Essays* (London: SCM Press, 1926), pp. 135–151.

59. Augustine, *Confessions* 1.1.

60. Calvin, *Institutes* 1.3.2.

61. Ibid., 1.1–6. Cf. Alvin Plantinga, "The Reformed Objection to Natural Theology," *Christian Scholar's Review* 11/3 (1982): 187–198.

62. Theodosius Dobzhansky, *The Biology of Ultimate Concern* (New York: New American Library of World Literature, 1967), pp. 4–5.

63. Daniel Bell, "The Return of the Sacred? The Argument on the Future of Religion," *British Journal of Sociology* 28/4 (Dec. 1977): 442, 443–444.

64. Barth, *Church Dogmatics* IV/1, pp. 358ff. Compare these words of Diogenes Allen: "Any disagreement that I may have with a particular presentation of the human condition does not constitute a repudiation of this kind of study per se, nor do I wish by any means to deny that many of men's needs as human beings are met by the gospel. But I wish to insist that there is a distinctive range of fears, hopes, and aspirations which arise only with a hearing of the gospel. Unless there is a distinctive range of needs, there is great force in the view that religious beliefs are psychological projections; a view that would undermine my thesis that the fulfillment of needs is a sound ground for religious beliefs. Thus I must here argue that there are two ranges of needs which are satisfied by the gospel: those which are part of the human condition, and those which are awakened by the scriptural portrayal of God" (Diogenes Allen, *The Reasonableness of Faith* [Washington, D.C.: Corpus Books, 1968], pp. 54–55).

65. Calvin, *Institutes* 4.1.2; 4.1.3.

66. John Calvin, "The Necessity of Reforming the Church," *Selected Works of John Calvin: Tracts and Letters,* vol. 1,

Tracts, ed. Henry Beveridge and Jules Bonnet, trans. Henry Beveridge (Grand Rapids: Baker Book House, 1983), part 1, p. 200.

67. Karl Barth, *Church Dogmatics* IV/2, p. 643.

68. Lord Eustace Percy, *John Knox* (London: Hodder & Stoughton, 1937).

69. John H. Leith, *Reformed Theology and the Style of Evangelism*. Originally published by Board of National Missions, Presbyterian Church U.S. Available from Continuing Education Office, Union Theological Seminary in Virginia.

70. *World Christian Encyclopedia*, ed. David B. Barrett (New York: Oxford University Press, 1982), p. 3.

71. Barth, *Church Dogmatics* IV/2, p. 645.

72. Greeley, *Religious Change in America*; Roof and McKinney, *American Mainline Religion*; Wuthnow, *The Restructuring of American Religion*.

73. Robert Wuthnow and Clifford Nass, "Government Activity and Civil Privatism: Evidence from Voluntary Church Membership," *Journal for the Scientific Study of Religion* 27/2 (June 1988): 157–174.

74. William Temple, *Religious Experience and Other Essays and Addresses* (London: James Clarke & Co., 1958), pp. 244–245.

Chapter 2: The Church and the Ministry

1. John H. Leith, ed., *Creeds of the Churches: A Reader in Christian Doctrine from the Bible to the Present*, 3rd ed. (Atlanta: John Knox Press, 1982), p. 129.

2. Paul D. L. Avis, *The Church in the Theology of the Reformers* (Atlanta: John Knox Press, 1981), p. 1.

3. Jeffrey K. Hadden, *The Gathering Storm in the Churches* (Garden City, N.Y.: Doubleday & Co., 1969).

4. Roland Bainton, "Interpretations of the Reformation," in *The Reformation: Material or Spiritual?* ed. Lewis Spitz (Boston: D. C. Heath & Co., 1962), pp. 1–7.

5. Lucien Febvre, "The Origins of the French Revolution: A Badly-Put Question," in *A New Kind of History, and Other Essays* [by Lucien Febvre], ed. Peter Burke and trans. K. Folca (New York: Harper & Row, 1973).

6. Steven Ozment, *The Age of Reform, 1250–1550* (New Haven, Conn.: Yale University Press, 1980), p. 204.

7. Febvre, "The Origins of the French Revolution," p. 60.

8. Ibid., p. 74.

9. Martin Luther, *The Babylonian Captivity of the Church*, trans. A. T. W. Steinhaeuser, rev. F. C. Ahrens and Abdel Ross Wentz, *Selected Writings of Martin Luther, 1517–1528*, ed. Theodore G. Tappert (Philadelphia: Fortress Press, 1967), 1:465.

10. Febvre, "The Origins of the French Revolution," pp. 74–75.

11. A. G. Dickens and John Tonkin, *The Reformation in Historical Thought* (Cambridge, Mass.: Harvard University Press, 1985), pp. 286–289.

12. Robert Kingdon, "Calvin and the Government of Geneva," in *Calvinus Ecclesiae Genevensis Custos*, ed. Wilhelm H. Neuser (New York: Frankfurt: Peter Lang, 1984), p. 51.

13. Ibid., pp. 53–54.

14. Jenny Wormald, *Court, Kirk, and Community: Scotland, 1470–1625* (Toronto: University of Toronto Press, 1981), pp. 76, 88. This study was brought to my attention by Alec Cheyne, Emeritus Professor of Ecclesiastical History, University of Edinburgh.

15. Ibid., p. 89.

16. Ibid., p. 90.

17. Ibid., p. 104.

18. Ibid., pp. 104–105. Quoted from G. R. Elton, *Reformation Europe 1517–1559* (New York: World Publishing Co., 1964), p. 52.

19. Wormald, *Court, Kirk, and Community*, p. 21.

20. Ibid., p. 120.

21. Ibid., p. 131.

22. Ibid., p. 135.

23. Ibid., pp. 134, 137.

24. Alexandre Ganoczy, *The Young Calvin*, trans. David Foxgrover and Wade Provo (Philadelphia: Westminster Press, 1987), p. 308.

25. Calvin, *Institutes* 4.5.9; 4.5.7; 4.4.6. See the Second Helvetic Confession, Ch. XVIII, for a brief but classic statement of the Reformed doctrine of the ministry.

26. Reinhold Niebuhr, *Leaves from the Notebook of a Tamed Cynic* (New York: Da Capo Press, 1976), pp. 64–65.
27. Daniel Jenkins: *The Gift of Ministry* (London: Faber & Faber, 1948), pp. 23–24.
28. Karl Barth, *Church Dogmatics* IV/4, ed. G. W. Bromiley and T. F. Torrance (Edinburgh: T. & T. Clark, 1936–62), IV/4, p. 201.
29. Calvin, *Institutes* 4.5.4; 4.3.7.
30. Quoted by J. L. Ainslie, *The Doctrines of Ministerial Order in the Reformed Churches of the Sixteenth and Seventeenth Centuries* (Edinburgh: T. & T. Clark, 1940), p. 37.
31. Richard Baxter, *The Reformed Pastor*, ed. William Brown (Edinburgh: Banner of Truth Trust, 1983), p. 88.
32. Ainslie, *The Doctrines of Ministerial Order*, p. 39.
33. J. K. S. Reid, ed., *Calvin: Theological Treatises*, Library of Christian Classics, vol. 22 (Philadelphia: Westminster Press, 1954), p. 32. See Ainslie, *The Doctrines of Ministerial Order*, pp. 41–45.
34. Church councils cannot make a preacher as the medieval church gave priests power in the sacrament. The church can only recognize the gift and ability to preach and authorize persons to exercise it.
35. See: "Draft Ecclesiastical Ordinances (1541)," in *Calvin: Theological Treatises*, p. 62; "Ordinances for Supervision of Churches in the Country (1547): Catechism," ibid., p. 77. Cf. Calvin, *Institutes* 4.3.4, "The pastoral office includes all these functions within itself."
36. "Draft Ecclesiastical Ordinances (1541)": "Of the Visitation of the Sick," "Of the Visitation of Prisoners," in *Calvin: Theological Treatises*, p. 68.
37. A study of the origin of local congregations, institutions, assembly grounds would reveal, I think, that they had their origin more in individual initiative than with councils or staffs.
38. Theodore Tappert, ed. and trans., *The Book of Concord* (Philadelphia: Muhlenberg Press, 1959), pp. 416–417.
39. See Andrew Landale Drummond, *The Church Architecture of Protestantism: An Historical and Constructive Study* (Edinburgh: T. & T. Clark, 1934), p. 45.
40. Calvin, *Institutes* 4.4.9.

41. Tappert, *Selected Writings of Martin Luther, 1517–1528,* 1:465ff., 438.

42. Ibid., 2:44.

43. T. W. Manson, *Ministry and Priesthood, Christ's and Ours* (London: Epworth Press, 1958), p. 38. Manson points out the diverse meaning of priest for Calvin and Luther. For Luther, Christians are all priests. For Calvin, they are all lay people. Manson as a New Testament scholar finds "that the priesthood of all believers lies in the fact that each believer offers himself as a sacrifice according to pattern laid down by Christ; and—what is essential—that all these individual offerings are taken up into one perpetual offering made by the one eternal high-priest of the New Covenant." See the Second Helvetic Confession, Ch. XVIII, for a clear affirmation of the priesthood of believers.

44. Marilyn J. Westerkamp, *The Triumph of the Laity: Scots-Irish Piety and the Great Awakening, 1625–1760* (New York: Oxford University Press, 1988).

45. Nathan Hatch, "Evangelicalism as a Democratic Movement," *Reformed Journal,* 34/10 (Oct. 1984): 11.

46. Karl Barth, *Church Dogmatics* IV/3.2, pp. 681ff. See James Bergquist, "The Identity of the Church in Light of Developing Ideas of Mission," in *The Church Emerging: A U.S. Lutheran Case Study,* ed. John Reumann (Philadelphia: Fortress Press, 1977), pp. 200–251.

47. Reply to Sadolet in *Calvin: Theological Treatises,* p. 228.

48. Sidney Hook, *Out of Step: An Unquiet Life in the Twentieth Century* (New York: Harper & Row, 1987), pp. 570–581.

49. I first heard this from George Forell.

50. *The Constitution of the Presbyterian Church (U.S.A.),* Part II: *Book of Order* (Louisville: The Office of the General Assembly).

51. It was in the 1960s that I first heard voices raised in support of strict construction of the *Book of Church Order* and loose construction of the *Confession.* I remember being startled when I saw this in print in a letter or a brief article (I think in *Presbyterian Life*) that I have been unable to locate. In recent years, the dominance of the *Book of Order* over the *Confession* is frequently seen in actions of presbyteries. In the 1930s, 1940s, and 1950s, the theological portion of the ordination examina-

tion was likely to be more crucial than questions raised about polity. In recent years this emphasis has been reversed.

52. E. G. Schwiebert, *Luther and His Times: The Reformation from a New Perspective* (St. Louis: Concordia Publishing House, 1950), pp. 490–491; "After the gathering had assembled, one of the masters, probably Agricola, started the fire. From one of Luther's letters, written around 10 A.M. that morning to Spalatin, it is clear that the *Extravagantes,* the *Summa Angelica,* and some of Eck's and of Emser's books were included in the list. But the principal collection of writings which Luther wished to destroy was the *corpus iuris canonici,* that body of Canon Law which gave the Pope all the extravagant powers which Eck, Emser, and others tried to defend. One after the other the various tomes were consigned to the flames. Finally, Luther unexpectedly drew a printed copy of the bull *Exsurge, Domine* from his gown and threw it into the flames with the remark: 'Because thou hast destroyed the truth of God, may the Lord consume thee in these flames.' . . . Luther, therefore, on this occasion impulsively burned the papal bull which threatened him with excommunication, but he intentionally destroyed the whole basic framework upon which the Roman Church had been built. After the burning of these books and the bull the audience sang the *Te Deum* and the *De profundis,* whereupon the faculty returned to the college."

53. Karl Barth, *Church Dogmatics* IV/1, pp. 650ff.; IV/2, pp. 618ff.

54. Emil Brunner, *The Christian Doctrine of the Church, Faith, and the Consummation,* trans. David Cairns (Philadelphia: Westminster Press, 1962), pp. 3–139.

55. *Calvin: Theological Treatises* contains Articles Concerning the Organization of the Church and of Worship at Geneva (1537) and Draft Ecclesiastical Ordinances (1541); James K. Cameron, ed., *The First Book of Discipline* (Edinburgh: Saint Andrew Press, 1972); James Kirk, ed., *The Second Book of Discipline* (Edinburgh: Saint Andrew Press, 1980); *The Confession of Faith . . . the Form of Presbyterian Government* (Edinburgh: William Blackwood & Sons, 1959).

56. Calvin, *Institutes* 4.3.15; J. H. S. Burleigh, *A Church History of Scotland* (London: Oxford University Press, 1960), pp. 277ff. Samuel Rutherford wrote that ordination was not nec-

essary in an emergency and that the election of the people would supply want of it. See James Walker, *The Theology and Theologians of Scotland, Chiefly of Seventeenth and Eighteenth Centuries* (Edinburgh: T. & T. Clark, 1872).

57. James L. Ainslie, *The Doctrines of Ministerial Order* (Edinburgh: T. & T. Clark, 1940), pp. 151–154. *The Constitution of the Presbyterian Church (U.S.A.)*, Part II: *Book of Order*, 1989–90 (Louisville, Ky.: Office of the General Assembly), G-6.0107.

58. Richard Hutcheson, Jr., *Wheel Within the Wheel* (Atlanta: John Knox Press, 1979). Hutcheson's excellent study is based not only on professional study but on much experience in church organization.

59. Charles Hodge, *Discussions in Church Polity* (New York: Charles Scribner's Sons, 1878), pp. 118ff.

60. John B. Adger and John L. Girardeau, eds., *The Collected Writings of James Henley Thornwell* (Richmond: Presbyterian Committee of Publication, 1873).

61. Hadden, *The Gathering Storm in the Churches*, p. 229; James Davison Hunter, "American Protestantism: Sorting Out the Present, Looking Toward the Future," *This World* 17 (Spring 1987): 64–65.

62. Calvin, *Institutes* 4.3.13–16.

63. Adger and Girardeau, *The Collected Writings of James Henley Thornwell*, p. 100.

64. Peter Berger, "Different Gospels, the Social Sources of Apostasy," *This World* 17 (Spring 1987): 6–17.

65. George Lindbeck, "Scripture, Consensus, and Community," *This World* 23 (Fall 1988): 5–24.

66. Ernest Trice Thompson, *Presbyterians in the South* (Atlanta: John Knox Press, 1963), 1:519ff.; 2:420ff.; Julius Melton, *Presbyterian Worship in America* (Richmond: John Knox Press, 1967), p. 113.

Chapter 3: Preaching

1. Henry W. Jessup, ed., *History of the Fifth Avenue Presbyterian Church of New York City, New York, from 1808 to 1908* (New York: Fifth Avenue Presbyterian Church, 1909), p. 169.

2. James Hastings Nichols, *Corporate Worship in the Reformed Tradition* (Philadelphia: Westminster Press, 1968), p. 51.

3. *Theological Dictionary of the New Testament,* ed. Gerhard Kittel (Grand Rapids: Wm. B. Eerdmans Publishing Co., 1964), s.v. "evangelizomai," by Gerhard Friedrich, 2:720.

4. John Calvin, *Letters of John Calvin,* ed. Jules Bonnet (Philadelphia: Presbyterian Board of Publication, 1858), 2:190–191.

5. John Calvin, Commentary on Isaiah 55:11; 50:10.

6. "If there be one day in the week reserved for religious instruction when they have spent six days in their own business, they are apt to spend the day which is set apart for worship, in play and pastime; some rove about the fields, others go to taverns to quaff; and there are undoubtedly at this time as many at the last mentioned place, as we here assembled in the name of God" (Calvin, Sermon on 1 Timothy 3:16).

7. Calvin, Commentary on 2 Corinthians 2:15; Commentary on Isaiah 6:10.

8. See Richard Stauffer, "Le discours à la première personne dans les sermons de Calvin," in *Regards contemporains sur Jean Calvin* (Paris, 1965). The following paragraph from the third sermon of Calvin on Jacob and Esau states a basic element of his doctrine of preaching: "When the Gospel is preached in the name of God, this is as much as if he himself did speak in his own person: and yet all come not to Jesus Christ. There are a great many that go back the more when they have heard the Gospel; for then the devil kindles them in such a rage, that they are more outrageous than ever before, and this comes to pass, because there is a two fold hearing: the one is preaching; For the voice of a man will not enter into the hearts of his hearers. I speak, but it behooves that I hear myself being taught by the Spirit of God: For otherwise the word which proceeds from my mouth should profit me no more than it does all others, except it be given me from above, and not out of mine own head. Therefore the voice of man is nothing but a sound that vanishes in the air, and notwithstanding it is the power of God to salvation to all believers (saith Saint Paul). When then God speaketh unto us, by the mouth of men, then he adjoins the inward grace of his Holy Spirit, to the end, that the doc-

trine be not unprofitable, but that it may bring forth fruit. See then how we hear the heavenly father: that is to say when he speaketh secretly unto us by his Holy Spirit; and then we come unto our Lord Jesus Christ." (John Calvin, *Thirteen Sermons* . . . [London, 1579], pp. 35–36.)

9. Calvin, *Institutes* 4.14.26. The Holy Spirit seems to have the same relation to the Word, both in scripture and in preaching, as it does to elements in the sacraments. See *Calvin: Institutes of the Christian Religion,* ed. John T. McNeill and trans. Ford Lewis Battles (Philadelphia: Westminster Press, 1960), 4.1.6 and 4.14.9–19. See also Hendrikus Berkhof, *Christian Faith: An Introduction to the Study of the Faith,* rev. ed., trans. Sierd Woudstra (Grand Rapids: Wm. B. Eerdmans Publishing Co., 1986), pp. 360–362; Karl Barth, *Church Dogmatics,* ed. G. W. Bromiley and T. F. Torrance (Edinburgh: T. & T. Clark, 1936–62), I/1, p. 56.

The Heidelberg Catechism, Question 65, defines preaching in a similar manner: "Q. Since, then, faith alone makes us share in Christ and all his benefits, where does such faith originate? A. The Holy Spirit creates it in our hearts by the preaching of the holy gospel, and confirms it by the use of the holy Sacraments." See the Westminster Shorter Catechism, Question 89.

10. Calvin, *Institutes* 3.24.12. In a sermon on Jacob and Esau the percentage is lowered to 10 percent.

11. Calvin, Commentary on John 14:26; Commentary on Ezekiel 2:2; Commentary on Isaiah 29:11.

12. Martin Luther, "Lectures on the Epistle to the Hebrews 1517–18," *Luther: Early Theological Works,* ed. and trans. James Atkinson, Library of Christian Classics, vol. 16 (Philadelphia: Westminster Press, 1962), pp. 194–195.

13. See Calvin's prefaces to the *Institutes:* "John Calvin to the Reader" (1559) and "Subject Matter of the Present Work" (1560).

14. Calvin, *Institutes* 3.6–10.

15. Donald R. Kelley, *The Beginning of Ideology: Consciousness and Society in the French Reformation* (Cambridge: Cambridge University Press, 1981), p. 103.

16. *The Westminster Directory,* ed. Thomas Leishman (Edinburgh: W. Blackwood, 1901), pp. 29–37.

NOTES 203

17. Calvin, *Institutes* 4.10.14, 19; 4.15.19; 4.17.43. See also *The Westminster Directory*, pp. 31–32, 35–37.

18. William Haller, *The Rise of Puritanism* (New York: Columbia University Press, 1938), ch. 4, esp. p. 135.

19. Ibid., p. 128.

20. William Perkins, "Treatise of the Duties and Dignities of the Ministrie" in *The Workes of That Famous Minister of Christ in the Universitie of Cambridge, Mr. William Perkins* (1609), 3:430.

21. Robert Baillie, "Letter to Mr. William Spang, (Postscript), 21st July," *The Letters and Journals of Robert Baillie, A.M.: Principal of the University of Glasgow*, ed. David Laing (Edinburgh: Robert Ogle, 1842), 3:258–259.

22. "The order and sum of the sacred and only method of preaching: 1. To read the text distinctly out of the canonical scriptures; 2. To give the sense and understanding of it being read, by the scripture itself; 3. To collect a few and profitable points of doctrine out of the natural sense; 4. To apply, if he have the gift, the doctrines rightly collected to the life and manners of men in a simple and plain speech. The sum of the sum: Preach one Christ by Christ to the praise of Christ" (William Perkins, *The Art of Prophesying*, in *The Work of William Perkins*, ed. Ian Brevard [Appleford, Eng.: Sutton Courtenay Press, 1970], pp. 325–349). Puritans attending the London Provincial Assembly of 1654 defined preaching in this way: "By the preaching of the Word we understand an authoritative explication and application of Scripture, for exhortation, edification, and comfort, to a congregation met together for the solemn worship of God, in the stead and place of Jesus Christ; and we desire that every branch of this description may be well weighed in the balance of the sanctuary. The subject of the preaching is the Word of God (Matt. xxviii, 19). . . . This work is the explication and application of this Word. . . . The end of this work is the edification and comfort of the Church. . . . The object of this work is a congregation met together for the solemn worship of God. . . . The manner of the doing of this work is authoritatively . . . in the stead of Christ. . . . 'He that heareth you, heareth Me.' " Quoted by James L. Ainslie, *The Doctrines of Ministerial Order* (Edinburgh: T. & T. Clark, 1940), p. 49.

23. Karl Barth, *Church Dogmatics* IV/3.2, p. 800.

24. Ibid., pp. 867, 869.

25. Karl Barth, *Protestant Theology in the Nineteenth Century: Its Background and History* (Valley Forge, Pa.: Judson Press, 1973), pp. 429–430.

26. See Calvin's prefaces to the *Institutes* and his insistence that true theology edifies. See also *Corpus Reformatorum: Ioannis Calvini Opera quae supersunt omnia,* ed. Guilielmus Baum, Eduardus Cunitz, and Eduardus Reuss (Braunschweig: C. A. Schwetschke & Filium, 1863–1897), 33:709.

27. Neil Postman, *Amusing Ourselves to Death* (New York: Penguin Books, 1988). An excellent, readable analysis. "Indeed, in America God favors all those who possess both a talent and a format to amuse, whether they be preachers, athletes, entrepreneurs, politicians, teachers or journalists. In America, the least amusing people are its professional entertainers" (p. 5). When preaching becomes amusing it approaches blasphemy.

28. Paul Tillich, *The Protestant Era,* abr. ed. (Chicago: University of Chicago Press, 1957), pp. 99ff.; and *Systematic Theology* (Chicago: University of Chicago Press, 1951–63), 3:122.

29. Robert Wuthnow, *The Restructuring of American Religion* (Princeton, N.J.: Princeton University Press, 1988), ch. 10.

30. Karl Barth, *Church Dogmatics* III/4, §155.3.

31. Louis Berkhof, *Systematic Theology,* 2nd ed., rev. and enl. (Grand Rapids: Wm. B. Eerdmans Publishing Co., 1941); Charles Hodge, *Systematic Theology,* 3 vols. (New York: Charles Scribner's Sons, 1911); Augustus Hopkins Strong, *Systematic Theology: A Compendium and Commonplace Book Designed for the Use of Theological Students,* 7th ed., rev. and enl. (New York: A. C. Armstrong & Son, 1902).

32. See the writings of William Perkins in Brevard, *The Work of William Perkins.* Also see J. Wollebius, "Compendium Theologiae Christianae," in *Reformed Dogmatics,* ed. and trans. John W. Beardslee (New York: Oxford University Press, 1965).

33. W. A. Visser 't Hooft, "Evangelism Among Europe's Neo-Pagans," *International Review of Mission* 66/264 (Oct. 1977): 349–360. See Marc H. Spindler, "Europe's Neo-Paganism: A Perverse Inculturation," *International Bulletin of Missionary Research,* n.s., 11/1 (Jan. 1987): 8–11.

34. James Davison Hunter, " 'America's Fourth Faith': A Sociological Perspective on Secular Humanism," *This World* 19 (Fall 1987): 101–110.

35. John Dewey, *A Common Faith* (New Haven, Conn.: Yale University Press, 1934). For a brilliant critique of "humanitarian modernism" see Robert L. Calhoun, "The Dilemma of the Humanitarian Modernism," T. E. Jessop et al., *The Christian Understanding of Man* (London: George Allen & Unwin, 1938), pp. 45–81.

36. Schubert M. Ogden, *On Theology* (San Francisco: Harper & Row, 1986); Hendrikus Berkhof, *Introduction to the Study of Dogmatics,* trans. John Vriend (Grand Rapids: Wm. B. Eerdmans Publishing Co., 1985).

37. Barth, *Church Dogmatics* I/1, pp. 248ff., and Paul Tillich, *Systematic Theology,* vol. 1 (Chicago: University of Chicago Press, 1951).

38. No contemporary theologian understands this problem better than Albert C. Outler, who in a remarkable way has combined the academic and the kerygmatic. See Albert Outler, *The Rule of Grace* (Melbourne: Uniting Church Press, 1982).

39. Robert Morgan and John Barton, *Biblical Interpretation* (New York: Oxford University Press, 1988), p. 169; see p. 171. "In a secular culture, to ignore the religious dimensions when handling religious texts implies acceptance of an alternative view of reality" (p. 277).

40. "In every Protestant form the religious element must be related to, and questioned by, a secular element" (Tillich, *The Protestant Era,* p. 214).

41. See Hubert Cunliffe-Jones, ed., *A History of Christian Doctrine* (Edinburgh: T. & T. Clark, 1978), pp. 11–13; Claude Welch, *Protestant Thought in the Nineteenth Century,* vol. 1 (New Haven, Conn.: Yale University Press, 1972). For an excellent current review see William C. Placher, *Unapologetic Theology* (Philadelphia: Westminster Press, 1989). Jeffrey Stout's comment concerning the preoccupation of theologians with methodology is to the point. Theologians who spend too much time on method "become increasingly isolated from churches as well as cultural forums" (Jeffrey Stout, *Ethics After Babel* [Boston: Beacon Press, 1988], p. 163).

42. Many of Jesus' contemporaries thought of him as the carpenter's son, as a blasphemer, as a teacher. For a good summary of New Testament teaching about Jesus Christ by Rowan Greer, see James L. Kugel and Rowan Greer, *Early Biblical Interpretation* (Philadelphia: Westminster Press, 1986), pp. 157ff.

43. Pluralism is used loosely in contemporary discussion with no clear definition of its meaning or its limits. See Will Herberg, *Protestant, Catholic, and Jew: An Essay in American Religious Sociology*, rev. ed. (Garden City, N.J.: Doubleday & Co., Anchor Books, 1960); John Murray Cuddihy, *No Offense: Civil Religion and Protestant Taste* (New York: Seabury Press, 1978); Robert N. Bellah and Frederick E. Greenspahn, eds., *Uncivil Religion: Interreligious Hostility in America* (New York: Crossroad Publishing Co., 1987); Martin E. Marty and Frederick E. Greenspahn, eds., *Pushing the Faith: Proselytism and Civility in a Pluralistic World* (New York: Crossroad Publishing Co., 1988).

44. No one has expressed this better than Walter Lippmann: "As a consequence of the modern theory of religious freedom the churches find themselves in an anomalous position. Inwardly, to their communicants, they continue to assert that they possess the only complete version of the truth. But outwardly, in their civic relation with other churches and with the civil power, they preach and practice toleration. The separation of church and state involves more than a mere logical difficulty for the churchmen. It involves a deep psychological difficulty for the members of the congregation. As communicants they are expected to believe without reservation that their church is the only true means of salvation; otherwise the multitude of separate sects would be meaningless. But as citizens they are expected to maintain a neutral indifference to the claims of all sects, and to resist encroachments by any one sect upon the religious practices of the others. This is the best compromise which human wisdom has yet devised, but it has one inevitable consequence which the superficial advocates of toleration often overlook. It is difficult to remain warmly convinced that the authority of any one sect is divine, when as a matter of daily experience all sects have to be treated alike.

"The human soul is not so divided in compartments that a man can be indifferent in one part of his soul and firmly believing in another. The existence of rival sects, the visible demonstration that none has a monopoly, the habit of neutrality, cannot but dispose men against an unquestioning acceptance of the authority of one sect. So many fruits, so many loyalties, are offered to the modern man that at last none seems to him wholly inevitable and fixed in the order of the universe. The existence of many churches in one community weakens the foundations of all of them. And that is why every church in the heyday of its power proclaims itself to be catholic and intolerant.

"But when there are many churches in the same community, none can make wholly good on the claim that it is catholic. None has that power to discipline the individual which a universal church exercises" (Walter Lippmann, *A Preface to Morals* [New York: Macmillan Co., 1929], pp. 75–76).

45. Wilfred Cantwell Smith, "Theology and the World's Religious History," *Toward a Universal Theology of Religion,* ed. Leonard Swidler (Maryknoll, N.Y.: Orbis Books, 1987), pp. 51–72; Wilfred Cantwell Smith, *Towards a World Theology* (Philadelphia: Westminster Press, 1981); John Hick and Paul F. Knitter, eds., *The Myth of Christian Uniqueness: Toward a Pluralistic Theology of Religions* (Maryknoll, N.Y.: Orbis Books, 1987).

46. Wilfred Cantwell Smith, "Idolatry: In Comparative Perspective," in Hick and Knitter, *The Myth of Christian Uniqueness,* pp. 53–68.

47. Gordon D. Kaufman, "Religious Diversity, Historical Consciousness, and Christian Theology," in Hick and Knitter, *The Myth of Christian Uniqueness,* pp. 8, 12–13.

48. Richard Rorty, *Philosophy and the Mirror of Nature* (Princeton, N.J.: Princeton University Press, 1980), pp. 389–394.

49. See Hick and Knitter, *The Myth of Christian Uniqueness:* John Hick, "The Non-Absoluteness of Christianity," pp. 16–36; also Wilfred Cantwell Smith, "Idolatry: In Comparative Perspective," pp. 53–68.

50. Allan Bloom, *The Closing of the American Mind* (New York: Simon & Schuster, 1987), pp. 313–335; Thomas E. Spahn, "Halls of Ivy, Walls of Glass," *Richmond Times Dispatch* (March 12, 1989), op-ed page; Chester E. Finn, "The Campus: 'An Island of Repression in a Sea of Freedom,' " in *Commentary* 88/3

(Sept. 1989): 17–23; George Will, "Liberals Want to Ban Free Speech on College Campuses," *Richmond News Leader* (Nov. 6, 1989), op-ed page.

51. John Knox, "The Identifiability of the Church," *Theological Freedom and Social Responsibility: Report of the Advisory Committee of the Episcopal Church* (New York: Seabury Press, 1967), p. 69.

52. Étienne Gilson, *The Philosopher and Theology*, trans. Cecile Gilson (New York: Random House, 1962), pp. 107, 204, 209.

53. Étienne Gilson, *Elements of Christian Philosophy* (Garden City, N.Y.: Doubleday & Co., 1960), p. 54.

54. William Bouwsma, "Calvinism as a Renaissance Artifact," in papers presented at a colloquium on Calvin Studies at Davidson College Presbyterian Church and Davidson College, 1985; also Bouwsma, "Calvin and the Renaissance Crisis of Knowing," *Calvin Theological Journal* 17/2 (Nov. 1982): 190–211.

55. The strong rhetorical tradition of preaching in Baptist and even Assembly of God churches persuades obviously highly educated modern persons, as is indicated by the statistics of these churches as well as their presence in affluent suburbs and in the vicinity of universities.

56. Reinhold Niebuhr, "Without Consensus There Is No Consent," *Center Magazine* 4/4 (July/Aug. 1971): 2–9. The presence of Islamic communities in Britain and America raises questions for a pluralistic society for which no adequate answer has been given. See Richard M. Merelman, *Making Something of Ourselves* (Berkeley, Calif.: University of California Press, 1984: "A politics of abstract individualism is not a fully successful democratic alternative" (p. 243).

57. Reinhold Niebuhr, *The Nature and Destiny of Man* (New York: Charles Scribner's Sons, 1943), 2:8.

58. H. Richard Niebuhr, *The Meaning of Revelation* (New York: Macmillan Co., 1941), p. 18.

59. James C. Livingston, *Modern Christian Thought: From the Enlightenment to Vatican II* (New York: Macmillan Co., 1971), esp. chs. 1 and 2. See Peter Gay, *The Enlightenment*, 2 vols. (New York: Alfred A. Knopf, 1966–69).

60. George A. Lindbeck, *The Nature of Doctrine: Religion*

and Theology in a Postliberal Age (Philadelphia: Westminster Press, 1984).

61. Ronald F. Thiemann, *Revelation and Theology: The Gospel as Narrated Promise* (Notre Dame, Ind.: University of Notre Dame Press, 1985), pp. 82–91; and idem, "Radiance and Obscurity in Biblical Narrative," *Scriptural Authority and Narrative Interpretation,* ed. Garrett Green (Philadelphia: Fortress Press, 1987), pp. 21–41.

62. Thiemann, *Revelation and Theology,* esp. chs. 4 and 5. Thiemann's exposition of Matthew is very persuasive, but in my judgment he exaggerates the novelty of his argument. Few theologians have ever conceived of Revelation in terms of knowing subject and object, certainly not Augustine or Calvin. I do not understand why anyone would be concerned with theological speech or with discipleship apart from the conviction that the faith is true, that it reliably affirms what is.

63. The decision of faith is not formally different from the decision to marry or to choose a vocation.

64. Dietrich Bonhoeffer, *Letters and Papers from Prison,* ed. Eberhard Bethge, enl. ed. (New York: Macmillan Co., 1972), p. 158; Milner S. Ball, *The Promise of American Law: A Theological, Humanistic View of Legal Process* (Athens, Ga.: University of Georgia Press, 1981).

65. Erich Auerbach, *Mimesis: The Representation of Reality in Western Literature,* trans. Willard R. Trask (Garden City, N.Y.: Doubleday & Co., 1957), pp. 11ff.

66. Cuddihy, *No Offense: Civil Religion and Protestant Taste,* pp. 191–207.

67. Karl Barth, *Church Dogmatics* IV/1, p. 737.

68. Augustine, *The City of God,* trans. Marcus Dods (New York: Modern Library, 1950), bk. 19, ch. 17, p. 696.

69. Calvin, *Institutes* 2.12.4.

70. This position is supported by Calvin's exposition of John 1 and his doctrine of the *extra Calvinisticum.* See Heiko A. Oberman, "The 'Extra' Dimension in the Theology of Calvin," in his *The Dawn of the Reformation* (Edinburgh: T. & T. Clark, 1986), pp. 234–258. See also E. David Willis, *Calvin's Catholic Christology: The Function of the So-called Extra Calvinisticum in Calvin's Theology* (Leiden: E. J. Brill, 1966).

71. Étienne Gilson, *Revelation and Reason in the Middle Ages* (New York: Charles Scribner's Sons, 1938), pp. 32–33.

72. Reinhold Niebuhr, *The Nature and Destiny of Man*, 2:6.

73. Karl Barth, *Church Dogmatics*, I/2, p. 17. See IV/1, pp. 116ff., for Barth's openness to words spoken in the secular world.

74. Emil Brunner, *Revelation and Reason: The Christian Doctrine of Faith and Knowledge*, trans. Olive Wyon (Philadelphia: Westminster Press, 1946), pp. 262–264, 270–271.

75. Hendrik Kraemer, "Continuity or Discontinuity," *The Authority of the Faith*, Madras Series (New York: International Missionary Council, 1939), 1:1.

76. Ibid. 3.

77. Hendrik Kraemer, *Why Christianity of All Religions?* trans. Hubert Hoskins (Philadelphia: Westminster Press, 1962), p. 79. Also see his *Religion and the Christian Faith* (Philadelphia: Westminster Press, 1957), chs. 22 and 23.

78. D. Dumaine, "Cool Cures for Burnout," *Fortune* 117 (June 20, 1988): 78–81.

79. See Stout, *Ethics After Babel*, p. 163. Stout with seeming satisfaction declares that theology is marginal in commanding attention "as a distinctive contributor to public discourse in our culture." He doubts that theology can speak persuasively "to an educated public without sacrificing its own integrity as a recognizable mode of utterance." Stout appears to identify "an educated public" with a university philosophy and religion department. Without denying much of Stout's criticism of "academic theology," his contention that theology is marginal to an "educated public" is refuted each Sunday in churches where Christian faith is explicated to highly educated "modern people," including the church adjacent to the Princeton University campus, indeed, the church out of which Princeton University came to be.

Chapter 4: Teaching

1. *Calvin: Institutes of the Christian Religion*, ed. John T. McNeill and trans. Ford Lewis Battles (Philadelphia: Westminster Press, 1960), 4.2.3; 4.2.4.

2. C. H. Dodd, *Apostolic Preaching and Its Developments* (New York: Harper & Brothers, 1944).

3. Edward D. Hirsch, *Cultural Literacy: What Every American Needs to Know* (Boston: Houghton Mifflin Co., 1987), p. 30. See Lynn V. Cheney, *American Memory: A Report on the Humanities in the Nation's Public Schools* (Washington, D.C.: National Endowment for the Humanities, 1987).

4. Hirsch, *Cultural Literacy,* p. 30.

5. Ibid., p. 8.

6. Ibid., pp. 7, 2.

7. John H. Westerhoff III, *McGuffey and His Readers: Piety, Morality, and Education in Nineteenth-Century America* (Nashville: Abingdon Press, 1978). A competent study of McGuffey and his influence, including material from the readers.

8. Ibid.

9. William J. Wolf, *The Almost Chosen People: A Study of the Religion of Abraham Lincoln* (Garden City, N.Y.: Doubleday & Co., 1959), p. 75; Hans Morgenthau and David Hein, *Essays on Lincoln's Faith and Politics,* American Values Projected Abroad Series, ed. Kenneth Thompson (Lanham, Md.: University Press of America, 1983).

10. In 1986, 12,501,000 Americans were enrolled in institutions of higher education; of these, 9,722,000 were in public institutions and 2,779,000 were in private schools (*Statistical Abstract of the United States, 1989* [Washington, D.C.: U.S. Department of Commerce, Bureau of the Census, 1989], p. 149). For a critique of the university from the traditional Christian perspective, see Walter Moberly, *The Crisis in the University* (London: SCM Press, 1951).

11. Allan Bloom, *The Closing of the American Mind* (New York: Simon & Schuster, 1987), p. 54.

12. Sydney E. Ahlstrom, *A Religious History of the American People* (New Haven: Yale University Press, 1972), pp. 349–350, 843, 1079.

13. Bloom, *The Closing of the American Mind,* p. 67.

14. S. Robert Lichter and Stanley Rothman, *The Media Elite and American Values* (Washington, D.C.: Ethics and Public Policy Center, 1982), p. 43. According to Lichter and Rothman, half of all media elites claim no religious affiliation; 14 percent

are Jewish, and 23 percent are Protestant, and fewer than 13 percent are Catholic. Only 8 percent attend religious services weekly, and 86 percent seldom or never do.

15. Quoted by Geoffrey Wagner, *The End of Education* (New York: A. S. Barnes & Co., 1976), p. 31.

16. Calvin, *Institutes* 1.1.1; 1.1.2.

17. Ibid., 3.7.1.

18. Paul Tillich, *Systematic Theology* 1:11ff. (Chicago: University of Chicago Press, 1951).

19. Karl Barth, *Church Dogmatics*, ed. G. W. Bromiley and T. F. Torrance (Edinburgh: T. & T. Clark, 1936–62), IV/1, p. 685.

20. Ibid., p. 694.

21. Calvin, *Institutes* 4.1.5. Calvin's insistence that the pastor is the teacher in the congregation probably contributed to the failure of the office of doctor to become established in Reformed churches.

22. Ibid., 4.12.2.

23. Ibid., 1.11.7.

24. Ibid., 4.19.13.

25. Lewis J. Sherrill, *The Rise of Christian Education* (New York: Macmillan Co., 1950), pp. 245ff. Rodolphe Peter, "L'abecedaire genevois ou catechisme elementaire de Calvin," *Revue d'histoire et de philosophie religieuses* 45 (1965): 11–45. This simple book of instruction in ABCs and in numbers contains the rudiments of the faith: the Lord's Prayer, the Apostles' Creed, the commandments, prayers, a summary of the faith necessary to participate in the Lord's Supper, a collection of scripture passages, prayers for small children, and a simple catechism. This instruction existed alongside Calvin's more advanced catechism. An English translation is printed in *Calvin Studies* V, available from Davidson College Presbyterian Church, Davidson, North Carolina. Cf. Werner Jaeger, *Early Christianity and Greek Paideia* (Cambridge, Mass.: Harvard University Press, 1961), p. 92: "As the Greek paideia consisted of the entire corpus of Greek literature, so the Christian paideia is the Bible."

26. George Lindbeck, "Scripture, Consensus, and Community," *This World* 23 (Fall 1988): 5–24.

27. Calvin, *Institutes* 4.8.8.

28. Ford Lewis Battles, ed. and trans., *Institutes of the Christian Religion: 1536 Edition* (1975; Grand Rapids: Wm. B. Eerdmans Publishing Co., 1986), Appendix, p. 374.
29. Westminster Confession of Faith, ch. I, 7.
30. Northrop Frye, *The Educated Imagination* (Bloomington, Ind.: University of Indiana Press, 1964), p. 110. See J. H. Gardiner, *The Bible as English Literature* (New York: Charles Scribner's Sons, 1906).
31. Karl Rahner, *Foundations of Christian Faith: An Introduction to the Idea of Christianity*, trans. William V. Dyck (New York: Seabury Press, 1978).
32. Hans Frei, "The Literal Reading of Biblical Narrative in the Christian Tradition: Does It Stretch or Will It Break?" in *The Bible and the Narrative Tradition*, ed. Frank McConnell (New York: Oxford University Press, 1986); C. H. Dodd, *The Bible Today* (Cambridge: Cambridge University Press, 1952), ch. 5; John Knox, *Criticism and Faith* (New York: Abingdon-Cokesbury Press, 1952), ch. 2; Herbert Butterfield, *The Origins of History*, ed. Adam Watson (New York: Basic Books, 1981), ch. 6; George Marsden, "Common Sense and the Spiritual Vision of History," C. T. McIntyre and Ronald A. Wells, *History and Historical Understanding* (Grand Rapids: Wm. B. Eerdmans Publishing Co., 1984); Martin Hengel, *Acts and the History of Earliest Christianity* (Philadelphia: Fortress Press, 1980), pp. 127ff. See William J. Abraham, *Divine Revelation and the Limits of Historical Criticism* (Oxford: Oxford University Press, 1982).

Herbert Butterfield's comment about history in general is also true for the importance of narrative for scripture. "We must have a political history that is set out in narrative form—an account of adult human beings, taking a hand in their fates and fortunes, pulling at the story in the direction they want to carry it, and making decisions of their own" (Herbert Butterfield, *George III and the Historians* [London: William Collins Sons & Co., 1957], p. 206).
33. See J. N. D. Kelly, *Early Christian Doctrines* (San Francisco: Harper & Row, 1978), pp. 60–79; see also Robert Grant, *A Short History of the Interpretation of the Bible* (New York: Macmillan Co., 1963), p. 83.
34. Cf. William Bouwsma, *John Calvin: A Sixteenth-Cen-*

tury Portrait (New York: Oxford University Press, 1988), pp. 113ff.

35. William Ames, *The Marrow of Theology,* ed. and trans. John D. Eusden (Philadelphia: Pilgrim Press, 1968). In his introduction (pp. 2–3), Eusden writes: "Ames wrote his *Marrow* not as a scholarly treatise but as a useful compendium for laymen and students. The text is divided into two books with chapters in numbered sections, providing even a neophyte a chance to discover quickly the Amesian answer on a particular point. More than a theological checklist, however, the book was a declaration of the Puritan position that theology was an art with its own rules and practice—an art for every man, not reserved for the expert or the *perfectiones.* Theology was for all men because it spoke not only to the intellect but to the common *sensus,* or man's feeling and emotions. . . . Ames wrote it in simple, late Renaissance Latin so that it could be read by anyone with a rudimentary seventeenth-century education, be he English, French, Dutch, or German." See John W. Beardslee, ed. and trans., *Reformed Dogmatics* (New York: Oxford University Press, 1965), pp. 11, 29–262.

36. James Gustafson, "The Vocation of the Theological Educator," *Austin Seminary Bulletin,* Faculty ed., 101/7 (March 1986): 15–16.

37. A theme of Calvin's prefaces to the *Institutes.*

38. Cf. Calvin, *Institutes* 4.3.16. Calvin was flexible as to ordination rite. Yet all Reformed churches are emphatic about the call and responsibility under God to scripture and to the faith of the church.

39. Alexander F. Mitchell, *Catechisms of the Second Reformation* (London: James Nisbet & Co., 1886); T. F. Torrance, *The School of Faith* (New York: Harper & Brothers, 1959).

40. Calvin's Farewell to the Ministers, *Letters of John Calvin,* ed. Jules Bonnet (Philadelphia: Presbyterian Board of Christian Education, 1858), 4:376.

41. Mitchell, *Catechisms of the Second Reformation.*

42. The Church of Scotland attempted a new catechism in 1955. This catechism along with others failed to gain general acceptance.

43. Augustine, *First Catechetical Instruction,* trans. and an-

NOTES   215

not. Joseph P. Christopher (Westminster, Md.: Newman Book-
shop, 1946), p. 6.
    44. Alan Richardson, *Christian Apologetics* (New York:
Harper & Brothers, 1941), ch. 10; Albert T. Mollegen, *Christianity and Modern Man: The Crisis of Secularism* (Indianapolis:
Bobbs-Merrill Co., 1961).
    45. John E. Smith, *The Analogy of Experience* (New York:
Harper & Row, 1973).
    46. Reinhold Niebuhr, *Faith and History* (New York:
Charles Scribner's Sons, 1949), ch. 10.
    47. Calvin's catechisms, for example, contained instruction
about sacraments, about worship and prayer. Model prayers for
use during the day were attached.
    48. Calvin, *Institutes* 3.3.16.
    49. Calvin emphasizes the transcendence of God, the
moral, and life in the world in contrast to mystical spirituality
and meditation. Also Calvin endeavored to eliminate "theatrical
trifles." Today church literature advocates such non-Reformed
usages as oil and candles at baptisms.
    50. Steven Ozment, *The Age of Reform, 1250–1550* (New
Haven, Conn.: Yale University Press, 1980), pp. 32ff.; John R.
Knott, Jr., *The Sword of the Spirit: Puritan Responses to the Bible*
(Chicago: University of Chicago Press, 1980); David F. Wright,
ed., *The Bible in Scottish Life and Literature* (Edinburgh: Saint
Andrew Press, 1988).
    51. Rush Welter, *Popular Education and Democratic Thought
in America* (New York: Columbia University Press, 1962),
pp. 15–18; William M. French, *America's Educational Tradition:
An Interpretative History* (Boston: D. C. Heath & Co., 1964),
p. 280.
    52. Richard A. Baer, Jr., "Cosmos, Cosmologies, and the
Public School," *This World* 5 (Spring–Summer 1983): 5–17.
    53. Rockne McCarthy et al., *Society, State, and Schools*
(Grand Rapids: Wm. B. Eerdmans Publishing Co., 1982).
    54. Paul F. Parsons, *Inside America's Christian Schools* (Ma-
con, Ga.: Mercer University Press, 1987), p. xiii. Enrollment in
non-Catholic religious schools rose from 561,808 in 1970 to
1,329,526 in 1980.
    55. Calvin, *Institutes* 1.1.2; 2.2.14; 4.3.11.

56. D. G. Tewksbury, *The Founding of American Colleges and Universities Before the Civil War, with Particular Reference to the Religious Influences Bearing Upon the College Movement* (New York: Teachers College, Columbia University, 1932).

57. John Knox, "The Identifiability of the Church," *Theological Freedom and Social Responsibility* (New York: Seabury Press, 1967), p. 72.

58. This is reflected in the quantifiable statistics of the denominations in which mainline and university seminary graduates preach. There is need for a study of the "success" of seminary graduates as pastors.

59. See Deana L. Astle, "Suicide Squeeze: The Escalating Costs of Scholarly Journals," *Academe, Bulletin of the American Association of University Professors* (July–Aug. 1989); Jay Amberg, "Higher (-Priced) Education," *American Scholar* (Dec. 1989).

60. Gustafson, "The Vocation of the Theological Educator," *Austin Seminary Bulletin* (March 1986).

61. See Robert Morgan and John Barton, *Biblical Interpretation* (New York: Oxford University Press, 1988), esp. ch. 5.

62. Stephen Sykes, *The Identity of Christianity* (Philadelphia: Fortress Press, 1984), pp. 262ff.

63. See note 15 to Preface.

64. Jeffrey L. Pasley, "The School for Scandal," *New Republic* (July 4, 1988).

65. Willard Sperry, *Reality in Worship: A Study of Public Worship and Private Religion* (New York: Macmillan Co., 1925), p. 200. See Dietrich Von Hildebrand, *Liturgy and Personality* (rev. ed. 1960; Manchester, N.H.: Sophia Institute Press, 1986).

66. William J. Bennett, "To Reclaim a Legacy: A Report on the Humanities in Higher Education" (Washington, D.C.: National Endowment for the Humanities, 1984), p. 6: "What characterizes good teaching in the humanities? First, and foremost, a teacher must have achieved mastery of the material. But this is not enough; there must also be engagement. Professor William Arrowsmith of Emory University described good teachers as 'committed to teaching what they have learned to love.' In one crucial way, good teachers cannot be dispassionate. They cannot be dispassionate about the works they teach—assuming that they are teaching important works. This does not mean they advocate

each idea of every author, but rather that they are moved and are seen to be moved by the power of the works and are able to convey that power to their students. Just as good scholarship is inspired, so must good teaching be."

Chapter 5: Pastoral Care

1. *Corpus Reformatorum: Ioannis Calvini Opera quae supersunt omnia,* ed. Guiliclmus Baum, Eduardus Cunitz, and Eduardus Reuss (Braunschweig: C. A. Schwetschke & Filium, 1863–1897), vols. 10–20.

2. Karl Barth, *Church Dogmatics,* ed. G. W. Bromiley and T. F. Torrance (Edinburgh: T. & T. Clark, 1936–62), IV/3.2, p. 885.

3. Herbert Butterfield, *Christianity in European History* (London: William Collins Sons & Co., 1952), pp. 14–15.

4. Nicolas Berdyaev, *The End of Our Time* (New York: Sheed & Ward, 1933), p. 29: "The division made by the Renaissance, the rift in the soul of man, is become the theme of modern history. *It is an unfolding of ideas and events wherein we see Humanism destroying itself by its own dialectic, for the putting up of man without God and against God, the denial of the divine image and likeness in himself, lead to his own negation and destruction; the affirming of paganism against Christianity means the denial and demolition of his sacred past.* The image of man, the image of his body and soul, is the work of classical antiquity and of Christ. Modern Humanism in breaking with Christianity departs from the ancient knowledge of what man is and changes his image." See Nicolas Berdyaev, *The Fate of Man in the Modern World* (New York: Morehouse Publishing Co., 1935), p. 22.

5. Peter Brown, *The Body and Society: Men, Women, and Sexual Renunciation in Early Christianity* (New York: Columbia University Press, 1988), p. 424.

6. A recently discovered letter of Augustine to Atticus; quoted in Brown, *The Body and Society,* p. 424.

7. Arthur F. Smethurst, *Modern Science and Christian Beliefs* (New York: Abingdon Press, 1955), pp. 146ff.

8. David Baltimore, "Can Genetic Science Backfire?" *U.S. News & World Report* (March 28, 1983): 52–53.

9. Reinhold Niebuhr, *The Nature and Destiny of Man* (New York: Charles Scribner's Sons, 1941–43), vol. 1, chs. 6–7.

10. Reinhold Niebuhr, *Love and Justice,* ed. D. R. Robertson (Philadelphia: Westminster Press, 1957).

11. Augustine, *Confessions* 1.1.

12. Karl Barth, *Church Dogmatics* III/2, p. 147; Eduard Thurneysen, *A Theology of Pastoral Care,* trans. Jack A. Worthington and Thomas Wieser (Richmond: John Knox Press, 1962), ch. 3, esp. p. 66.

13. Peter Brown, *Augustine of Hippo* (London: Faber & Faber, 1967), pp. 348ff.

14. See Gerald Bonner, "Augustine and Pelagianism in the Light of Modern Research," in *God's Decree and Man's Destiny* (London: Variorum Reprints, 1987); Robert Evans, *Pelagius: Inquiries and Reappraisals* (New York: Seabury Press, 1968).

15. Brown, *Augustine of Hippo,* p. 348.

16. Ibid., pp. 340ff.

17. Max Weber, *The Protestant Ethic and the Spirit of Capitalism,* trans. Talcott Parsons (1930; New York: Charles Scribner's Sons, 1958), pp. 98ff.; Ernst Troeltsch, *The Social Teaching of the Christian Churches,* trans. Olive Wyon (London: George Allen & Unwin, 1931), pp. 609ff.; Bonner, "Augustine and Pelagianism in the Light of Modern Research."

18. Brown, *Augustine of Hippo,* p. 342; W. H. C. Frend, *Saints and Sinners in the Early Church* (London: Darton, Longman & Todd, 1985), pp. 118–140.

19. Brown, *Augustine of Hippo,* p. 348.

20. Ibid., ch. 21.

21. Augustine, *Letters* 157.

22. Augustine, "Nature and Grace," *Nicene and Post-Nicene Fathers of the Christian Church,* ed. Philip Schaff (New York: Christian Literature Co., 1887), 5:132.

23. Quoted by Brown, *Augustine of Hippo,* p. 351, *De bono viduitatis.*

24. Gerald Bonner, "*Libido* and *Concupiscentia* in St. Augustine," in Bonner, *God's Decree and Man's Destiny.*

25. Cf. Reinhold Niebuhr, *Love and Justice.*

26. T. S. Eliot, *The Complete Poems and Plays 1909–1950* (New York: Harcourt, Brace & Co., 1952), p. 142.

27. Albert Mollegen, a professor at Virginia Episcopal Seminary and an able preacher, once carried out this experiment in his own preaching. His conclusion has been confirmed in my own experience.

28. Brown, *Augustine of Hippo*, pp. 365ff.

29. Evans, *Pelagius, Inquiries and Reappraisals*, p. 111.

30. Augustine, *Sermon* 131. See Peter Brown, *Augustine of Hippo* (London: Faber & Faber, 1967), p. 365.

31. Gerald Bonner, *St. Augustine of Hippo: Life and Controversies* (Norwich: Canterbury Press, 1963), pp. 276ff.

32. Calvin, *Institutes* 2.9.4.

33. Ibid., 2.7.1–17.

34. Karl Barth, *Church Dogmatics* IV/2, pp. 499ff. See IV/3.2, pp. 506ff. on the problems of attempting a psychological and biographical description of the evolution of a Christian.

35. Gordon Rupp, *Methodism in Relation to the Protestant Tradition* (London: Epworth Press, 1954).

36. John H. Leith, *John Calvin's Doctrine of the Christian Life* (Philadelphia: Westminster Press, 1989), pp. 82ff.

37. Calvin, *Institutes* 4.1.1.

38. Huldrych Zwingli, *The Shepherd*. See G. R. Potter, *Zwingli* (Cambridge: Cambridge University Press, 1976), p. 135.

39. Martin Bucer, *On the True Care of Souls and the Proper Role of the Pastor*. See David F. Wright, "Martin Bucer 1491–1551: Ecumenical Theologian," *The Common Places of Martin Bucer*, trans. and ed. David F. Wright (Appleford, Eng.: Sutton Courtenay Press, 1972), p. 21. John T. McNeill calls this the outstanding early Protestant text on pastoral care in *A History of the Cure of Souls* (New York: Harper & Brothers, 1951), p. 180.

40. Calvin, *Institutes* 4.1.1.

41. See Hendrikus Berkhof, *Christian Faith: An Introduction to the Study of the Faith,* rev. ed., trans. Sierd Woudstra (Grand Rapids: Wm. B. Eerdmans Publishing Co., 1986), ch. 40.

42. This is a characteristic Reformed theme with its emphasis on the transcendence of God and the distinction between Creator and creature.

43. Schmalkald Articles (1537), Art. III, in Theodore Tappert, ed. and trans., *The Book of Concord* (Philadelphia: Muhlenberg Press, 1959).

44. Seward Hiltner, *Preface to Pastoral Care* (Nashville: Abingdon Press, 1958), p. 49.

45. See Thomas Oden, *Care of Souls in the Classic Tradition* (Philadelphia: Fortress Press, 1989). See also Albert Outler, *Psychotherapy and the Christian Message* (New York: Harper & Brothers, 1954).

46. James Hasting Nichols, *Corporate Worship in the Reformed Tradition* (Philadelphia: Westminster Press, 1968), p. 32.

47. The Word of God is gracious and pastoral. See Robert Moats Miller, *Harry Emerson Fosdick, Preacher, Pastor, Prophet* (New York: Oxford University Press, 1985), pp. 115ff.

48. Daniel Day Williams, *The Minister and the Care of Souls* (New York: Harper & Brothers, 1961), pp. 110ff.; Gordon Allport, *The Individual and His Religion* (New York: Macmillan Co., 1950), chs. 5 and 6.

49. See "Draft Ecclesiastical Ordinances (1541)," in J. K. S. Reid, ed., *Calvin: Theological Treatises*, Library of Christian Classics, vol. 22 (Philadelphia: Westminster Press, 1954), pp. 68ff.

50. Richard Baxter, *The Reformed Pastor*, ed. William Brown (Edinburgh: Banner of Truth Trust, 1983), pp. 88f., 90, 100, 235-236.

51. Emil Brunner, *The Divine Imperative* (New York: Macmillan Co., 1942), p. 286, "A person who 'reveals' love is more successful—in the last resort—than one who does loving actions."

52. The only competence ministers can have that is not exceeded elsewhere in society is as theologians. Until the world respects the competence of ministers as theologians it is not likely to respect ministers as they engage in other activities.

53. D. James Kennedy, *Evangelism Explosion* (Wheaton, Ill.: Tyndale House Publishers, 1971).

54. The church can humanize services that are increasingly professional and commercial. Many church hospitals as well as programs for housing illustrate this. The history of church hospitals illustrates how difficult this ministry is.

55. For the role of the church supper in the New Testament see Acts 2:42; 1 Cor. 11:17-22.

56. Westminster Confession of Faith, ch. XXIV, 3.

57. "Draft Ecclesiastical Ordinances (1541)," in *Calvin: Theological Treatises*, p. 68.

58. Karl Rahner, "Ideas for a Theology of Death," *Theological Investigations*, trans. Lionel Swain (New York: Crossroad Publishing Co., 1983), 3:169–186.
59. Oden, *Care of Souls in the Classic Tradition*, ch. 1. See E. Brooks Holifield, *A History of Pastoral Care in America* (Nashville: Abingdon Press, 1983).

Chapter 6: The Christian Witness in the World

1. David J. Bosch, *Witness to the World: The Christian Mission in Theological Perspective* (Atlanta: John Knox Press, 1980), p. 15.
2. Karl Barth, *Church Dogmatics*, ed. G. W. Bromiley and T. F. Torrance (Edinburgh: T. & T. Clark, 1936–62), IV/3.2, p. 874.
3. Quoted by David B. Barrett and Harley C. Schreck, *Unreached Peoples: Clarifying the Task* (Birmingham, Ala.: New Hope Publishers, n.d.), p. 45. See Justin Martyr, "Dialogue with Trypho, a Jew," 39, 117, for variant translations.
4. Barrett and Schreck, *Unreached Peoples*, p. 46. See Origen's *Commentary on Matthew* 24:9 and *Homily* 9.10, quoted in Adolf von Harnack, *The Mission and Expansion of Christianity in the First Three Centuries*, trans. James Moffatt (New York: G. P. Putnam's Sons, 1908), 2:11.
5. Karl Barth, *Church Dogmatics* IV/1, pp. 643ff.; IV/2, pp. 614ff.
6. Cyril Richardson, ed. and trans., *Early Christian Fathers*, Library of Christian Classics, vol. 1 (Philadelphia: Westminster Press, 1953), pp. 216–217.
7. William Telfer, ed., *Cyril of Jerusalem and Nemesius of Emesa*, Library of Christian Classics, vol. 4 (Philadelphia: Westminster Press, 1956), p. 186.
8. Augustine, *The City of God*, trans. Marcus Dods (New York: Modern Library, 1950), 19.17, pp. 877–878.
9. Figures provided by David B. Barrett, editor of *World Christian Encyclopedia* (New York: Oxford University Press, 1982) and mission researcher for the Foreign Mission Board, Southern Baptist Convention.
10. Martin Kähler, *Schriften zur Christologie und Mission* (Munich: Chr. Kaiser, 1971), p. 190.

11. In 1960 the Presbyterian Church U.S. and the United Presbyterian Church U.S.A. had a total of 1,785 missionaries. In 1988, reunited as the Presbyterian Church (U.S.A.), they had less than 400, including term missionaries. See *Minutes of the 200th General Assembly, Presbyterian Church (U.S.A.), 1988,* Part I: *Journal,* pp. 723–725.

12. See the debate on missions today in *International Bulletin of Missionary Research* 12/4 (Oct. 1988).

13. Martin E. Marty and Frederick E. Greenspahn, eds., *Pushing the Faith: Proselytism and Civility in a Pluralistic World* (New York: Crossroad Publishing Co., 1988).

14. For divergent views, see documents in John H. Leith, ed., *Creeds of the Churches,* 3rd ed. (Atlanta: John Knox Press, 1982), pp. 658–696.

15. Ernst Troeltsch, *The Absoluteness of Christianity and the History of Religions,* trans. David Reid (Richmond: John Knox Press, 1971); Ernst Troeltsch, "The Place of Christianity Among World Religions," in *Christian Thought: Its History and Application,* ed. Baron F. von Hügel (New York: Meridian Books, 1957), pp. 53–63.

16. Quoted by Bosch, *Witness to the World,* p. 136.

17. John Hick, "The Non-Absoluteness of Christianity," and Rosemary Radford Ruether, "Particularism and Universalism in Search for Religious Truth," in John Hick and Paul F. Knitter, eds., *The Myth of Christian Uniqueness* (Maryknoll, N.Y.: Orbis Books, 1987); Torben Christensen and William R. Hutchison, eds., *Missionary Ideologies in the Imperialist Era: 1880–1920* (Arhus, Denmark: Aros, 1982); William R. Hutchison, *Errand to the World* (Chicago: University of Chicago Press, 1987), p. 204. "Several responses seem warranted by the history of American mission thought and activity. The first is an acknowledgment that if 'imperialism' be defined with the breadth and depth most historians now consider appropriate, the American missionary movement takes its place as an active contributor. To be sure, if one were to define the term more traditionally that would be far less true, since missionaries and their sponsors often stood in an equivocal relation, at most, to colonialism and to military or commercial expansionism. But if 'imperialism' connotes the attempt to impose one's ideas and culture on another, and the

possible instruments of imposition are not limited to guns and power politics—if the tools of the trade include, for example, ordinary persuasiveness backed by vastly superior resources— then the missionary movement unquestionably qualifies as an arm of this broader sort of imperialism."

18. Donald Anderson McGavran, ed., *Eye of the Storm: The Great Debate in Mission* (Waco, Tex.: Word Books, 1972).

19. Peter Beyerhaus, *Mission: Which Way?* (Grand Rapids: Zondervan Publishing House, 1971).

20. David B. Barrett, "Annual Statistical Table on Global Missions: 1989," *International Bulletin of Missionary Research* 13 (Jan. 1989): 20–21; also explanatory materials circulated in mimeographed form.

21. Ibid. 20. For documentation of the above figures, see *International Bulletin of Missionary Research* 12/1 (Jan. 1988): 16–17; 13/1 (Jan. 1989): 20–2l; Barrett, ed., *World Christian Encyclopedia*, pp. 3–19.

22. Hick, "The Non-Absoluteness of Christianity," pp. 16ff.; Pearl Buck, *The Good Earth* (New York: John Day Co., 1931).

23. Barrett, ed., *World Christian Encyclopedia*, p. 3. See also updated report listed in note 20.

24. Gordon Rupp, *Six Makers of English Religion 1500– 1700* (London: Hodder & Stoughton, 1957), pp. 53–73.

25. David B. Barrett, "Annual Statistical Table on Global Mission: 1987," *International Bulletin of Missionary Research* (Jan. 1987), pp. 24–25.

26. Kenneth Scott Latourette, *A History of the Expansion of Christianity* (New York: Harper & Brothers, 1939–45), 7:494, 499ff.

Epilogue

1. Gertrude Himmelfarb, *The New History and the Old: Critical Essays and Reappraisals* (Cambridge, Mass.: Harvard University Press, 1987), p. 35.

2. Ibid., p. 36. See Simon Schama, *Citizens: A Chronicle of the French Revolution* (New York: Alfred A. Knopf, 1989), for a similar emphasis on history as narrative.